DEPARTURES

DEPARTURES

Memoirs
Paul Zweig

Introduction by Morris Dickstein

1817
HARPER & ROW, PUBLISHERS, New York
Cambridge, Philadelphia, San Francisco, Washington
London, Mexico City, São Paulo, Singapore, Sydney

Portions of the work originally appeared in the *American Poetry Review* and *TriQuarterly*.

Grateful acknowledgment is made for permission to reprint:

Lines from "The Natural History of Death," "Afraid That I Am Not a Poet" and "I Pay with Hunger" from *Against Emptiness* by Paul Zweig. Copyright © 1977 by Paul Zweig. Reprinted by permission of Harper & Row, Publishers, Inc.

Excerpts from *Eternity's Woods* by Ruthellyn Weiner. Copyright © 1985 by Ruthellyn Weiner. Reprinted by permission of Wesleyan University Press.

Lines from "The Waste Land" in *Collected Poems 1909–1962* by T. S. Eliot. Copyright 1936 by Harcourt Brace Jovanovich, Inc. Copyright © 1963, 1964 by T. S. Eliot. Reprinted by permission of Harcourt Brace Jovanovich, Inc. and Faber and Faber, Ltd.

Photo on page 5 courtesy Robert Mahon

FIRST EDITION

Designer: Abigail Sturges
Copy editor: Robert Hemenway

Library of Congress Cataloging-in-Publication Data

Zweig, Paul.
    Departures: memoirs.

    1. Zweig, Paul—Biography. 2. Poets, American—
20th century—Biography. I. Title.
PS3576.W4Z464 1986   811'.54 [B]   86-45166
ISBN 0-06-015650-3

86 87 88 89 90 HC 10 9 8 7 6 5 4 3 2 1

For Vikki

INTRODUCTION

WRITERS who die young are the very stuff of legend. Their foreshortened lives, reshaped into sad parables, compete with their work for the attention of posterity. Keats lingered on for a century as a figure of pathos and fragile sensibility; F. Scott Fitzgerald and Hart Crane became bywords for self-destructive dissipation. To us art is always an endangered activity, and this makes us all too ready to sentimentalize writers who were actually made of sterner stuff. It's a curious sensation to see this mythmaking apparatus crank up in a small way around the life of a close friend, to be reminded how history can be subtly rewritten in the presence of the survivors.

Paul Zweig died in August 1984 at the age of 49, not exactly young but a person of exceptional vitality, very much at the height of his creative powers. For six years he had suffered from lymphoma, a cancerous condition of the lymph system, eventually complicated by leukemia. Paul had always been a prolific writer, but in his last years he burned with an especially bright flame. Before his illness he had published two wide-ranging, unclassifiable works of cultural history, *The Heresy of Self-Love: A Study of Subversive Individualism* (1968) and *The Adventurer* (1974); two volumes of poems, *Against Emptiness* (1971) and *The Dark Side of the Earth* (1974); a study of the French poet Lautréamont, based on his Sorbonne dissertation (1967; revised in English as *Lautréamont: The Violent Narcissus*, 1972); a strangely oblique but eloquently composed volume of memoirs, *Three Journeys* (1976); dozens of scattered translations and essays, and innumerable reviews of poetry and prose, always glitterly well-written.

Paul's early books of prose, especially *The Adventurer*, were brilliantly idiosyncratic, full of suggestive flashes of insight and

7

intuition. They were great performances, in the best sense of the word, before it became fashionable for critics to strut and fret at center stage. But they were far surpassed by the more subdued work he did in his last years, including his much-acclaimed critical biography of Whitman, which appeared a few months before his death, his third book of poems, *Eternity's Woods* (1985), and an extraordinary new book of memoirs, virtually complete at the time of his death, to which his publisher has given the very appropriate title *Departures.* It never ceased to amaze me, as I read early drafts and manuscripts of each of these books, that Paul's writings, like Paul himself, had become so focused and incandescent under the threat of fatal illness. But this is different from the well-meaning myth that surfaces in reviews of these books that they were the work of a man haunted by the imminence of death.

One of the arresting things about Paul's biography of Whitman, as about so many of his poems and a good deal of *Departures,* is that they give so little indication of his condition or his recurrent bouts of anxiety at the time he wrote them. To say, as Alan Helms did in *Partisan Review,* that "Whitman's life during the Civil War is perhaps so moving in Zweig's account because Zweig himself was close to death as he finished the book" is to substitute a poignant fiction for the vigorously healthy book we are actually reading. (The same false note was sounded in the glowing *Times* review of *Eternity's Woods.*) Paul talked quite frequently about his illness, but in the most natural way imaginable, without a trace of self-pity or desperation. He was extremely well informed about the medical side and realistic about his slim chances of survival, which he never exaggerated and never wholly abandoned.

In the end his death was startlingly sudden, after a week or two of fever at the stone farmhouse he loved in the Dordogne. He died in Paris, on his way back to America, but even the day before his death he told his friend C. K. Williams that he had finally "cracked" the structure of his next book, a study of prehistory. In most ways his outlook was that of a healthy man, certainly of someone with an undiminished interest in life. Writing *was* life to him, for all the concern with death we find in his work. Nearly everything he wrote was in some way autobiographical but hardly confessional: he was never given to maudlin self-dramatization. When he lost his capacity to imagine a future he turned his eye toward the mysteries of the past: to prehistory, a subject on which he did a mountain of

8

research, to the murky origins of Walt Whitman, self-made man, to the ten years he himself had spent in Paris after graduating from Columbia in 1956, and, in poetry, to the Jewish family he thought he had left behind during those Paris years.

Fearing he was running out of time, Paul focused on the time he had already had, yet lived in the present with remarkable intensity. Formerly quite detached, he now seemed to lend a different quality of attention to the ordinary business of living his life. While researching his illness, grappling with his fears, and shaking off the effects of toxic chemicals, he went on being a father, a lover, a teacher, a colleague, a traveler, a son and brother, a friend, and a writer. Always a great talker, he now became a good listener as well, never succumbing to the self-absorption of the seriously ill. For many years my friendship with Paul had been one long, exhilarating conversation; in these last years it became something deeply personal as well. Illness rendered him more vulnerably human without reducing him in any way, and he could now talk about the life around him with the same bemused concentration he had once reserved for books and ideas. The change crept up on me: I was surprised at the gaping hole his death left in my life. There were subjects I no longer cared to talk about, streets and cafés I now instinctively shunned, books that took on a melancholy aura. For more than a year, a beautiful day on Riverside Drive left a pang of agony. There was simply a terrible absence where there had once been an immensely vivid presence.

Paul and I first met a few weeks after his return from Paris in 1966. He had the look of a poet—slight but well-built, dark, with wild, thinning hair and fiery eyes, a deep, nimble voice, perfect for reading aloud, and a temperament at once taut and relaxed. We were both freshly minted English instructors at Columbia, sharing a small office with Paul Delany, who had already been teaching a year or two. We were an odd threesome, not obviously destined to become fast friends: Delany, a quickwitted, taciturn Englishman who had lived in Canada and come to New York by way of Berkeley; Zweig, mysteriously cosmopolitan for a Jewish kid from Brighton Beach, who had first arrived at Columbia on a track scholarship, studied engineering for three years before deciding to become a poet, and spent ten years in Paris exploring *la vie de bohème* in its late existentialist phase; and me, budding intellectual, already published in *Partisan Review*, as arrogant as I was inexperienced.

Talk was the perpetual buzz that kept our lives humming. We were just then teaching the Great Books four times a week in the same Humanities course where we had cut our own teeth a few years earlier. Just down the hall were the offices of Lionel Trilling, Fred Dupee, and other mentors of my undergraduate days. The charged air in Hamilton Hall was thick with what passed for Socratic dialogue but was actually the anxious display of untenured intelligence. Thrown into an appalling, unspoken rivalry with each other, we managed remarkably to form friendships that endured.

With his silver tongue and easy manner and endless curiosity, Paul was always a pleasure to be with. Though we both loved the play of ideas, Paul's speculative fancy often brought out my teasing sense of fact. His role was to fly off, mine to tug him gently back to earth, to keep him tethered to something real.

With his genius for making wide cultural connections, Paul found the contemporary world too small for his taste. The bickering of cultural factions, the ebb and flow of reviews and opinions, mainly amused him. Institutional arrangements, including the ones that had brought him back to New York, seemed to hold no interest for him. Even before the famous uprising he was oblivious to the campus hubbub at Columbia. In 1968 the university exploded, the whole nation exploded, but Paul essentially went his own way. He taught his classes, saw students in the office, walked across campus commenting on the best features of every good-looking girl we saw, and started reviewing a steady stream of poets for Helen Yglesias at *The Nation*, reviews which showed me a new way of approaching contemporary poetry.

A few years earlier he had gotten to know Robert Bly, not yet the portentous figure he later became but already a gruff, combative observer of the poetry scene. Paul became Bly's man in New York for a time, and also grew friendly with several of the exciting new poets Bly was promoting in his lively magazine *The Sixties*, including Galway Kinnell, David Ignatow, Louis Simpson, and James Wright. Like Bly these were poets who had turned their backs on the dense, witty academic verse of the 1950s to cultivate simpler language, surreal imagery, and a more expressive personal voice. In polemical essays and reviews, Bly also attacked the confessional verse of Lowell and his followers, pointing instead to Neruda and other Spanish and South American poets, who themselves had been strongly influenced by Whitman, D. H. Lawrence, and other alternative voices in the Anglo-American poetic tradition.

For a short time Paul remained a protégé of Bly's. He wrote antiwar poems and personal poems in the style of Neruda, Vallejo, and Bly. In his poems and reviews he joined the campaign to free American poetry from the shackles of formalism, to make it more spiritual but also more political, with highly dramatic, even incongruous images that were charged with unexpected emotion. This was an imitative period in Paul's work; the language he used was more rhetorical than poetic, and the emotions often seemed unfelt. One of his best early poems, "The Natural History of Death," was a kind of opaque, discontinuous story of his life as if seen from beyond the grave. It begins,

> I decided at birth to go on living,
> Not even my parents convinced me I was wrong.
> When the mistake was pointed out
> I excused myself,
> Alleging my extreme youth.

Paul uses surrealist mimicry to explode the solemn gestures of autobiography. This isn't so much the language of metaphor as a language of paradox. Though Paul eventually developed a tremendous gift for metaphoric writing, especially in prose, his early poems rely on the kind of prose poetry he had encountered in Paris, particularly the surreal storytelling and heightened verbal violence of Lautréamont and Baudelaire. Until his last volume Paul had an uncertain ear, which he tried to offset with caustic wit, compression, or charged repetition:

> When they pried open my life
> They found
> Mechanical toys and a taste for pure light;

> They heard a voice calling backward
> In the fibers of the body. . . .

> When they pried open my life
> They found
> A memory twisted as old iron,
> Ice-age fingers innocent as murder.

The language of Paul's early poems rarely achieves a feeling of inevitability, yet I remembered these lines very well after fifteen years. But they do fall at times into prosaic flatness ("I excused myself / Alleging my extreme youth"), arbitrary line divisions, or a pat violence inviting a predictable reaction ("innocent as murder"), as if certain code words, especially those connected with death, could always be expected to jolt the reader.

The main problem with Paul's early poems is that the rhetoric is part of an evasive action that conceals what it pretends to reveal. This is autobiography without any coherent sense of self, indeed, haunted by a fear of inner emptiness that Paul would later make a key theme of *Three Journeys*. He finds himself "Afraid that I am not a poet, / Yet willing to write / Even about that," and concludes,

> How can I be sane with borrowed faces?
> When the fears and pleasures
> That tumble my words
> Like seasons harvested in love,
> Are only empty mirrors,
> Images floating in a dry sea?

In another poem against emptiness, Paul writes, "I am a plant / Without roots, and that's all. / For my mobility I pay with hunger." The last section of "The Natural History of Death" is about how words and feelings invariably elude each other, as if language and inner experience each had trajectories of their own:

> At thirty, a man discovers that he has told
> A secret. His eyes whisper, while the shouting
> In his head goes on, too quick to understand.

> The wasted minutes hang
> Like a halo of lines around his face.

> Words become human as they sink out of reach,
> Already bored with being said,
> But sweaty,
> Expectant. His words listen to themselves,
> Like an eye gradually closing,
> Making the body-ruins transparent,
> But who is there to be seen?

The unrelieved grimness of these lines suggests something between a modernist conceit—Conrad's "The horror! The horror!"

or Eliot's echoes of it in "The Waste Land" and "The Hollow Men" —and a deeply felt personal anxiety. After sleepwalking through his undergraduate years, Paul had turned Paris into his university, modern literature into his graduate curriculum. The writers he read spoke to him of the emptiness of modern life—"What are the roots that clutch, what branches grow / Out of this stony rubbish?" —a message that echoed through the corridors of his own imagination.

The Paul I knew always radiated self-confidence and revolved smoothly around his own center of gravity, but in his work his deepest fear is that no one was home, that "my life was organized around a core of blandness which shed anonymity upon everything I touched." One of the most terrifying passages in Paul's prose comes just before this point in *Three Journeys,* near the beginning of his evocation of his Paris experiences:

> I think I would like to write an autobiography in which there would be no people, although people would keep stumbling into it with an expression of surprise, as if they had stumbled on a shameful scene behind a bush. And yet nothing would be going on behind the bush, the grass wouldn't even be trodden down; no one would be there, or would have ever been there. It would perhaps be the only place in the world of which this would be so. I would write the autobiography of the place behind the bush where no one ever was.

Paul thought enough of these lines that he planned for a time to reprint them as a prose poem in his next collection. For all his mobile fluency, especially his facility with language, Paul imagined at some level that his adult life was a series of impersonations— brilliant but not quite believable performances as grownup, lover, husband, Frenchman, poet, political militant, critic, teacher, piano player, and so on. A good friend who knew him early in his Paris days told me he was frightened at how rapidly, how flawlessly Paul was acquiring French—with none of the clumsiness of the other Americans but also without a motivating center. It was never clear what impelled him to such a feat of impersonation.

Paul's troubled evocation of an inner vacancy was meat and drink for Christopher Lasch, who quoted copiously from *Three Journeys* in *The Culture of Narcissism.* In the Paris segment of the book Paul refers to himself throughout in the Mailerian third person as "the boy," highlighting his immaturity, his distance from the person he had been, and, indeed, that person's distance from himself. He attributes the "inner core of blandness" to his upbringing as a well-behaved, obedient Jewish kid from Brooklyn, the son of cultivated parents, just as Mailer in *The Armies of the Night* was distressed to notice behind his multitude of personalities "a last remaining speck of the one personality he found absolutely insupportable—the nice Jewish boy from Brooklyn."

Mailer was one of the few contemporary prose writers who genuinely interested Paul. Their affinity for existential risk and adventure was built on the same base, the same self-aversion. Mailer turned himself into a wild man, a would-be conqueror, filling his life and work with a series of dazzling self-projections that turned egotism into high-wire literary performance. Paul, whose bravura and egotism could rival Mailer's, chose flight over public visibility. He shared Mailer's need to turn his life into raw material for writing. He set out for Paris, for the Sahara Desert, for India, in an effort either to become another, fuller person or to yield himself up to a larger solitude than the one he inwardly felt. "How can I be a writer when I don't have any biography?" he asks himself.

To some extent this question is a literary conceit, a theme Paul uses to tie the disparate strands of his life together. Yet his many incarnations were living testimony to the restlessness of the modern self in its hunger for meaning. The one certain thing was that, as with Mailer, whatever he did would eventually reappear as writing. Many writers actually dislike writing, a lonely occupation at best; what they enjoy is having written. Paul felt most fully engaged when he was writing. It was another form of self-transcendence, a way of living on a plane higher than that of "the boy" doing his brave impersonations. During his years of illness, when his will and concentration might well have faltered, when he might have wondered, "What for?," Paul could always refocus himself in his work, even when the subject was his own dying.

If Mailer turned his egotism into celebrity, Paul turned his into cultural history. His almost reclusive detachment at Columbia was partly explained by the first book he published in English, *The Heresy of Self-Love*, a wildly original history of narcissism that preceded Lasch's more hostile polemic by a full decade.

Though Paul could only wonder when the college's influence had seeped in, this was also very much a Columbia-style book, since Trilling and his students had long since made the self a privileged subject through which modern literature and culture could be uniquely understood. Paul had the impression that Trilling, the author of *The Opposing Self* and *Beyond Culture*, considered his book "too private," but he was pretty well armored against what other people thought of his work. Unlike most writers, he loved critical comments, even on his poetry, that would help him in the endless task of revision. This was because he did not depend on the gaze of others to ratify his existence. To a degree unthinkable to me, Paul lived contentedly within his own mind. Though his spectrum of concerns was strikingly broad, it was hard to interest him in a book he couldn't somehow use. He was immune to trendy topics. He could talk brightly about anything, even things he knew nothing about, but he reserved his passion for the handful of matters that expressed him and fired him up, the things he wrote books about. Yet on almost any subject he could plunge in anywhere, learning as he went on, barreling past his ignorance until some large essential point came into view. This too was a piece of Morningside Heights that Paul had assimilated in Paris: a delight in the play of ideas for its own sake, along with a contempt for the niceties of pettifogging scholarship and narrow specialization.

The sheer range of subjects in *The Heresy of Self-Love* was immense, from the Gnostics to the nineteenth century. There was hardly a chapter that was in any way definitive, not even the wonderfully eloquent chapter on Rousseau, who was at the heart of the subject (in every sense), but each chapter threw out intuitions and connections only Paul could have made. The book was too meditative, perhaps too dithyrambic to succeed fully as criticism, but as with its sequel, *The Adventurer*, the whole was greater than the sum of its parts. These books created a tradition, explored a way of looking at the world. They found "objective" materials that conveyed Paul's deepest sense of personal reality. They expressed his rejection of the social, the domestic, the purely rational, the urban and the civilized— in other words, the world he actually lived in. *The Adventurer*, in particular, concerned itself not with the social order of epic or fiction but with the demonic world of myth and adventure, rooted in shamanism and magic, and with the modern writers who explored the same spiritual terrain.

In the games he played in conversation, Paul often cast me as a reader of novels, content to live in society, and as a family man— stable, rational, domestic—the good son, husband, father—all the things he felt he could never be. In later years, when he had become all those things himself, when he lived by a routine as unvarying as that of Immanuel Kant, he said he once had been amazed that we had ever become friends, since I reminded him of everything he had run off to Paris to escape. This was one of the few times I was mildly hurt by something Paul said. *I* certainly didn't see myself as an anchor of stability, though I much preferred densely textured social novels, full of intricate human motives, to the boyish fantasies of adventure fiction. (This was why I learned so much from Paul's books: they delved into a tradition that had scarcely interested me.) Neither was I a nice Jewish boy from Brooklyn, though I was still Jewish enough to find Paul's involvement with Muktananda, the Indian guru, faintly distasteful, if not downright laughable. ("Isn't this the most perfectly realized human being you've ever seen?" he once asked, showing me a picture of the brown-bellied swami. "What about Muhammad Ali?" said I, grinning.) Yet I grudgingly relished the essay he wrote about it in *Three Journeys* for the way he remained outside the experience, objective and dispassionate, even in describing exactly how he had lost his head.

This was a subject on which I no doubt said some hurtful things myself, for we never could discuss Muktananda without some trace of mockery slipping into my voice. My early years of orthodox Judaism had made me allergic to orthodoxy of any kind, certainly to the idolatrous idea of abasing one's will before that of another man. Yet after the initial fascination, which was virtually total—an "emotional avalanche," he called it—Paul managed some-how to recover his balance, to put "Baba" on the back burner even after he'd become a key publicist for the man's teachings. He even convinced me that this guru was very much what one made of him —a figure of transference rather than mindless adulation, whose message was to live your own life, to attend to your real needs and desires whatever they were. For Paul's Western mind Muktananda offered an alternative form of psychoanalysis, with a message of self-acceptance that was sensible and this-worldly.

In his introduction to a collection of Muktananda's writings he edited in 1976, Paul wrote that even on first impression "his very presence seemed to cry out that there was no spiritual life separate from a worldly life; that the activities of one's normal existence, the pains and pleasures, tragedies and successes, were the one field which every man ploughed and reaped according to his acts. The field was spiritual or worldly as one chose to make it." This sounds like pop psychology. In a sense, adherence to Muktananda offered spirituality and inner peace on the cheap. It asked no one to give up his daily life or worldly wealth to follow him to his ashram in India. In fact, more like a classic shrink than a Chassidic *rebbe*, Muktananda rarely told anyone what to do; he merely urged them to find their own bent. What a perfect message for Emerson's American offspring!

It was typical of Paul to make a circuitous journey to an exotic source to uncover such simple truths. Paul never surrendered his personal autonomy in this process, but the *idea* of doing so, the feeling that for moments at least he *had* done so, was deeply gratifying to him. Starting with *The Heresy of Self-Love* and continuing through all his books, self-creation was Paul's great theme, but, as *Three Journeys* showed, it was also his deepest source of anxiety. *The Heresy of Self-Love* and *The Adventurer* were a diptych on the antinomian strain in Western culture, the need to escape from the cities of men—from their rational as well as social constructions, from all the prescriptive demands of religion, family, and citizenship. In *The Adventurer,* a more straightforward, solidly grounded critical performance than its predecessor, the exemplary figures for such an escape from social bonds stretched from Odysseus and Gilgamesh to T. E. Lawrence and Malraux, including one chapter on "the flight from women"—an essential feature of adventure stories—and another, "The Great Escape," on the self-enclosed world of the Gothic novel, which was like the horrific underside of the kind of social fiction Paul disliked.

But in *Three Journeys* Paul shows that the adventurer's self-making, his "automythology," is a flimsy bridge over the chasm of his own vulnerability. The dark side of the earth, which the adventurer explores, is also the dark side of himself, the horror and emptiness of Mr. Kurtz, the weakness inherent in ordinary human needs and heightened by the fear of death. In Muktananda Paul seemed to find a form of selfhood that was an emptying-out of self, a relief from the pressure of narcissism and egotism. In the guru he saw a man who had "surpassed his personal ego by replacing it with the steadiness and needlessness of his master, to whom he has surrendered his thoughts." What Baba tells him is that "your goal —inner autonomy—is correct, but your method—defensive egotism—is wrong, because no matter how good you become at defending yourself, you'll never conquer your own vulnerability." Muktananda seemed to offer him the promise of reversing, yet paradoxically fulfilling, the whole subjective pattern of his life and work.

This self-indenture to Muktananda was the most spectacular of Paul's departures, the only one that threatened for a time to alter his personality beyond recognition. Ironically, it occurred after he had become a far more social being than ever before. After being turned down for tenure at Columbia while spending a sabbatical in France, Paul taught for a year at MIT, during 1970–71, then returned to New York to chair the new comparative literature department at Queens College. I had taken a job at Queens myself a few months earlier, and remembering Paul's isolation at Columbia I wondered whether administration was his cup of tea. In the far less tense atmosphere at Queens, however, a new man emerged, not for the last time—affable, gregarious, shrewd about institutional constraints, and adept at handling the levers of academic power. Especially in those first years, when his department was expanding and bright young teachers could be hired, he managed to do a first-rate job without expending too much time. His writing life prospered. Many of the pieces he did then were hasty and careless—he remarked without boasting that he could review books of poetry while watching the Knicks on TV—but in his many friendships, in the relative calm of the early years of his second marriage, and in his summer world of Paris, the Dordogne, and Venice (a city he never tired of revisiting), Paul appeared to have reached an equilibrium which the convulsions of the mid-70s would soon belie. Muktananda, who seemed at first like another faddish enthusiasm, was the temporary answer to problems I didn't even know he had.

Paul's preoccupation with Muktananda itself became a source of conflict in his life. It was bitterly resented by his wife, who saw part of her bedroom turned into a shrine, and who once even accompanied him to India to confront the powerful rival who had so engrossed her husband's emotional attention. In the first year or two after this redirection of his life, Paul also saw his poetry dry up, as if the practice of meditation had blurred and diluted his inner conflicts. Certainly it was not because he now walked around in a perpetual state of bliss. Far from it: as Paul became a father for the first time at the age of forty, and as his marriage devolved into a desperate attempt to avoid open hostilities, Paul found that the guru's presence had not transformed him as much as he had hoped, that life itself, as long as you continued to live it, had a way of playing tricks on you. The real disappointment came, I think, after 1978, when Paul's illness was first diagnosed, and he found that Baba, much as he still admired him, could not offer him much help in dealing with it. The fear of personal extinction, which Muktananda himself had seemed to overcome, still plagued the sleepless hours of his would-be acolyte, who wrote in one of his last poems, "I don't know if I can bear this suddenly / Speeded up time."

The personal metamorphosis which Paul had failed to achieve in the Sahara Desert or in his relation to Muktananda now took place over a six-year period as a result of his illness. It took years for Paul's friends and family to realize how much he had changed, but long before he died there could be little doubt about it. Though he continued to go to France each summer, this journey was a way of coming home rather than going away, for Paris and the Dordogne were by this time home to him. Like New York, they were places where he could live and write in predictable ways, see people he'd known for a long time, and, in the country especially, work up a healthy sweat that might keep death at bay. His marriage broke up shortly after the discovery of his illness, and he drew closer to his young daughter, Genevieve, from whom he had once been remote. This new role drew him closer to his own family—to his sister and her children, who helped him through the difficulties of fatherhood, and perhaps to the parents he had long since left behind.

The quality of Paul's friendships shifted slowly but definitively. He developed a new kind of interest in other people's lives. Each of his friends imagined he had simply gotten closer to them; only after his death did they realize he had imperceptibly altered his way of knowing everyone. After a time he entered into a difficult but intensely serious love affair with Vikki Stark, who had two young children of her own—a relationship that continued to grow and ended only when he died. I had always assumed that people with serious ailments became more wrapped up in themselves, that terminal illness could only erode or sour one's interest in life. Self-involved earlier, Paul became far less so now. His last years were nothing short of a lesson in life, an evangel of how the self could function in the teeth of its extinction. This never ceased to amaze me, but I didn't really understand it until I read Paul's essay on his illness, which now stands as the concluding part of these memoirs. It shows Paul's singular way of spinning out minute perceptions into general ideas. In the forge of a new self-knowledge, won at terrible expense, even personal tragedy could turn white hot with eloquence:

> Normally we live in a double sphere of consciousness: a near shell reverberating with needs and hopes, full of urgency, heavy with the flesh of our lives; and a far, attenuated hood of thoughts and projects which spin us years into the future where we pretend that there is time. The near shell is tribal and blood-real; the far, attenuated shell is glorious, flimsy; it is man's experiment with immortality without which books would not be written and buildings would not be erected to last centuries. It is the lie of endlessness. . . . I was released into uncertainty. My outer shell of time had been broken; I would never give my thoughts to it again without an undercurrent of disbelief. Only tribal time was real to me, and tribal time was a kind of eternity.

This describes, though it scarcely explains, how Paul was able to live so full a life in his last six years. The adventurer's contempt for the banalities of daily life gave way to a precious feeling for all that was palpable and immediate. Paul never ceased planning remote and ambitious projects. His biography of Whitman, despite the epigrammatic ease of its style, was an enormous labor of research, the patient work of many years, written with the kind of mastery of detail and confident scholarship that had never previously appealed to him. Poems, reviews, and autobiographical prose seemed to flow from his fingertips, and he took a particular delight in reading things aloud to friends.

Never had writing and sociability seemed less in conflict. More than ever, his work seemed written for the voice, conceived rhythmically, and he was its best performer. The world of his early poems, with their somewhat mechanical evocations of death, was bare and grim. But the sense of "speeded-up time" makes his last poems overflow with a sense of dying ripeness that recalls the juncture of death and fruition in Keats's final ode, "To Autumn." In the best of these poems, which Galway Kinnell read at Paul's funeral, a gravely injured farmer looks unblinkingly at his own death:

> "*Ça y'est, cette fois.*" This is it, I know it.
> To know it all deeply; to have it press up
> Like earth-blood out of the crooked old peach tree
> In front of the house, propped up on sticks,
> But nursing its peaches year after year
> Until it seems to hunch lower and want to lie down,
> And the peaches swell with long-cooked sweetness,
> Orange, yellow and pink.

The farmer celebrates the world he is leaving by accepting the principle of death inherent in nature. By adopting the farmer's stance as his own, Paul recreates the pattern of the great Romantic poems of personal crisis and self-recognition, from "Tintern Abbey" and "Dejection" to the odes of Shelley and Keats. Yet Paul's poem is not the least bit embarrassed by such imposing models. Sadly, it took the spectre of death to bring out Paul's full talent as a poet; happily for him and us, he proved equal to the challenge. *Eternity's Woods* is a book to read and reread; its limpid, direct style was a hard-won achievement, the work of the same man who could talk so openly about his illness—or not talk about it, if the conversation took other turns. I'll never forget sitting in Paul's flat high above Riverside Drive, reading one of the many versions of "The River," another Romantic recognition poem. Much of it is addressed to his young daughter, though Paul knew it would be years before she could make much sense of it:

> When my daughter was an hour old, flailing
> In the aseptic glow of the hospital cradle,
> Her eyes squeezed shut, already bruised by light,
> She made thin, rasping sounds,
> As if some creature were trapped behind her gums.
>
> Genevieve, one day
> You will remember someone: a glimpse,
> A voice, telling what I never told
> —What the living never say—
> Because the words ran backward in my breath.

The name brought me up short because Paul, with his curious reticence, almost never mentioned actual people in his poetry; with a sudden chill it hit me that despite Paul's usual optimism about surviving, this was a message in a bottle, a piece of posthumous poetry. Genevieve was the posterity he cared most about. Concern for her future cast a long shadow over his years of illness; for her sake more than his, he grew wild at the thought she might grow up without him. As she matured he began to see the adult already projected in her, and his desperation gradually subsided. In this poem he saw her as still half-formed:

> My daughter comes halfway up my thigh,
> A thin, serious little girl, but already
> She has her secrets. Because her face has no past,
> She is still only partly human. . . .

In *Departures* he writes of the curious mesh between his own fate and the freshness of his daughter's life: "In a peculiar way, my daughter and I were equals; neither of us had any time, and the irony was terrible, for I had lost mine, and she hadn't acquired hers yet. Therefore we had each other." This may seem like a flip remark, yet they really did grow very close.

Paul could spin out epigrams at the edge of an abyss, but this is not what most of his late writing is like. In poems about his Aunt Lil, about observing a friend teaching a class, about his father, his daughter, and above all in a powerful sequence about his old stone house in France, even his verse took on a novelistic immediacy he had once defensively scorned. The prose of his Whitman biography and of these final memoirs is thick with a new social and human density. The mystery of self-creation remains his deepest theme, but now it is enacted against the churning background of Whitman's New York in the 1840s—full of sleazy journalists, politicians, promoters, and phrenologists—of New Orleans at the end of the decade, of the Civil War hospitals; or, in Paul's own case, the student life of Paris in the 1950s and 1960s. This writing was the precise equivalent of Paul's new focus on friendship, family, and everyday life. It was not that the adventurer had been domesticated —his last project on prehistory was as exotic as anything he'd ever undertaken—but "tribal time" had become infinitely richer to him, so that even his own past seemed worth saving.

We cannot doubt—though neither should we exaggerate—the

connection between Paul's final memoirs and the growing shadow of his illness. As Paul came to know that most of his time was behind him, he felt the urge to recapture the most extended of his flights, his decade in France. He had never been quite happy with his summary treatment of this period in *Three Journeys,* and he had often talked of rewriting that section of the book. Above all, he wanted to exorcise a traumatic sexual episode barely mentioned in the earlier work. Paul had already returned to Paris in a number of short autobiographical pieces. Now, without thinking as yet of any new book, he began a piece of sexual autobiography which, to some extent, would enable him to live vicariously in his past while giving it permanent form. But these opening pages are suffused as much with death as with sex: we hear of a dying man who, with Paul's connivance, sleeps with his lover, Claire; a dead friend whose wife—half dead herself—comes to Europe to haunt him; and a penis that plays dead, shattering Paul's brittle sense of himself, leaving him with a feeling of nameless dread that foreshadows the terrors of his illness. When the sexual equipment begins to fail him, the writing can turn comical rather than steamy. Often it brings to mind Henry Miller's Odyssey of sexual boasting and Philip Roth's Iliad of the Jewish boy's anxieties about his penis. (There's even a serio-comic visit to an analyst—who can explain everything, since he's very French.)

The initial immersion in sex, as Paul describes it, is as anonymous and exhilarating as deep-sea diving. It's an escape into another medium, dark, wet, and amorphous, that has no resemblance to his life: it's like an earlier, amphibious stage of the chain of being. Always in flight from the heavy drag of his own identity, Paul pursues sex in a spirit of exalted self-forgetfulness. It is all in keeping with "a life lived in another language, airy and curiously empty, insulated from the gut demands of words uttered since childhood." Shades of Samuel Beckett! But since the boy he was can never wholly be canceled, the sex is etched with anxiety. The self-imagined man is in a state of perpetual arousal with a woman he scarcely knows, but it is a dreamlike, fragile kind of transcendence.

Sexual failure throws him back to images of his boyhood in Brooklyn and an isolation different from the kind he relishes: "I felt numb, alone with my lanky thighs, my belly that was already a little domed, my chest hairs and my clotted curls of pubic hair;

alone with my penis that had retracted and become insignificant, like one of those marginal outcast boys with fat unhealthy faces in my classes in elementary school. We knocked them over without caring, and left them out without noticing." In place of the soaring and diving he seeks, Paul is reduced to the physical limits of his own retracted self, which he can later recall in punishingly apt images: "My penis was playing dead . . . shrinking to the size of a small doughy monument; it was a laughable tombstone, a bit of nameless flesh, sticking out of some grass." Since Paul will soon be returning to New York, this episode marks the end of a ten-year idyll in the weightless space of another culture, another language, free of all childhood associations. A woman "had shattered my laboriously constructed foreignness; she had penetrated my code. The body, it seems, knows only one language."

Paul wrote this at a time when the language of the body was speaking to him of a different kind of failure, telling him of a sleepy, mysterious, almost incomprehensible rebellion in his cells. Yet he never falls into an elegiac tone about the life he has lived. Until the final essay on his illness, written with a self-searching lucidity that takes one's breath away, Paul's memoirs never give the impression of a sick man talking. Yet most of the Paris memoir was written *after* the account of his illness, which had been commissioned as a magazine article but never appeared. As Paul loops back from his last months in Paris to his early years, as he moves from Claire, his sexual Waterloo, to her older sister Arlette, his first serious French lover, and then to his stormy six-year affair with her volatile friend Michèle, a painter, whom he eventually marries, the book turns into one of the most vivid portraits of existentialist and bohemian Paris I have ever read.

Much has been written about the expatriate Paris of the 1920s, from *Exile's Return* to *A Moveable Feast,* from Gertrude Stein to Sylvia Beach, from the novels of Hemingway and Fitzgerald to the antinovels of Henry Miller. But we have no comparable picture of the bohemian/student world of the postwar years, which was still pulsing with seedy vitality when I passed through briefly in 1961 and 1964. Already it was being suffocated by the puritanism and bourgeois conservatism of de Gaulle's Fifth Republic (which was more like a return to the pretensions of the Second Empire, not the old Babel of party squabbles and intellectual ferment). When Paul moved in with Michèle he also linked up with her fierce Communist politics and with her family, which included a father who had died in the Resistance, a mother, Julianne, memorably portrayed here, who "would keep her husband's death alive, not by mourning for him, but by living his sacrifice over again," and good-looking brothers who make Paul feel small, ugly, and American—a man whose "very presence mocked the family myth." The nameless father, another of the dead and dying who play key roles in this memoir, presides over their politics as his picture peers out at their love-making, as a "spirit of high purpose, but also a judge at whose feet our tangled lives struggled helplessly."

From the recesses of the heroic past this mythical father also gazes down at the "silent war" between the impassioned, emotionally exigent daughter and her stony, inaccessible mother, who fascinates Paul as the France he will never quite get to know, a France that exists in and of itself, not simply as a stage of his personal odyssey:

> I felt awe and compassion for stony Julianne who often seemed girlish and unworldly behind her quiet willfulness. During all the years Michèle and I lived together, from our angry beginnings to our improbable marriage five years later, to that cold afternoon only a few months after our marriage when, already separated, I had begun my solitary life and, as a first act of solitude, sat with Julianne in a café on the Rue Soufflot: she asking me, like an old-fashioned matriarch, to give an account of myself; me, tearfully unable to, but feeling a grudging love for this intensely solitary, untalkative woman —during all these years, Julianne would be a sort of Alp in my life: sharp, cold, beautiful, fine, although implacable when Michèle threw herself against her with embraces that were almost assaults, and assaults that were almost embraces.

These passages, quite different from anything in *Three Journeys*, show how Paul could subdue his gift for paradox, epigram, and metaphor into a portraiture of human relationships that had usually eluded him.

As Wordsworth does in his great autobiographical poem *The Prelude*, Paul presents his earlier self as a creature whose deepest bent is toward solitude, whose yearning reaches out toward a kind of cosmic emptiness that echoes the inner vibrations of his own being. "Already, as a small child, I had lived with my foot half out the door, a vacant, elsewhere sort of boy, whose only fullness of feeling came when he was alone. . . ." As in his poems, he recollects a Wordsworthian incident that occurred when he was nine or ten:

> I got out of bed and went down to the basement. The cement floor was covered with a layer of coal dust that was soft and fine to my naked feet. The furnace loomed in a corner, cold and black; it was summer. I took my pajamas off, and felt the cool night air all over my body. My penis rose like a small, thin bone, and the darkness wheeled about me slowly, peacefully, and a wild contentment ran down my legs. After a few minutes, I put my pajamas back on, and went to bed. Such were my moments of true living: cosmic, blank, impersonal.

There are other Wordsworthian touches to this autobiography: a gradual shift from personal history to the politics of the age; the writer's reflections not only on the past but on the very act of recapturing it. The intensity of his youthful appetite for experience made Paul sharply remember almost everything that had happened during his ten-year stay. "Soon virtually every street over a vast area of the Left Bank and parts of the Right Bank, too, contained a multitude of impressions one on top of the other, like emotional transparencies, a trick photography of the mind."

By the time he came to write about it, this palimpsest of memories, this inability to forget, gave the whole period "a curious feeling of unreality," so that these years were remote and present at the same time. Wordsworth described this indelibly in the second book of *The Prelude:*

> A tranquilling spirit presses now
> On my corporeal frame: so wide appears
> The vacancy between me and those days,
> Which yet have such self-presence in my mind
> That, sometimes, when I think of them, I seem
> Two consciousnesses, conscious of myself
> And of some other Being.

Despite his Proustian attention to every wrinkle of private memory and personal association, Wordsworth's aim was to wean himself from solipsism to a communal consciousness, to show the way from love of solitude and nature to love of man. It was the French Revolution that drew his mind away from the Alps, and helped him to see even the Alps in apocalyptic terms. The equivalent for Paul was the Algerian war, which continued to tear France apart even after de Gaulle made peace in 1962, sowing bitterness among those who had put him into office a few years earlier. One of my most chilling memories of Paris in 1961 was the sight of *gendarmes* with submachine guns at many of the Métro entrances, and I well remember the reports of Arab bodies found floating in the Seine, as well as the implacable anger of the *pieds-noirs* who left Algeria and sometimes turned to terrorism.

Paul's involvement with Michèle brought him into the orbit of the leftists and intellectuals who worked for Algerian independence, and even formed underground networks which sheltered FLN agents, at considerable risk. Paul, Michèle, and her family joined a support group and for several months became minor conspirators by taking in an Algerian operative named Daniel. It's hard to know how to take this story, which Paul had already told in some detail in *Three Journeys.* Their life in the flat soon revolves completely around this polite, mysterious guest. The games of love and family warfare give way to a mildly exhilarating sense of revolutionary solidarity. The continued ordinariness of their lives, now dotted by moments of fearful apprehension and comic absurdity, begins to smack of scenes from Conrad's *The Secret Agent,* with its ironic account of the confused motives and methods of amateur conspirators. For his part, Paul, with his longing for adventure, comes to identify with Daniel. "He belonged to an idea, an action": heady stuff for a boy from Brooklyn who has read Malraux. He sees Daniel like himself as a creature of isolation, a fictional character made up by the man himself, as he would later portray Walt Whitman.

When I got to know Paul shortly after his return from Paris, he was in no way a political person, though he became moderately active in protests against the Vietnam war, including the march on the Pentagon, the antidraft demonstrations, and numerous poetry readings against the war organized by Robert Bly. He looked back on his period as an honorary French Communist as a remote oddity, another way of jettisoning the personality he had brought with him to Europe. For all the urgency and justice of the cause, it was the *frisson* of politics that attracted him, the new identity and education it offered. The Algerian revolution provided him with a sense of excitement and high purpose, "although I lived only on the edge of action, a voyeur." He wonders whether "outside of his idea, Daniel too was a voyeur." Only much later does he think it significant that the members of his support group all happened to be Jewish. Paul's account wonderfully conveys the turbulent, murderous, electrically charged atmosphere of Paris during the Algerian struggle, but his own commitment seems curiously literary: a case of the errant self, the wandering Jew, in search of an idea to give it meaning—a quest that would eventually lead Paul back to America, to the Sahara, to India, and to the Dordogne, whose painted caves enclose part of the enigma of prehistoric man.

Even if Paul's political passions remain a question mark—evidence more of a wish to feel committed than of a deeply felt commitment—he gives us a strong evocation of Paris during the Algerian war. Compared to the briefer account in *Three Journeys*, this one has greater personal and social texture—the very qualities Paul was quietly pursuing in his life at the time he wrote it. This becomes evident in *Departures* long before he reaches his belated discovery of the political crisis. Shafts of insight light up his references to his grandfather, whose farm he visited as a child; his father, a precise, taciturn man who, like his son, preferred "empty spaces to the anxiety of relationships"; Anna, the drugged-out widow of his writer friend David, who lives on amphetamines and tells Paul that she too is dead; and Raymond, a benign sage, gradually going blind, who guides Paul through the maze of French literature and politics, and whose knotty integrity and near-anonymity embody something very special in French intellectual life.

Paul devotes some powerful pages to the sheer madness that impelled him to devour all the books around him—an account that reminded me of the terse intensities of Sartre's *Les Mots*. Like Sartre he begins to live in words, plummeting frantically from book to book in search of a second skin. Trying to read through all of French literature when he barely knows the language, he writes, "I felt that I had surreptitiously broken into a building full of unlived-in rooms, corridors and back stairs. . . . I was a burglar in my solitary castle, a cat-man wrestling with words, naturalizing them with an anxious attention that resembled meditation." It is yet another flight from family and self, from some inescapable Brighton Beach of the mind.

Paul's last flight was one that brought him ineluctably home. He researched his final illness with the same galloping thoroughness and clarity with which he read French literature or did research on Whitman or on prehistory. He spoke to doctors all over the country, followed the progress of every form of experimental treatment, and eventually submitted to punishing bouts of chemotherapy. Though we spoke several times a week, I never heard from him when the drugs or his fears had got him down. Always he managed to get on top of them, mastering himself as he'd learned to master so much strange scientific information. A day or two later I might learn that he'd had a bad time, only after it was safely behind him. Then he could once again assess his illness in an open-eyed way, or ignore it completely to carry on with his life.

Gradually, his friends realized that something remarkable was happening, that Paul's behavior had become a quiet example of how to live one's life on borrowed time, without the least assurance of having a future. Paul's great fear was that he had no center that bound together his many passions and enthusiasms. Who could have predicted that in the face of death the center would hold, that Paul would be able to summon up such resources of equanimity and purpose, or that he would reach out to people so nakedly in his life and writing? With great emotional strength and intellectual stamina, he somehow robbed death of its power over him. His mind never became the stricken reflex of his illness. Without trying to do any more than get along or get his work done, he became something of a hero to many of us, a model of how to look death in the face with fear and hope but without panic or illusion, a precious instance of a man who went on conjuring with words the way the rest of us breathed, not from vanity or self-love but out of an elemental need. His writing became so focused and intense that it seemed to feed on the fuel of his own being.

All this is present as a silent undercurrent in Paul's last three books, bright and buoyant as they genuinely are, but it is most nakedly there in some of Paul's last poems and in the amazing final section of *Departures*, where Paul deals directly with his illness as he so often did in conversation. This essay fits a little oddly into the book itself, for it is more a fierce self-examination than a memoir —a piece of writing unique of its kind, in a prose that gives the illusion of pure immediacy, a prose from which all the consolations of rhetoric have been burned away, in which every metaphor strikes home like the simplest truth. In its utter nakedness it is the furthest thing from where his writing life began.

Paul must have asked himself why he had chosen to write this essay, as he must have wondered why he was trying to finish his books. This piece was finally about writing itself, which was the way he had chosen to live and die, and his answer was that "writing was my best self. It was, internalized, the view from my window, or my stone house on a hilltop in southwestern France. It was the cohered tensions of living made deliberate and clear." It was escape too, but also self-reconciliation, the place where his gifts and limitations best came together. Finally, it was a way of living, and a way of living on—a crystallization of the life within. "A work is not a life, but writing is living, and now especially I wanted to live with all my might."

The Paris sections of *Departures* may have been Paul's way of buoying himself up by returning to a past rich with moments that could ignite a brilliant language of memory. But this last departure was something indescribably brave. The reveries of adventure, like the masks of "automythology," have been left behind, along with the vacant "place behind the bush." Had it appeared during his lifetime, as he expected it would, this essay would have marked him in his readers' eyes as a sick man, in his own words as "a member of a heavy tribe, those who walked minute by minute into a blankness which ate the near distance." Appearing now, it becomes a posthumous marker of the final quality of his self-recognition and the words he found to give it enduring shape and life.

MORRIS DICKSTEIN

EDITOR'S NOTE

PAUL ZWEIG was preparing the manuscript of *Departures* for publication at the time of his death. Parts I and III were more or less finished. Much of Part II was in a revised typescript, but the final section (pages 166–194) was still in its original draft in Zweig's handwriting. Dorothy A. Riesman, Zweig's secretary, C. K. Williams, his literary executor, and I have attempted to establish an appropriate text from this draft.

TED SOLOTAROFF

The names and identifying details of certain people who intimately figured in Zweig's life have been changed or removed.

PART ONE

I

I DON'T remember how I met Claire for the second time. She was
living in a maid's room at the end of a hallway lit by a single bare
light bulb, on the Boulevard Richard Lenoir near the Bastille.
The room was tall and narrow, with suitcases piled on top of each
other and a flowered sheet hanging from some nails to form a
closet. She had a hot plate, a few books, an overexposed photograph
of her mother and sister pinned to the wall; it was more like a base
than a place to live in. I'm pretty sure we never made love there.
Mostly I remember the contrast between its tall clutter, always a
little damp and chilled, and Claire's almost childish grace, her
innocence even, or so it appeared to me then.

I remember the trestle table at a restaurant on a hilly street
behind the Pantheon. The paper tablecloths were covered with
purple rings from the wineglasses. There were wicker baskets filled
with rounds of baguettes, and swirls of sawdust on the floor. Voices
echoed harshly from the walls and the low ceiling. Claire wore a
plaid dress that had been washed so often it looked flimsy and
faded, as if without any effort she could shrug herself out of it and
become naked. She was the sort of woman who often seemed half
out of her clothes.

This was our first date, and we must have had a lot to say to
each other, but I don't remember any of it. For after a few helpless
minutes, we seemed to be falling into each other's faces, feeling
under the table for our knees and skin, like two blind men. Claire
was an actress, I knew that much about her. She carried around
purple Larousse pamphlets of Racine or Marivaux. There was a
fullness in her voice; a kind of low throaty echo, full of timbres and
trills. It was a voice full of carnality, like a dress flopping open for

35

a minute to reveal the crushed tip of a nipple, and the bone deeply hidden between the breasts.

For weeks after that, we made love almost anywhere we could get our clothes off. In my bedroom on the Rue des Ecouffes, over-looking the orange chimney pots and gray patches of crazy-quilt walls of the Jewish neighborhood; in my car on a windy empty industrial street near the Canal Saint Martin; on last year's crisp leaves in the overgrown park of the Abbaye of Royaumont, north of Paris; on my narrow balcony late at night, jammed against the forged iron grate, and looking out at the lit dome of Sacré Coeur in the distance. When we made love, Claire would seem to bend into a depth, holding her breath and reaching, and then, with a helpless gulp, find what she had been reaching for, and expand. At that moment, I felt that I had spooned something rich and sweet from inside a deep cup and drunk it, and had become her as she had become me. It was that interchange of selves I reached for; to cast myself away and receive in my place another me, a woman-self whose body took in, took in endlessly.

I never found out much about Claire. She seemed to have no ties, no recent past. In the morning she would smile at me, a sort of tremolo at the corners of her mouth, and kiss me goodbye. In the late afternoon, I would pick her up at her room, or we would meet at a café near the Palais Royal, or in the Luxembourg Gardens near the pond where children in blue school uniforms shoved model boats out onto the gray water. She would be waiting for me in a metal lounge chair, with her acting books and her full twisty back that loomed through whatever she wore.

Claire was the younger sister of my first lover in Paris, ten years before. Her older sister, Arlette, had been educated at a Catholic convent school, the famous academy of Les Oiseaux; sin and guilt were companionable traits in her, and they gave her an icy fascination for me. She would come to my hotel room on the Rue de Tournon as to a flaying, and I would fall at her feet, awed that this saintly woman was willing to take her clothes off and get into my bed with a hop, permitting me to make a kind of reflexive love to her, full of unconsciousness. For a few weeks in the spring of 1957, Arlette had even moved in with me; she had brought a paper bag, with some clothes, her vaginal jelly and a copy of Simone Weil. We had been chilly lovers, befuddled by intimacy; we rarely even held hands. Then, weary of my all-American good will and my devotion to doing the right thing, if only she would be so good as to point it out to me, she left me.

In those days I had a brown motorcycle that I rode all over France. During my summer peregrinations, I visited Arlette at her parents' chalet on the outskirts of Megève in the Haute-Savoie. She seemed happy to see me, and for a few days we climbed up and down the flowering slopes above the treeline. Her younger sister, Claire, was a skinny kid of thirteen or fourteen, younger to me, a rigid and fearful twenty-one, than she would have been ten years later when I was able to recognize the nymphet allure of very young girls as one of nature's miracles. I hardly noticed her. But mostly I remember her stepfather, a man cured by old age to a length of gristle and bone. He walked slightly bent over, as if lost in himself. The girls and he seemed like strangers to each other. I recognized Arlette's superior vacancy as a flow of renunciation that came to her from this superbly solitary mountain man. When I left, Arlette, ever my nettle and my daimon, watched me sputter down the looping road, appearing to see not me vanishing behind a hill but some chilly tomorrow full of sacrifice.

Arlette renounced me, but she haunted me. A year later, she renounced me again, introducing me to her best friend, Michèle, whom I lived with for six years and eventually married. And now here was her kid sister, Claire, not a nymphet any longer, but a woman who had acquired mystery. Her Paris was a map of sexual memories. She lived for that grateful gulp at the bottom of her flesh; and I adored her. The loops of time spin strangely. Arlette had ruled over ten years of my life. Her sister was a sexual goddess, but she had Arlette's smile: an enigma of withheld amusement that was a fault line in time, making me teeter, as if Claire, like Arlette a decade before, were disappearing in my arms.

Arlette's smile had contained the irony of a partial saint; Claire's, however, contained erotic corridors, sheets thrown back in small rooms; a world of chandeliers hanging from splotchy ceilings, of tree branches spinning in horizontal wheels over a woman lying on leaves with a man heavy upon her. There was something abstract about her; she was a tremolo of a person, flexible and naked. I didn't question her; didn't think of penetrating beyond her spry allure of glossy brown hair, slim freckled forearms, and her long-legged stride that swung along beside me as if the world were watching. She had freaky leaps of tenderness; she liked to put her hand under my pants while we walked, and play down along my back, into the cleft of my buttocks. There seemed to be nothing she didn't know about sex: once, she smeared honey on her cunt for me to lick off; her spontaneity embarrassed me while it drove me wild; it made me feel foolish and stiff, a prude whose body had been kidnapped by the total erotic attention of a ruthless, tender, tricking, and inventive woman.

Almost immediately we began the crazy plans of lovers. Claire's room was left to its dampness. She arrived one morning, as her sister had arrived ten years before, carrying a shopping bag full of underwear and spring dresses, and her Larousse pamphlets. I was planning to go back to the United States in a few months. Ten years had passed in my inadvertent exile, and my past had grabbed hold of me. As an American I was still the inhabitant of a large country. Such a person needs more space; even his mistakes have muscle and scope. When he thinks, he needs to run out line without snagging it on borders. I had seen expatriate Americans in Paris, fugitives from racism or McCarthyism, who had become over the years diminished and shrill, as if some essential nutrient of their being had been removed. I didn't want that to happen to me. Besides, I had begun to crave my own language. When I heard it spoken, by strangers, I found myself aching for its elaborate vowels and thick consonants. I could feel my lips pout when I spoke French, which I had mastered with disturbing ease as if, deep down, I possessed a mobility that could thrust me into any character but the abandoned one of a boy born in Brooklyn who, in his flight from home, had gone too far; who always seemed to go too far.

My apartment on the Rue des Ecouffes was furnished with imitation Empire lamps and an Oriental rug worn to a kind of mud color. There was an enameled gas heater of florid design. The wallpaper, of tiny multicolored flowers, had long since faded to something like late autumn. It was a place out of another century. Zola and Balzac prowled in its faded décor. In winter, the smoke from dozens of chimneys rose like skywriting from the adjoining buildings. My bed sagged in the middle, and that's where Claire and I ended up in the morning, rolled into the gulch of the old feather mattress. Yves Montand used to sing an old folk song about a bed so broad and deep that a river flowed through the middle of it. All the king's horses couldn't cross it, or drink it up, but the lovers played solemn love games there, and slept or made love until the end of the world. My mattress with its deep crevice was our river. There Claire gulped with amazement; there I was a spectator to my body's nervous ability to engender this quicksand of a trance which drew me down, and yet—was I imagining it?—seemed to exclude me. Claire, freckled and wild, was like a chick, its mouth unhinged and gaping for a worm. I deposited the worm over and over again; I was inexhaustible. I wondered if I would become dehydrated from loss of body fluids.

One morning I woke up with the impression that I was locked under a thickness of glass. The impression was so strong, I could virtually see the glass a few inches from my face. It was like a waking dream; I *saw* my feelings instead of experiencing them, as if my kidnapped body had excreted from it this secret of sidereal space, this smothered distance, which now flowered into one of those overused images the psyche loves: a glass dome. I had become a man in a cage. When I spoke, I was tempted to raise my voice so as to be heard on the other side. I was making breakfast in the kitchen, while Claire showered in a tin stall next to the stove. The glass was so thick it seemed to have a double surface, reflecting yet also transparent. I felt a little foolish, wondering how to get out again, yet vaguely aware that our sexual play had somehow generated this dazed place of glass, hermetic and fictive, but almost real enough to touch.

When Claire stepped out of the shower, I saw her body through the glass—a sculpture of pink dream, with a modest black patch under her belly—and wondered with a surge of panic if she too could see this stolid surface between us. For weeks now the plan had been for her to come to New York with me at the end of the summer. She was going to go down to the embassy to see about a visa. She would learn English of course so as to pursue her career as an actress, now with an irresistible accent. She would be one of those French sweethearts, innocent but seductive, a child of manners. Although the vision faded after a few minutes, I kept glancing gingerly to see if it was still there. I felt abashed and wary. I wasn't used to these mental events that seemed to say: Don't worry, there are more surprises to come. I didn't like these surprises. I preferred to think of my mind as a serviceable recording and filing system. But here was proof that the mind had generative powers of its own, like a lizard growing back its tail. I suppose I should have guessed that the fictive glass and my inexhaustible penis were part of the same surprise. Claire had bewitched my tail, and it kept on growing back.

Before I met her my life with women had been a campaign of marches and countermarches. I had lived with Michèle for six years, and then, in a kind of daze, I had let things go sour between us. Let them go sour! Had watched her get involved with a painter until, almost imploring me to stop her, she left me for him. I didn't know how to stop her. I was frozen, glued to the spot. In the months that followed, I observed the aloneness, like a never-before-known space, swirl around me: a world of furnished rooms, late-night cafés; classic old movies on the Rue Champollion, with the waiting line strung out along the sidewalk listening to buskers bawling out folk songs and whanging on their guitars. My life resembled a montage of night streets, nameless tensions, women met in movies, bookshops and cafés.

My nose sniffed out solitudes amid the walls of used books in my friend George Whitman's bookstore across from Notre Dame or in a café that stayed open late on the Rue Saint Jacques, full of drug pushers and insomniacs. It was an adventure, but joyless, confused, as if my penis and I had different aims in life, which put me at a disadvantage, for I didn't know what I wanted but my penis knew unerringly what it wanted. It fished in the pink neon of the Café des Deux Ponts, and left me, after a groping and clumsy night, to say goodbye. I was bad at saying goodbye: it caught in my throat and made me anxious, as if I were doing mysterious harm to this person whose name I was already forgetting. So it had gone for almost three years. On late afternoons, when the sky matched the mottled gray of the buildings on the Rue des Ecouffes and the cries of vendors drifted into my room along with the sharp, arguing voices of the street, inhabited now by North African Jews, a people who lived at the top of their lungs between the grocery store, the Tunisian café and the storefront synagogue—on those late after-noons, I would think about the night hours that were coming; the streets of the Latin Quarter filled with couples; the cafés with their neon embroidery. And a feeling of wounded impatience would come upon me. I would start calling old phone numbers, new phone numbers; numbers that had been exhausted but now revived, as if my penis had detected some new angle of interest.

Into this nervous shuffling of numbers had come Claire. I don't remember how. She didn't have a telephone. Our ending has wiped out our beginning. She simply appeared on that wicked evening in the doorway of her cluttered room on the Boulevard Richard Lenoir, a slender freckled girl with chestnut hair and a tremulous withholding smile. She wore a faded frock, and she was not the skinny child I had last seen nine years before. She made the clothes wilt from my body. She was pure heat. It was the damndest thing. All I could do was fall toward her kamikaze body.

It was unreal to start with. Maybe Claire was simply poaching on her older sister's past, taking revenge on Arlette's monopoly of saintliness by becoming the family nymph. She was an actress, remember that. She could spin out attitudes. And I was an innocent American. Under it all, I was frightened at the sexual peeling away that rendered me voiceless and made me vanish.

One morning Claire received a phone call from "some friends" she had given my number. By now we were pretty much living together. Her room had become little more than a letter drop. I had a feeling that Claire had done this before. She moved so easily between the parts of her life that I hardly noticed the bold strokes of the separations. I simply assumed that my part was the center, and the others were left over from some previous life I never asked about. I was too fascinated, too helplessly tangled in her sexual charm, to allow her a past.

The phone was on the mantel of a blocked-off fireplace in my living room. Claire stood beside it, leaning her head against the receiver. She wore a pale cotton shirt and corduroy slacks. There was a kind of waxen shine about her, as if the gravity of her thoughts had made her transparent. She left after the phone call; but there were other calls; men's voices asking for Claire in grave, lilting accents, solemn, urgent, a little desperate. These men had rights to Claire, their voices were saying. She received the messages as if she were receiving blows, and became more waxen.

She became childlike, grave. Our love-making became slow. She reached for ledges and depths of the river that flowed in the crevice of our bed but could not cross it or drink it up. Her sexual swimming caught me. I swam harder, while she plunged beneath me to the thick jelly at the bottom, and gulped and became real.

Several days passed, and then she told what the phone calls were about. The year before, she had become friends with a group of political exiles from South America. She hadn't seen them for some time, but now they were trying to get in touch with her. One of the group had just found out that he had lung cancer. The doctors wanted to operate, but he wouldn't give his consent. He seemed to have given up, preferring death to hope with its nightmare of uncertainty. Now his friends were trying to find a way to give him a taste for life again, *le goût de vivre*. They thought Claire could help, if she would go to him, talk to him.

"I can't do it. I won't do it."

She sat in a stiff armchair facing the *portes-fenêtres*—the window-doors—and the narrow balcony that ran around my apartment. The windows were open, and the slanting line of sunlight cut across the balcony. It was a cool May morning. Trails of smoke rose from the orange chimney pots that were bunched together like the chromatic reeds of a flute of Pan. She seemed bewildered, angry. A man was dying, and she was being asked to pull him back from the edge; not to save him, but to give him a new kind of pain: hope, the will to go on living when life was exhausted in him.

I sat on the ledge of the window trying to understand Claire's anger and her panic. Waxen and quiet, her mouth contracted, at last she gave in. For what could she do? How could she not go to this man? I managed not to see what I suppose was plain enough. The man had been Claire's lover. She had left him, and now she was with me. Yet she was no more mine, probably, than she had been his a year before. Claire lived lightly, floating into and out of men's lives. She lived by her men; she lived by me, but gave me only her disposable self.

I'm saying more than I knew at the time, but I must have known something; must have sensed, at least, that Claire was panicked less by the thought of death—what could a twenty-three-year-old woman glowing with health and sex know of death?—than by an ugly, heavy call to become real; to stop her weightless floating and retrace her steps deliberately, accepting the weight of what was being asked of her.

A few days later I drove to the Latin Quarter with her, and sat in a café at the Carrefour de l'Odéon while she went up to his room in a residence hotel around the corner. I felt a nerveless indifference, trying to repress the thought that a man was dying in a hotel room around the corner and that Claire was bringing him *le goût de vivre*, packaged in her delicious body; that maybe while I sat there he was taking it, letting go of his despair for a day, an hour, so that life would flood forward in him again, with or without his consent.

An hour later, Claire crossed the street and stood beside my table. She wanted to leave right away. She seemed to be holding her breath as we walked to my car.

"Drop me off at home," she said.

We drove across Paris, circled the verdigrised pylon in the middle of the Place de la Bastille, and turned into the wide empty boulevard where Claire's building was located. Claire hummed quietly to herself and looked out the car window, yet she seemed to be struggling, almost in pain. Neither of us wanted to talk, and our silence filled the car as it rattled over the cobbles, and darted with neat, insectlike stabs through the traffic.

Ignorance can be a tool; lack of feeling a kind of receptacle for feeling. I have known little, and then, all at once, I have known too much. For example, I knew that my life was being wrenched into a new form that afternoon, sitting in my car in front of Claire's two-story gray building on the Boulevard Richard Lenoir. Suddenly she frightened me; I frightened myself. A chain of events was beginning that I seemed to have been waiting for all my life.

That night we rolled in the hollow of my feather mattress. We seemed to be under water; the shadows shimmered on the wall, like high-water marks. My bed thumped against the wall, as Claire reached ever deeper for her gulp of release. I had never understood how demanding a woman's orgasm was, how fragile. I nursed it, called it to me with sucked-in breaths.

At the same time I was thinking that a man was dying. What was his name? I imagined him taller and older than I was; not a boy, not always out of his element. There is no death, only me dying, says a character in one of Malraux's novels. I coaxed Claire's body, but my penis and I hardly seemed connected. Something had come between Claire and me. It resembled indifference, but was not; it was as if, internally, each of us had become too busy for the other.

A few days later, I read in the *Herald Tribune* that a friend of mine had died—of lung cancer too. He was a novelist whose books often had a radical slant. One of his novels had even dealt with a revolutionary group in Latin America. This too would have a bearing on what followed. The mind doesn't accept coincidences; it refuses to believe that two similar events can occur randomly, so

43

it casts them into shadows on its wall that become connected and in this case malevolent.

I had been reading the paper in an empty classroom at the school I taught at, when I came across the item, a short paragraph in the obituaries. I knew that David had been seriously ill, but in those days I didn't think of even serious illnesses as being fatal. Suddenly death was working overtime in my life. I tried to remember David's voice, his walk. I saw him in a bathing suit on his terrace in New York, a little chubby, a little manic, but always soft-spoken and incredibly kind. I realized that I didn't know what it meant for someone to be dead. It was so peculiar. There was no place for death, yet it came by subtraction. Someone wasn't there, and would never again be there. He wasn't on a trip, or living in some other city. Gradually the strata of memory images which had been his substance within us become blurred and begin to crumble until the images seem like isolated forms of unknown origin. It would take time for my memories of David to absorb this peculiar fact, that they weren't substitutes any longer for my friend who lived in New York, ready to be scattered at any moment by his actual presence. Now the whole burden of his being lay with them, and already they were tired; it was a burden they couldn't sustain.

2

THAT afternoon, Claire and I talked about my dead and her dying friend. We stood leaning against the wrought-iron grill of the balcony outside my living-room window. Montmartre peeked above the rooftops; across the street a lattice of heavy beams held up the side of a building. It was as if a distance had broken in on us. Until now death had been a remote game; a kind of hide-and-seek of youth. But now it was all around us; I saw it in the flat white gleams of the sun on the rooftops which made me feel vulnerable, as if suddenly my body were in an element beyond its control. Claire's mouth had become thin; she seemed to be smiling, but without pleasure; and again, as so often, I saw her sister: private, inflexible. There was a kind of childish willfulness about her. For several days now, the phone calls had stopped. I don't think I actually asked myself if Claire had visited her dying friend again. I didn't want to think about him. I wanted to will him away, make him disappear, and I think she did too. But now there was David; again, death had come between us. "I don't even know what I'm feeling. Look out at the rooftops," I said. "It's not grief; more disbelief, I think, as if dying were a dirty trick. It's absurd, suddenly I can't understand why everyone isn't dying. I mean, so many things can go wrong."

There was a look of distaste on Claire's face. She was angry. She liked to think the body was something you could always fix. The shopping bag when she moved in had been full of drugs and Oriental powders. She loved to read the sheet of clinical data that came in my boxes of pills and suppositories and colored syrups.

She went back inside, and when I followed her, a few minutes later, her mood had changed. She was fingering her blouse, covering her breasts absent-mindedly. She smiled lazily, as if to bring an end to our conversation.

Claire and I usually fucked more than we talked, and we did it now. She unbuttoned her pants, and lifted her sweater over her head. Again she was sad and slender, mute, giving but imperious. And I swelled inside her. We'd done this so often in the weeks since we had met. Yet it still seemed so incomplete, so perilous. There was a freckle on the head of my penis, which I called my one-eyed bandit; but it saw nothing, it dived and was blind. And now, as we made love, I felt my mind lift away, as if under the pressure of a gas. My erection seemed to freeze and then, like ebbing water, to recede. At first it was imperceptible; from my interior perch it seemed not to be happening. I worked harder, but it was useless. Claire looked up at me, her chestbones visible between her breasts, her hair stuck to her forehead by sweat. She seemed hurt as she dragged herself up against the headboard. I don't think I understood right away. We lay on the slope of my bed, barely touching, vast between us a distance that seemed alternately an illusion and an abyss. Claire spoke softly, with a tone of self-control in her voice.

"Don't worry, ça arrive; things like that happen."

A word hung between us that I tried not to think about, but it insinuated itself into my mind and made me nauseous: *impotent.* As we lay in the flashy afternoon light that filtered through the orange curtain, Claire seemed unconcerned, almost playful, as if letting me know that she was an experienced woman who knew all about the eccentric penises of men. But an anxious solitude possessed me. I felt numb, alone with my lanky thighs, my belly that was already a little domed, my chest hairs and my clotted curls of pubic hair; alone with my penis that had retracted and become insignificant, like one of those marginal outcast boys with fat unhealthy faces in my classes in elementary school. We knocked them over without caring, and left them out without noticing. But they were always around, wanting to play if only we would let them. And when they tripped over their feet, we didn't even snigger, because they didn't exist; or maybe because they did exist, with their thick glasses and their inexpressive bodies, because they were what we weren't, we who horsed around and were strong. They were our loneliness, they were the secret knowledge that we too were probably lopsided and hurt. And this gave them a power which we never acknowledged or referred to. As they hopped along the sidelines, they drove us a little wild; they were the salt of our games.

As we lay beside each other in the bed, I tried to be as unconcerned as Claire, but my body flickered with uncontrollable sensation. Several times I became hard, but it didn't last, and I was thrown back into my solitude, haunted by a word that was like a sentence pronounced long ago: *impotent.* I was the boy who couldn't play, the one who hadn't been fooled by those hundreds of erections in the living rooms of my girlfriends and the bedrooms of my lovers; in my own bed or in the bathroom masturbating; or wherever I had snuck off as a boy to read *God's Little Acre, Tobacco Road,* or *Topper.* I hadn't been fooled by all those spry liftings, all those proddings.

We tried again for several days, afternoon and evening, but the result was the same. My penis was playing dead; it saluted David and the unknown South American by shrinking to the size of a small doughy monument; it was a laughable tombstone, a bit of nameless flesh, sticking out of some grass. One day I came home from work and found Claire standing silhouetted against the window in the living room. It was an extraordinary picture: the afternoon sun brightening the ancient facade of the building directly across the street; a slice of sky indented with chimneys and slanting zinc roofs. Claire, naked to the waist, was half turned to outline the cheerful tilt of her breasts and nipples. Already the top button of

46

her pants was loose, her hand played inside the waist. She smiled thoughtfully, and her lips looked thick and full. Everything about her was slow, unspoken. She wasn't offering me only sex, she was offering me life. I dropped my briefcase and started to get undressed. This was strong medicine. It was also pure theater and I was the audience, me, and the fanciful other strangers whom Claire seemed to conjure up, with her body and her marvelous face. My underpants hung around one ankle. Claire smelled of perfume, her mouth tasted of toothpaste; nothing had been left to chance. She sank against me with a light, sagging pressure, and my penis sprang up like a soldier. Alone it stood above the trenches calling out, Here, you bastards, here! The horizon, the enemy guns; my window, with the rooftops and the facing curtains in strong light. But by the time we reached the bed, I could feel a premonitory deadness. Already. The soldier was crawling back into the trenches without firing a shot, but he had felt the pressure of death flowing toward him: a man without a name, dying in a cheap hotel room, the faded flower pattern of the wallpaper, a small sink in a corner with a *douche* next to it; dusty lace curtains like mine; maybe a linoleum floor, with a small polyester rug next to the bed; the bed sagging, rented beds always sagged in France. There would be a pile of political tracts and newspapers. Maybe his window faced onto a *passage* with a couple of artisans' shops in it: a metal worker's, a plumber's storeroom. I knew that *passage*. Or maybe he looked out onto the Rue de Buci, reverberating with the voices of the market. I could see everything, but I couldn't see him, the man Claire had fed life to, *le goût de vivre,* as she was feeding it to me now.

Suddenly the accumulated failure of the past days stifled me; I had trouble breathing. A wild anxiety raced through my stomach and legs. Claire gave a loud laugh, and I looked up at her. She was sitting on the edge of the bed with her knees spread apart, angry or maybe merely contemptuous. I understood that this afternoon had been the final test and that I had failed. Perhaps she was humiliated, or even scared, because my impotence had wiped out the bed, the trick of forgetting. She looked like an irritated boy.

"Mon dieu, que c'est pénible," she said in a pinched voice. "Well, I'm not going to lie here while your prick makes up its mind. What's going on in that head of yours? Your problem is that you think too much."

I could hear her phrases: they were like empty boxcars rattling along a track. But who was I to say? As she walked around the room picking up her clothes, she flaunted herself ironically, glancing over to where I sat, pulled up against the headboard, still naked (what did I have to hide?), as if to make sure I was watching. Again I realized how little Claire and I had to say to each other. We had been intimate, but we were strangers. I watched her pull her jeans on, and tuck her breasts into their drooping cups. Her movements made me wince. By now I had gotten a pair of shorts on. We were in the living room. Claire went around stuffing her things into a bag. I followed her around the room. "I'm sorry; I don't understand what's happening," I muttered like one of the damned.

Claire took her time leaving. She stalked about the room, humming to herself. Then she started to sing an obscene song, at first softly and then in a loud voice. She stood with her hands on her hips and bawled it out. In a castle in Brittany, Queen Anne fiddled with her cunt, tralee trala. She got peasants, blacksmiths and the village idiot to do it to her; she got dogs, stags and a snake to do it to her, tralee trala. It was one of those ballads full of lugubrious rhymes that medical students sing in the *salle de garde* of hospitals when they're on night duty. It was an assault, an obscene onslaught, ruthless and strange. I felt that Claire my lover had become a killer, malicious and spiteful. I accepted the change, almost welcomed it, as an appropriate response to my failure. It occurred to me dimly that Claire was a little crazy, and should be spanked, but there was something about her wildness that transfixed me; I almost admired her.

At last she clicked the door shut, with ironic solicitude, and I was alone. The apartment looked shabby in the slanting light. I could see dust on all its surfaces. The fake Empire lamps on the mantel seemed homely and out of place. It was an appropriate setting for the anxiety that quivered inside me like the physical hysteria of someone who is falling from a great height—life is speeding up, in an instant you will be dead.

Claire hadn't said anything about coming back. Did I want her to? I felt like an invalid, a man with a fractured back.

I have a photograph of me taken only a few years before this. I am staring off to the side, my face expressionless yet somehow tense. I have a crew cut, and my clothes hang loosely off my hips and shoulders, as if the person in the photograph isn't aware that he has a body. He gives the appearance of a sort of strength, but it is unconscious, without experience or wisdom. His strength seems to keep everyone out, even the camera. The photograph disturbs me because, looking at it now, I seem to see where it all came from. I see the old man in the young man; the squelching of strong feelings; a life squeezed into a small space, like a man floating over a Hieronymus Bosch landscape in a transparent balloon.

Claire kept calling me on the phone. Sometimes she simply abused me. Other times she wanted me to pick her up at her room. We would go out to eat and then sit in my car in front of her building. She seemed to be afraid to go in alone. She needed company, but the sight of me drove her wild. She sang dirty songs in the car and slapped her knee, like an army sergeant.

As the days passed, I went to sleep with my anxiety and woke up with it. I had the numbing feeling that I had been waiting for this all my life: until now I had been a pretender, but this was real. I tried to talk about it to a few friends: the impotence, the dead and dying men, Claire's suddenly vicious behavior.

But Claire had become unreal—a sour little boy. Sometimes her face would be thin and tight, and I'd think: She's going to cry. But she never did. The two of us were like scorpions, except that my stings were passive, apologetic. I had no stinger, I was impotent. After a while Claire's calls became less frequent, and we saw less of each other. As we did, my anxiety began to lose substance. It became more like actual pain.

I called up a couple of former girlfriends, and explained what was happening: I needed reassurance. Would they come over, and make some friendly love?

"O.K.! Tomorrow afternoon is great; I'll be there after lunch."

They came on many afternoons, as devoted as nuns. They were happy when my penis heated up. The bed too was happy, creaking and groaning, and the white sky, the rooftops with their slopes, and angles, the chimney pots, the voices of the street five stories below. But in my bright room under the eaves, I discovered that even nuns, even friendly girls happy to be of service, couldn't allay my anxiety, which had become inviolate and abstract. In ways I couldn't grasp, I was still a sexual fool, a partial man. My personality had become unraveled.

I taught school early every morning, and the classroom of intense, shabbily dressed boys, simmering with sexual mischief, drove me a little wild. After lunch, I wrote for a while, and this was

the only time when, for an hour or two, I felt normal and whole.
The wound stopped hurting. Apparently my pen was dependably
erect.

Early one evening I met Claire on the iron bridge between the
Ile Saint Louis and the Ile de la Cité. We leaned over the railing
and watched a long barge slide underneath us. The water was
shining and gray. Lovers walked along the water's edge or stood
jammed together in the angles of the huge river wall under the iron
boat rings. Everything around us was in movement: the slapping
waters, the lights, the people, the clouds swooping and tumbling
overhead. Claire wore one of her flimsy dresses. But there was no
sexual playfulness now, only a hurt preoccupation, tinged with
irritation.

Neither of us wanted to be there that evening, but we still
functioned desultorily as a couple. As we had been bound together
in love, we were bound now in destructiveness and fear. This time
we decided not to go to dinner. Claire had a headache, she said, and
preferred to go home. She spoke without emphasis, looking straight
ahead, as if her words were a nervous reflex. That was fine with me.
We stood for a few minutes more, and then said good night.

I never saw Claire again. She dropped out of my life completely. I have never heard news of her. Years later, on a visit to
Paris, I bumped into her sister Arlette, back from Africa, but,
incredibly, forgot to ask about Claire. That evening of gray lights
and water, with fast clouds overhead, removed her from my life;
although it did not cure my wounded self and my mysteriously
willful penis—the panic that had expanded into a ball of hurt at the
center of my flesh.

3

A ROUND this time, two things happened. I got a letter from
David's widow, Anna: "Thank you for writing, Paul. David's
death was both terrible and joyous. During the last weeks we had
a nonstop party, and there was sex everywhere. It was unbelievably
desperate and swell. People fucked in every room. David lay in bed,

with me on one side and another woman on the other. We did things to him, and he laughed. He never got out of bed; his bed was the center of the party. It was uncanny, there was so much love."

I had visited David and Anna in the East Side brownstone, and I tried to imagine the brightly colored rooms; their friends climbing the narrow stairs with drinks in their hands, the men unshaven, the women dazed and motherly; everyone feeling a diffuse warmth from too much liquor mingled with too much grief. I imagined David, witty and out of breath, with Anna on one side of him wearing green nail polish, green eye shadow and a whore's underwear, and some other woman on the other side, David nuzzling first one, then the other, in a zany farewell. David had been a small-town boy from New Hampshire, awed and a little shocked by the brassiness of the big city. This party was his apotheosis, his swinging bad end.

Anna's letter threw me into a strange state. I had never imagined that grief could be mingled with such insane fun. While David was dying in his bed, his friends stumbled deliriously to the limit of themselves, as if to scout out the way for him. It occurred to me that I would have been an awkward guest at David's party: the owner of a dead penis; the appendage of an anxiety that, even then, was seeping and expanding. Maybe sex and death could be full of love: but with me it had been different. I had been defeated by them. I could not even mourn properly for my friend.

Shortly after receiving Anna's letter, I made up my mind to see a psychoanalyst. In those days, Americans had the reputation of going to see a shrink anytime they felt a twinge of anxiety, as if worry were a medical problem, and therefore curable. The French found this laughable. To them psychoanalysis was still a hidden practice, close to voodoo or alchemy. Jacques Lacan was already publishing the maddeningly difficult essays which, within the next decade, would make him the most famous man in France. But in 1966, Frenchmen on the whole had no truck with tinkering with the psyche, and I had been living in France long enough to be a Frenchman on this point. *La liberté* meant freedom to be a little crazy too. It meant freedom to suffer and drink cheap wine, and chew garlic in public. It meant freedom to have a face with wrinkles like claw marks, and deep-set eyes, like the writer Arthur Adamov whom I used to see, full of private horror, at the Old Navy Café on the Boulevard Saint Germain; freedom to sit with predatory patience at a round café table, with several large books piled in front of you as bait for girls, like Lucien Goldmann, whom I also used to run into in those days at cafés in the Latin Quarter.

But I had begun to think of my anxiety, which occupied an area in my stomach, as a kind of illness, at night affecting my lungs as well, and making me sweat; it felt like a sick loosening of the muscles. Claire was gone. Yet the anxiety persisted, irascible and mindless, resistant to thought, obsessive. I suppose that's why I thought about seeing a doctor. Maybe a doctor would be able to take care of this woundedness. Anna's letter decided me.

Toward the end of the winter, I had met a psychoanalyst named Michel de M'Uzan at a dinner party. He was a short man with curly black hair and a quiet, robust manner. I had been especially impressed by his wife, the writer Marthe Robert. That evening she had been like a flow of heat; ideas and laughter erupted from her. She had dark skin and a voracious mouth. Later I thought: it takes a large-souled man to live with such a woman.

I looked up Michel de M'Uzan in the phone book. Yes, he remembered our meeting. Yes, he would see me professionally. We made an appointment for several days later. His office was not far from the Moslem mosque, in the neighborhood behind the Jardin des Plantes, and I stopped off to have some tea in the mosque's interior garden before going to see him. The little courtyard was filled with the odor of mint and jasmine. I sat at a small table, listening to the fountain that bubbled out of a cluster of green shrubs in the middle of the café. I had no preconceptions about our meeting. The mosque's insular peacefulness, its pink walls and splashing fountain, contrasted with my "illness," which throbbed like an old enemy, a faint presence filling my whole being, uncontrollable and blind, a mechanism of fate.

De M'Uzan's office was spare and gray. He greeted me with a few barely social words. Before I could get my bearings, I was sitting opposite him, waiting for him to tell me what to do. Instead, he waited silently in an enormous wooden chair, his hands poised on the armrests as if at any moment he might get up and leave me alone in the room. His face was gray and still—like a death mask, I thought. The silence was like a suction, and I felt myself being pulled into it. I began to talk and to explain. I smiled and crossed my legs, and as I did, his face seemed to get even grayer and stiller. He looked very small to me, in his tall Gothic chair, almost a dwarf;

there was something bleak, even threatening about him. I was offering him my soul, and in return he was giving me this pure monotony, this blankness, like a wall, but a wall that listened, for his eyes watched me unswervingly for the whole hour.

I told him the entire story, every thread of it: the dead man, the dying man, my impotence, Claire's wild fright, her bitchiness, her killer instinct. It was a good story, and I told it entertainingly. I understood that I had a license to tell everything. I was to spare nothing, above all not myself. For the pleasure of this man with a gray face, this wall, I placed myself in every ludicrous posture; I described every naïveté, every innocence, every adolescent selfishness. I took hold of myself and shook, all for the sake of the tale. Was I a secret homosexual? Did I have suppressed suicidal urges? I opened up my psyche, and became a clown, a gypsy; I played my flute.

It took almost an hour, and when I finished I felt elated. I had turned my sick confusion into a story, with transitions, themes, branches and trap doors, and double meanings. It was hilarious, a kind of sick joke, and I was the author, full of irony and drama, with little flourishes that said: "Gentlemen, look at this unusual item, and this one." It turned out that I was telling one story, however, and de M'Uzan was listening to another. My performance had been in a vacuum. His face was resistant and hard; I could have been talking into my sleeve. This gave a nervous edge to my elation. Maybe I had simply made a fool of myself.

"How old was the man?" he asked abruptly, referring to Claire's dying friend.

"I don't know. Older than I am, I think; in his mid-forties."

"And how old was your friend who died?"

"The same."

He made a bridge with his fingers, and then looked blandly at me.

"In other words, you took this older man's woman away from him."

I looked at him without understanding. He looked as if he had a stomachache. Was this all he had to say to my story? For a minute I wondered if he had been listening. And then, as if to fill the uncomfortable silence, the whole tangled, desperate tale rose before me. I saw it all. I saw what had happened. I saw what I had done: all the tenuous threads, all the myths, all the lies full of echoes and muted howls.

It wasn't true. I hadn't taken his woman away. Claire had left him before she ever met me. She had probably never really been his woman anyway. But, in a stroke of appalling vision, I understood that my unconscious didn't care about these details. My unconscious knew, with the stubborn knowledge children often have, that a man was dying, and a boy had stolen his woman, and fucked her deliriously. Then David had died, and the two men, the one I didn't know and my friend, my older mentor, had come together and weighed upon me with all the heaviness of the blows I had struck with my killing tool, my penis. What could I do but fail, but die?

It was like a picture sketched in lines of light: the coincidences and the oedipal fantasy, the impotence. I saw it all, and started to laugh, a low, giggling sound that dribbled and sputtered. Still giggling, I looked at my watch. De M'Uzan was moving about grumpily in his chair. The hour was over.

I kept thinking to myself: so that was it, and, sputtering softly, I put my check on the table, shook hands with the doctor, who had become almost human again. We agreed that I would come back in a few weeks, and I left.

During the hour, dusk had begun to fall. I walked through the gray streets, feeling the cobblestones underfoot. Everything was empty and transparent, like an enormous indoors filled with the muted echo of cars and an occasional voice. These were the semi-deserted streets toward the 13th arrondissement, lined with artisans' shops and little factories. A *passage* crossed the Rue Mouffetard, scarcely wider than a sidewalk, that still used gaslights. The lamplighter, a plump old man in worn blue overalls, walked ahead of me, turning the lamps on, one by one. The blue-white flames winked on and burned with a motionless light. I felt that I was walking in the past. Time had not finished its job here. As I walked I giggled softly. I couldn't stop, didn't want to stop, as if a tremendous interior pressure had been released. The giggling spilled into the Rue Tournefort and the Rue de l'Estrapade. I took only the empty streets heading toward the river. I wanted to be alone with this gentle mirth, this ridiculous, tender flow bubbling out of me like water from the spring of springs.

4

THE story has a postscript. Weeks passed, and the emergency faded. Tiny blossoms snowed from the horse-chestnut trees and blew into white drifts along the bridges. The sky was full of tumbling clouds that seemed to skim the church spires. I spent hours on the hard slatted chairs of a *buvette* under the trees in the Luxembourg Gardens, or in an antiquated café specializing in wines, next door to my building on the Rue de Rivoli. The walls of the café were papered with round colored signs advertising morgons, médocs, graves, white wines from Pouilly or Sancerre, all by the glass. The traffic rumbled past, but the café seemed frozen in its outdated decor. I tried not to think about going back to the United States, at the end of the summer, or about Claire or her dying friend, even about David. I was exhausted, almost happy. "Almost," because present to every waking moment was a desultory pain, the sharp end of a memory jabbing me inadvertently, as if probing for a tender place.

For one unforgettable evening after telling my story to Michel de M'Uzan, I had felt like one of those martyred Christians who snapped their fingers and giggled as they leaped into the flames. My adventure with Claire, the murderous fairy tales in my mind, had dissolved, and I was free. Then everything blurred.

What happened that evening in the psychoanalyst's office? I had learned that a worn-out oedipal tale was at work in my psyche. That the psychology textbooks had not forgotten me, and therefore I was all right: not a mutant or a hopeless freak, but a man in the grip of a noble tale. I had learned that the mind, for all its staggerings and blanknesses, was composed of a spiritual substance that could be altered only by knowledge. And then I had forgotten. My anxiety remained, a stealthy throb. My sexual self was still breakable.

For ten years, Paris had been a map of encounters. I had been married and divorced there. I had been a revolutionary, waiting for terrible events that would bring capitalism down around my ears:

economic depression, Third World revolution, urban guerrilla warfare. Alas, when the revolution came it was dreadfully personal, an irreversible event. There were more goods than ever in the store windows. The streets were lined with new cars, lovers kissed in doorways and ran their hands under each other's clothes.

A few years ago physicists invented a bomb that mainly harms people, not objects. Such a bomb had fallen, but it had harmed only me. And I too went about my life as if nothing had happened. I packed my books and shipped them to the United States. I wrote, talked obsessively to my friends; I tried to cure my anxiety by making love as frequently as possible. Fucking became a form of exercise, an erotic jogging.

One day, it must have been in early May, I got a letter from David's widow, Anna. She and her daughter were thinking of coming to Europe for a few months: France, Italy, maybe Greece. Could I find a place for them to stay in Paris, and help them with their plans? I wrote back immediately: of course I would help. I hadn't been there for David's death, hadn't even really mourned for him, unless my impotence had been a form of mourning (the flag at half mast). Here was a chance for me to do something. It didn't matter that Anna had always frightened me. She was a suave New York lady who smoked too much and dressed in flashy clothes. Anna was a few years older than I was, and that had always maintained a distance between us, so that her shiny leather slacks, her pointy breasts falling half out of her blouse, didn't appear to be aimed at me.

Anna wrote me again. Did I plan to do any traveling this summer? Maybe she and Jane could tag along. I agreed to that too. She could come with me to Venice, where I was planning to visit friends, and then to a little town near Viareggio, on the other coast of Italy, where a friend was going to lend me a beach house.

This was not the farewell to Europe I had wanted. I had seen myself driving alone across France, climbing in the high meadows above the snow line in the Alps, walking along smelly green canals in Venice. I would sit at Florian's on the Piazza San Marco with my friends Domingo and Monin, who were surrealist painters and jewelers, longstanding inhabitants of Venice, with whom a tenuous mystery could be preserved, without saying very much. Then I would drive slowly across the hills of Tuscany: Florence, Siena,

San Gimignano. I would visit Lerici on the coast, with its medieval castle where I had lived for three summers when it functioned as a youth hostel and I had been young and poor. My summer was to have been a farewell to youth. But now there was this grating pain; this miasma of sex and failure that rose in my throat and threatened to stifle me.

Around this time, I had lunch with my ex-brother-in-law, Lucien, whom I hadn't seen for several years. He had recently separated from his wife, he told me, and on an impulse he had called me. That in itself is a story. People are never who we think they are. Lucien and his wife had lived with Michèle and me for six years in the family apartment we all shared. He was tall and well built, with a shock of blond hair falling into his eyes and an indolent swagger that seemed the natural counterpart of his incredible good looks. Women turned around to look at him in the street. Although he was only a teenager when I first met him, he already possessed the aloofness and the self-contained, almost indifferent grace that one associates with very beautiful women. Most of the time, Lucien seemed to disdain me as a bug, a mere creature. He was going to be a writer, and took an elegant pen name. He wrote in beautiful notebooks. When he was around, I felt ugly and boring. The cigarette dangling from the corner of his mouth seemed designed to flick ashes on me. While Michèle and I wrote and painted and talked revolutionary politics, across the hall Lucien and his wife had sexual parties full of new combinations: boy with boy and girl with girl, the husband with his friend's wife, and then with his friend. At one point, Lucien vanished for a few months. It turned out he had been traveling as the intimate companion of a Hungarian count. From his blond height, the world seemed golden and ripe; and his soft voice—a voice that had said everything, understood everything—gave an impression of boredom.

Across his golden youth came puzzling dissonances. One summer, alone in the apartment, he had swallowed a bottleful of pills. It didn't seem real; a kind of lazy experiment, not a suicide attempt. When he was drafted, during the Algerian war, he decided to get himself thrown out of the army, as a mental case. For months, he pretended to be clinically depressed, a vegetable. His officers must have been stupefied. At last, as a crowning touch, he slit his wrists in the barracks bathroom, and they let him go. He returned home, a skeleton, with sores on his face and eyes that winced when they looked at you. But it wasn't long before he was a golden boy again, with his beautiful notebooks and his pen name.

It was odd for Lucien to be calling me, and when he showed up at the little Tunisian Jewish restaurant on the corner of my street, the oddness increased. With his jacket slung over both shoulders, and his cigarette stuck in a corner of his mouth, he could have stepped out of a Fellini movie.

He was still everything I could never be: sexy, uninhibited, physically beautiful and blond. There was a sadness around his mouth, as if he knew more about everything than he chose to say. I, on the other hand, was dark and thin; I was already a little bald. My clothing didn't fit, my green tweed jacket was embarrassing. I was obsessive, joyless; twinges of sexual pain made me nauseous.

As we talked, Lucien seemed almost shy. He had called me, he said, because I had always represented something for him. I worked, I earned a living, when I said I was going to write I actually wrote. I had come to Paris and made a whole life for myself. All things he had never felt capable of. I was free, he wasn't; I was a grownup, he was stuck in some thankless adolescence. So when he found himself living alone, full of guilt about his marriage, wondering what to do next, he thought about me.

It was sad and hilarious at the same time. What do we know about people? From morning to night, they tell us who they are; they talk and we listen, and also the reverse. But something entirely different turns out to be the case. Half the time, it turns out, we were living in a script, and writing everyone else's part.

The funny thing was that Lucien's extraordinary confession didn't change anything. The parts we had played for each other were something more than a reading of each other's character. The golden boy was still there, although he wasn't a boy any longer. The smile creases around his eyes were permanent now, his skin had coarsened. My anxiety—that old friend—was buzzing furiously, like a hive that's been poked with a stick.

Our conversation didn't come off. We tried different subjects; we reminisced gingerly about the apartment on the Montagne Sainte Geneviève, overlooking half of Paris, although it was habitually so packed with tension, it could have given onto a brick wall much of the time, for all we noticed the view. The less we had to say, the more I talked. I told Lucien about my merry widow, and we joked about the summer. The summer frightened him, he said. All that empty time. He could have my widow if he wanted her, I said; and I wrote out the address near Viareggio on a corner of the paper tablecloth. We were both a little embarrassed. We laughed, and talked about other things.

The spring stretched out; the sky took on its summer tint of hazy white. On the Rue des Ecouffes, the voices spiraled up, filling my room on the top floor. With the approaching heat, they seemed wilder, more irritated, as if to fend off a memory of North African summers when the sirocco had cast a pall, and everyone drank spirit tea in the thick-walled houses without windows. My anxiety—sputtering and rusty—accompanied me on walks over toward the Rue Beaubourg and the empty lots beyond, where whores fucked standing up on warm nights against the retaining walls and the enormous wooden beams that kept the few houses remaining from falling down. I liked to have breakfast in a café on the Rue Saint Merri. The walls of the café were hung with myriads of richly decorated porcelain plates, the owner's proud collection which, all together, formed a pattern of vigilant eyes on the walls.

I had already shipped most of my belongings back to New York. My bookshelves were empty. The walls showed pale squares where paintings had been hung. A photograph of Rodin's marble lovers was still nailed to one end of the bookcase; their smooth white limbs interpenetrated and clung, as if the lovers were melting.

I had finished teaching now. The talk among my friends was of Provence and Italian beaches and the yellow desert of Castile. The summer migration was being prepared, the yearly flight away from friends and the city. These were the nomad months, a combination of bright, hot spaces and the relentless intimacy of a few chosen companions or lovers, from whom there would be no escape until the thunderstorms of late August signaled the end of summer. For me, it was the end of the only life I had known since leaving college. A life lived in another language, airy and curiously empty, insulated from the gut demands of words uttered since childhood. Already, Claire had shattered my laboriously constructed foreignness; she had penetrated my code. The body, it seems, knows only one language.

At the end of August, I would drag this body back to New

York, where language was wild, fat and rancid, frighteningly naked and rich. New York was sending me David's widow. I climbed the five flights of stairs to my rooms, which had become just another half-naked furnished apartment. I slept in the arroyo of my bed, which was an insomniac furrow now, not a river. From it I saw the metallic dawns, and the bloodless moon of the late hours, when an occasional car blubbered over the cobblestones on the Rue de Rivoli, or a worker shuffled to his four o'clock shift under my window.

On a Wednesday in the third week of June, I got up early and took a shower. I sat in my armchair, the window open, drinking instant coffee and tearing at a *tartine* of day-old bread. I was in a hurry, but I couldn't seem to get going. Anna and Jane would be arriving at Orly in an hour. They were probably over London now, a skinny thirteen-year-old with granny glasses and a heart full of grief; and Anna, my dead friend's widow, whom I could not imagine or even think about, whom I did not know.

At last I left the apartment and walked downstairs, passing the bright red door of Madame Rose, the palm reader, who had once offered to read my palm for free, if she could use my bathroom for a few days when her plumbing broke. I never collected my free reading. Palm readers and astrologers make me nervous; not that I believe in their ability to foretell the future, but words have an irreversible effect on me. If Madame Rose, in her dim nineteenth-century parlor, with the lace table covering, had told me that I was doomed, that my palm hooted at her with ghastly forebodings, the words would have sunk within me and quivered there. Let time alone, I say, as I longed to let it alone that very morning, walking unconsciously down the five flights, into the Rue de Rivoli and around the corner to my car.

I drove across the Seine with Notre Dame off to the right, looking from behind like a squat porcupine. The old Halle aux Vins was straight ahead. Crackerbox buildings of metal and glass were scattered about it to house the new science university. The Avenue des Gobelins sloped up gently past dark, noble stone buildings. There wasn't much traffic. Cars looped around the Place d'Italie into a star of avenues. Then came the autoroute passing through a gimcrack suburb of tile villas and cramped gardens.

The shining cigar shape of a 707 whined overhead. I was inside the Orly arrivals building. The vast hall was almost nauseatingly

60

hot. Everywhere lunging valises, and travelers with disoriented eyes; and there, emerging from a passport control booth, was Anna. She cleaved the crowd like a fin, her face oval and tan, her eyes vast under an awning of artificial lashes. Jane trailed behind her, lugging an oversized flight bag, her small thin face frowning with concentration.

"You're here," said Anna, in a nasal voice that trembled and developed trills even in these few words.

"Planes terrify me," she said, "I threw up after we took off. But Jane's been taking care of me. I made it on vodka martinis, although Jane doesn't approve. She's been lecturing me, but I won't listen."

This little Jane looked exhausted and motherly. She insisted on dragging her worn flight bag as we went down the escalator to the baggage retrieval area, and then, hauling two flapping red canvas bags through the revolving doors, onto the sidewalk. The air was hazy with exhaust fumes. A keen scent of jet fuel cut through the odor of gasoline. Anna and Jane waited in front of the terminal while I went to get the car. The asphalt in the parking lot was puffy with heat, and my shoes stuck slightly. With every step I felt the anxiety that had become my inner music.

When I pulled up, Anna took a look at my old unwashed car —a light blue Simca—and laughed girlishly as if an adventure were beginning. She stood out vividly beside the faded car. She wore black, and her lips flashed a dark painted red that she kept moist by running her tongue over them. We looped around the airport and cruised onto the autoroute crawling with eight lanes of traffic. Paris spread out ahead of us. Off to the left, the Eiffel Tower stood hugely on end, its base concealed by the swell of the outer arrondissements.

Anna kept moving around in her seat, calling me "honey." She exclaimed at the ornate end-of-the-century apartment houses with their carved granite cornices and wrought-iron balconies that lined the avenues heading north across the city. We had first met in Paris several years before. David had been at the center of our group; and Anna, ironical, outrageously feminine, had smoldered in silence like a tropical bird. The Algerian war had just ended, and David had been fascinated by my small role in it of providing a safe house for FLN rebels. But now politics and revolution were far away. Capitalism, it turned out, was doing fine; I was the one who was breaking down.

Anna leaned across the seat and touched my leg while she talked about the summer. She wanted Jane to see Italy and Paris. They were going to window-shop and sit in cafés. Anna's hand shook. Her bright talk and her sharp, knowing face made me feel clumsy and slow. Did she and Jane mind sleeping on the floor for a few days, until we got going? I asked, a little embarrassed. She laughed with that rich, nasal voice of hers. Like my car, the idea seemed quaint, and she wanted me to know how reckless and young she was feeling.

"I'm Jane's age. We're like sisters. Have you noticed it?"

It was true. Her miniskirt and ponytail were curiously adolescent, although an adolescence that had been worked to a high sexual polish. As we rumbled over the cobbles of the Boulevard Saint Michel, Anna seemed to have forgotten she was in Paris, she was so busy talking, casting her voice about me in loops and trills and titters. I sensed that Anna's gaiety was fragile. She seemed to be saying: Don't make me stop; let me bewitch you and frighten you, let me be a water spirit, a sexual fairy; for there is nothing else. "I'm dead," she was to say often during our weeks together: "David took me with him when he died, and now I'm incinerated, charred. I have no life."

5

A NNA may have been dead, but the little white pills she took were an afterlife: amphetamines. She had crossed the Atlantic on speed and martinis; she was speeding in my car. I could see that I was going to have to talk to her, tell her about my anxiety, my wound in the dark that was like another self: I wasn't material. I'd heard that expression from a West Indian yogi I'd known years before. I'm not material, he would sigh, rolling his soft, dark eyes, while his huge wife stood behind him. And the phrase had become a whimsical refrain, accompanied by Yogi Clemdour's doe eyes and his immaterial body, his seemingly boneless arms and legs that he bent into disgusting knots: I'm not material. Only now did it dawn on me that my yogi friend had not been talking only about spiritual matters. He had meant that he was impotent. "Unfortunately," he was saying, "I'm not a man, but a bendable creature that my wife, in her rotund vastness, can fold up and put in her pocket."

"Anna, I'm not material," I moaned silently, as we crossed over the Seine. The golden needle of the Sainte Chapelle gleamed above the Palais de Justice. The flower market spilled flaming dahlias, daisies and zinnias onto the sidewalk. A froth of tiny purple and yellow blossoms shone under the green awnings or leaned from buckets of water.

We climbed up the five dark flights, past the heavy red door of Madame Rose; past the neighbors whose radios seeped tinnily through my floor every Sunday, the day of rest. On this late June morning, accompanied by Jane's speechless sadness and her mother's manic despair, there would be no rest. Between Claire and Anna ran a thread that snagged me. I was hooked by the mysterious power of women I didn't understand; women who wanted something from me, women who were bright and sensuous with their paralyzing demands. I opened the door to my apartment and stumbled in, as if propelled by Anna's brittle speed and Jane's passiveness.

I saw the apartment differently now. Too many lives had been rubbed into its walls. It was small, a dull privacy.

Jane was exhausted. I showed her the bedroom, and she was asleep in a few minutes. Anna stood on the narrow balcony; she held on to the railing as if she were trying to keep from jumping or flying. From behind, her hunched shoulder blades looked like the nubs of wings. She had changed into a black pants suit, with a red belt and red trimmings. Her hair was straight and black, with a red elastic holding the ponytail in place. She didn't seem so formidable now. I could see the silent plea in her wing bones and her long neck. What did she see out there? A skyscape of zinc roofs and orange chimney pots? Or was she seeing something that wasn't there: David's face, his male softness, his absence that wouldn't end.

The fatigue of the trip had undermined Anna's amphetamine high. She swayed as she stepped into the room again and looked around at my bare walls, my sagging armchair, my bookcase of unpainted wood.

"Let's go for a walk," she said. Her cheerfulness seemed slower now, more unsure of itself.

We went downstairs. As always at this hour, the Rue des Ecouffes was crowded and noisy. There were lines at the kosher butcher and the bakery. People walked in the middle of the street with shopping baskets over their arms; cars crept along behind them flashing their headlights or honking futilely. Halfway down the block was a storefront synagogue. A loudspeaker in front of a music store blared a song by Enrico Macias, a North African Jewish singing star, whose photograph was plastered all over the store window. Anna took my arm in both her hands and leaned against me as we walked. It was comfortable, a letting go. I knew that I would have to have my talk with Anna soon. I would have to tell her about my sexual catastrophe, my impotence which had become a ghost of another sort. I would have to tell her that I was not material.

We walked around the Marais, with its tiny groceries painted green and red, the verdigrised facade of the public bath on the Rue des Rosiers, a dark little kosher restaurant down a flight of stairs on the Rue des Blancs Manteaux, the street Sartre had once written a revolutionary song about: It was early morning, the guillotine was oiled and ready; and the heads rolling gaily into the dust, the applauding ladies in their finery, on the Rue des Blancs Manteaux. Overripe fruit from the market wafted a heavy perfume. It was not a street on which history was made; and now my own history walked among the parked cars and the crowd coming from the market, with a woman leaning on my arm, a woman I did not know, sparkling with sexual electricity; an older woman who was also a Lolita, full of overwhelming needs. Anna's hurt made my own problems seem inadequate. Could I possibly put my needs before hers? And yet I knew that I had to. Because the penis doesn't lie. If I didn't speak, it would speak for me. As we walked, I started to tell Anna about my bizarre spring, and my own little death; the homunculus of anxiety that was like a fire inside me. I told my story apologetically. I can't be your ghost, I was saying.

We were on the Rue Payenne, in front of a small building squeezed between decrepit palaces. A sculpted portal, an air of grime and neglect: it was the Temple of Reason, the shabby cult of an old faith, Positivism, Auguste Comte; now a piece of crumbly real estate on a quaint street in the Jewish neighborhood. I hadn't gotten far with my story when Anna stopped and looked at me. She passed her hand over her face, as if to wipe out an irritating detail.

"Why are you telling me this, Paul?"

She looked frightened, as if a loud noise had just woken her up. I was scared because I was crying out for protection. Ever since I had received Anna's letter, I had known what she wanted and now she was casting her strands about me, drawing me to the center of her net, and it was not even a conquest. She was taking what she needed, as if we had agreed on it long ago. But I hadn't agreed.

"You mean you don't want to fuck? Is that it?"

"I can't fuck, Anna. It's been a terrible spring; I'm sick."

I stopped, thinking of David's sickness. Was I comparing my anxiety to it? The provocation was this sharp-eyed woman with pouting lips and peach-colored make-up, who looked at me with a combination of surprise and indifference.

"I'll take care of you and Jane," I said, speaking quickly now. "We'll go to Venice. We'll do everything we planned. I want to help you, Anna, but I'm in trouble."

She wasn't listening. She seemed lost in herself, and then, slowly, she began to sag. She leaned against the wall of the Temple of Reason, and started sliding toward the sidewalk. I grabbed her under the arms and let her down onto a stone step.

It's the trip, I thought, and amphetamines. Her slumped shoulders and her small white face expressed a desolation so absolute, it was like a death. It was a look I came to know during the weeks ahead. Anna's face would go blank, as if she weren't seeing the jagged Alpine peaks as we crossed over the Simplon into Italy; the switchbacked road; the grass of the high meadows glistening with sunlight; not seeing the Chinese-like islands floating in the early morning mists of Lake Como; or the wretched back canals of the Dorso Duro in Venice. Her looks then were bleak flickers, loomings that came and went. Otherwise, Anna was girlish and unstoppable. Her laughter sizzled like a gas under pressure. She moved in a dazzle of black and red, her favorite colors; and always those sharp breasts bursting her too-tight blouses; her soft stomach; her movements that came out of perfume advertisements and fur coat advertisements: promising and rich, and, slyly, terribly demanding.

Yes, I had given in. From his niche over the doorstep where Anna fainted, Auguste Comte, with his marble mustache and his pigeon-bespattered bust, had blessed us, and I had accepted the inevitable. Hovering over Anna, I had thought: Death makes imperious demands, life must meet them. David was my friend; I must do this for him.

I will say this for Anna, she was an expert, a technician. In another life, she could have been a temple whore or a geisha. There seemed to be nothing she didn't know about how to do it, and where to do it; what perfume to wear and the jewelry; the sheer, subtly patterned underwear; her voice, like a sexual bass fiddle, accompanying our love-making. She could be businesslike, tender, vulgar, girlish. She was a sexual encyclopedia; she had advice for everything, and she was willing to work for her ecstatic moment. Above all, she knew how to make my flagging penis work well enough for her to take her pleasure. I was like an old car, and she was the mechanic. I needed daily tune-ups. Every day little parts broke down, but Anna's fast fingers plunged under the hood and worked their miracle. I was kept together on spit and glue. It was uncanny, desperate, and funny, but I wasn't laughing.

In our peculiar way, we were a family, window-shopping together on the Frezzaria in Venice, or sitting at Florian's on the Piazza San Marco full of tourists in Bermuda shorts and plaid shirts, and draped with pigeons for the millionth snapshot from the millionth camera. We sipped tall white glasses of orzata, and wrote postcards. Anna's fierce, playful eye roved over the Piazza. She was looking over the men, whom she seemed to consider carriers of ecstatic merchandise, sperm merchants she might buy from. Now she was buying from me; and I was selling, grudgingly. The hard flame of anxiety flickered untouched in my belly.

We stayed at a pension on the Giudecca across the lagoon from the Doge's Palace and the enormous pink brick column of the Campanile. A froth of white statues danced on churches across the water. Naked boys swam in the greasy billows of the wide Giudecca canal. Taxi boats gave off a rich throb. *Vaporettos*—Venetian buses—chugged and wallowed with their load of passengers. The Casa Frollo occupied a Palladian palace, with a series of gardens stretching behind it and a thin odor of cats penetrating everywhere. It was a gloriously inefficient place. Vast hallways wandered, full of angles, old carpets, and dim yellow lamps. Most of the rooms were tiny, resembling monks' cells. A few of them, however, were three stories high and large as ballrooms, decorated with streaked antique mirrors and flamboyant frescoes of indeterminate age, representing women with bursting breasts, fiercely bearded heroes, and a fretwork of Oriental dragons and lions. It was pure, overdone Venetian self-display.

I'd been coming to Venice for years. I'd spent Christmases here, wandering in thick fog pierced by streaks of sunlight that gleamed on church domes. Once a procession of gondolas emerged from the fog into a patch of sunlight, rowing their silent black cargo to the cemetery. I'd sat in Florian's at nightfall, watching the winter rain sweep across the Piazza. In April, the sheer blue sky and the washed light gave the city a mineral sparkle. Shadows seemed painted on the pavements of the *campos*. The faded pastel walls and crazy-tilted columns of the sinking palazzos were so clear and clean, they seemed breakable.

Venice had become my city. I walked here, sat in desultory cafés; wandered into outlying neighborhoods where the canals stank, the churches sprouted weeds along their rubbly brick facades, and clothing was strung out on lines overhead in the narrow alleys.

My Venice seemed to resemble time itself: a labyrinth of meanders, overlaid with faint tracings. There wasn't a straight line in the whole city. Walking here was like rummaging in my past. I met myself in sunbaked courtyards or on little arched bridges looking into the littered mirror of a canal. Anywhere in Venice was only a step from the unfamiliar. I would turn left or right, and find myself strolling along a canal full of rowboats and parked gondolas. A delivery boy unloaded milk cartons from a barge onto a rubber-wheeled dolly. Large women in black dresses leaned out of windows and shouted across the alley to their neighbors. Children played soccer on a church square. The ball thunked against the massive wooden door of the church, as if God's knuckles were reverberating in the empty space paved with limestone blocks, resembling a game board because of the grass growing in squares around each block.

This is where I took my "family": Jane with her sad motherliness; Anna who seemed to see so little because of the grief she was afraid to name and the loneliness she couldn't speak; Anna, tender and fast, ruthless, kind. In the slow summer heat, her amphetamine speed took on a mad festiveness. Her whole being was a carnival mask, illuminated by panics and night terrors.

During the day, I could escape across the lagoon into the crowded *calles* near the Piazza, and then into deserted neighborhoods where I could sit at a café and read or write beside a marble- and onyx-encrusted church. But the nights were Anna's. She came into my room and perched on my high narrow bed. A window framed the lighted Doge's Palace across the lagoon. It was time for my lesson. She would spit into her hands and caress me. She had the touch of a night breeze, the white, twining persistence of a fish. She was warm, she was cool. The room was illuminated by her movements, which were curiously surgical and clean. She was a nurse, a doctor. Sometimes it didn't work. The anxiety trickled into my penis; my eyes hurt with it. I felt helpless; my semi-erections were flags of surrender.

And yet, on those hot Venice nights, awash with reflected light from the lagoon, behind yard-thick walls that muted the yowling of cats mating on the garden walls or on the waterfront stone steps, just above the slapping tide—on those nights, I felt myself live. I felt a secret willingness. Anna pulled me between her legs, or climbed on top of me. She took her gulps of pleasure. But for all her zany narcissism, she was generous whenever her speed-ghosts let her alone.

We were like castaways adrift on a raft of coarse white sheets. We hadn't chosen each other, but our ship had gone down, and here we were together trying to salvage ourselves. Anna buoyed me up with her pure, nervous will.

"I'm already dead, Paul," she would say. "I'm not here, not alive."

Yet she brought into my whitewashed room overlooking the water a claim I wanted to meet: for more life, more feeling. All day I walked around Venice feeling squelched and sad. The decaying city tilting into the water was my own image. I was impotent, flotsam. The secret was out. But Anna, cooing her nasal appeals, turned it all into a Roman circus, full of suicides and incense. Impotent? What a joke! Come here, I want my medicine, I want my sperm pill, and she held on to me tenderly, chuckling, as if to prove a point. It was all against my will. But our nights, full of reluctance and need, had made us bizarrely into a couple.

After a few weeks in Venice, we drove south toward Via-reggio, on the opposite coast of Italy. The house we were to occupy was on a sandy street in a nearby beach town that resembled a bungalow colony: rows of wooden boxes surrounded by succulent plants and pine trees. The street was full of children on tricycles, and mothers wearing flowered housecoats. I had the impression of stumbling into my Brighton Beach, the Brooklyn neighborhood where I had been brought up. The beach was an equalizer. It wiped out personalities, language, replacing them with universal sunburn and bare skin, sand stuck to red patches of back and shoulders.

Immediately, we were just another family, walking down the sandy street to the beach; watching the blue scallops of the Mediter-ranean pour toward us and break in monotonous lines of froth. We had our routine: beach, and then lunch; and then, still sticky with salt, an afternoon roll in bed. Jane was "our" child, her loneliness a silent accompaniment to our domestic games.

In the evening, we drove over to Viareggio and walked along the main street, full of palely lit shops. David was our companion on those evenings. He walked beside us; Anna held on to his waist, my waist. We played a game—their game—of "buying" whatever struck our fancy in the shop windows. We furnished penthouses and country houses, bathrooms, poolrooms. We bought baroque wicker chairs and brightly colored hammocks; closets full of feather dresses; pink, blue or green underwear; Panama hats; gilded kitchen fixtures; smoked hams and salami; baskets full of black grapes and golden pears, green speckled fists of artichokes. Then we would sit on the pier and eat ice cream, while the moist wind poured against us. We were the holy family, a trinity of refugees from death, helplessness and impotence, holding hands on the edge of the black ocean.

We leaned against each other for warmth, for sympathy. And yet we were not a family at all. Each of us was sealed into a different grief. Jane slipped through the days, rarely speaking to me. She accepted me as she accepted her father's death: by giving as little hold as possible to life and its derangements. I see her sitting on the beach, her skinny legs folded between her arms, looking out at nothing, while Anna in her stringy bikini waded in the water up to her knees, amid the hungry glances of Italian husbands and the yelping of boys who weren't above pinching her as they ran past. They were all roosters, and Anna was the queen of the barnyard.

Jane kept a nervous watch on her mother, as if, like everyone else in her life, she might suddenly disappear. To Jane, I was of no consequence; at best, a flimsy tether that kept Anna from running completely wild. Jane seemed to want to be invisible. I kept wanting to say: "Jane, tell me, what's the matter?" but what was the matter was desperately clear and irreparable. I couldn't get my mind around it. It was obvious that nothing made much sense to her—Italy, the beach, the glowing sky, me, even Anna; we were inert, barely present in her numb little world.

And there was Anna, popping those tiny white pills; slipping in and out of bed like an eel, flexible and cold, sexual, indifferent. Our little family had a secret. Anna was still living with David; the body in bed next to her was his; life made sense only because David with his sly humor and his soft-spoken wit said so. Anna was haunted by something inescapable and cruel: an absence, a crazy tilt out of orbit that had sent her reeling across the planet on an amphetamine spree, alone with David's impossible death and her own death that was like a glare on the water, hurting her eyes: As much as she tried, she couldn't help looking at it. Sometimes I wondered if, one morning, wading along the beach with her languorous hips and her slender breasts half rolling out of her tiny black halter, she would walk straight out into the ocean followed by a splashing line of naked boys.

And there was me, the "father" of this family, who was no one's father, no one's lover; stirred into reluctant, yet incredibly needy fits by Anna's educated body. I was the keeper of the nightmare. I stood guard over Anna's ghosts, helped her to keep them at bay. But there were my own ghosts.

One day late in July, I took a walk after lunch. The sandy street was empty. The beach was empty. The pine trees rustled in the summer gusts. Where were the children on their tricycles and the mothers with their soft, flapping breasts? Where were the teenage boys who usually congregated in front on the beach café on their Vespas, whooping whenever a girl walked past? I felt disoriented by the vacancy of the afternoon, which expanded, hissing with wind, into the tall pine trees, the white strip of beach, the ocean with pleats of foam rippling in.

The strain of the previous month seemed to evaporate, becoming the gusts of wind, the boxy houses set back from the street surrounded by pools of succulent plants, and the low crashing of waves on the sand. I gulped nervously and felt free. Free! I imagined myself walking back to the house, getting into my car, and never looking back. I imagined the solitary smell of the car; the switchbacked roads over the coastal mountains, heading nowhere. People did that: shed their lovers, wives, children, vanished and erased their past, as I was going to anyway in a few weeks, when I got on the boat at Le Havre.

A faint sound reached the street with each gust of wind, coming from the television sets and radios in several dozen living rooms scattered under the pine trees. I had forgotten. The World Cup Soccer Championships were on. Team Italy was playing today. That explained the empty streets and beaches. Everyone was watching the game.

I understood I wouldn't leave Anna and Jane. It wasn't even a possibility yet. My tether was short. I was tied to Anna by my own inertia and by a sort of mechanical obedience; maybe by loneliness too.

In a few weeks, I would drive to Paris, pack the rest of my belongings into a couple of cheap metal trunks, and sail back to America. Already my ten years in Paris resembled a fragment lifted out of my life. I was trying to remember a dream from the outside, from nowhere. As I trudged over the soft ruts toward the house, the emptiness had the feeling of a catastrophe that had left these dusty streets lifeless and frozen, except for the wind lisping in the pine boughs that laddered up to slender gray-green tufts. The television cheers petered out in the open sunlight. I could hardly hear them. As long as the game went on, the world was mine. I trudged past my battered Simca into the driveway. Anna was probably taking a nap. Jane would be sitting in the living room with the blinds down. She wouldn't say anything when I came in. I would sit with her in the living room for a while, reading, then tiptoe into the bedroom and lie down. Anna, feeling the mattress stir, would turn over and touch me. My anxiety would flare up; but my penis, that alien, that muscle with a will, would become hard and hopeful.

6

WHEN I saw myself at all in those days it was in isolation, a fugitive, or a planet without neighbors. This was probably the result of living for so long in a foreign country. For ten years I had lived within an elusive circle defined by an unshared childhood; by the daily effort, like an extra pressure of the will, required to speak this uncannily familiar language which fit me like a second skin, without ever being mine. As a foreigner, I felt my connections to others were flimsy, unserious. I could choose to set aside this labored character who spoke French, and lapse into my secret otherness as a boy from Brooklyn, living near that other beach, Brighton Beach, where the language that escaped me wasn't Italian or French but Yiddish.

It was a brave story full of Romantic attitudes. Behind me were the grim bohemians of an older Paris: Lautréamont, scuttling along the Rue Vivienne like an oversized bat, or Rimbaud, that provincial thug, who made outrageous scenes at a third-rate hotel on the Rue de l'Ecole de Médecine, in the Latin Quarter. I believed that a man possessed a homunculus self who abhorred love, friendship and family. I had had friends, lovers, but there had been a core self—impregnable and clear, like a yogi in a cave—that was beyond their reach.

It was a kind of youthful dishonesty. It was also part of a modern theory that isolates self, while ignoring the forlorn exchanges of substance that weld us to others. In truth, we are not *ourselves—je est un autre*, Rimbaud had written—but a yelping and tender chorus, a "barbaric yawp." Each of us is a crowd strolling out into a chaotic, lovely, slightly dangerous neighborhood: a throng of faces, oversized and shifting, recreated by love, by fascination. Passion is a Pygmalion's knife, molding features that change every day.

At the time, I didn't see any of that; I longed for something minimal. My motto was Live less. But it rarely worked, because there were surprises: Claire, Anna. During my last summer in

Europe, the anxiety was an echo of collapsing walls. My yogi's cave had vanished. There was a helplessness, a feeling that life had escaped me, left me impotent.

Yet there had always been surprises. Coming to Europe ten years before had been one of them. All through college I was going to be an engineer. Security! Technology! Engineers had been the heroes of my youth. Were you frightened by loneliness, death? Build a suburb, or a jet plane; invent the ballpoint pen, television; construct highways of clerical black asphalt, gleaming structures of glass and aluminum. I wanted very much to be an engineer, but something had happened.

Without knowing why, I had begun to haunt the streets of Greenwich Village and the East Village in the evening. I stared shyly at the hunched men and beaded women who seemed like moral adventurers, living in Lower East Side tenements with bathtubs in the kitchen and ancient gas heaters hissing in the living room. They stayed up all night, and wandered red-eyed into the dawn streets. They sat in the long, dimly lit cafés, and I sat there too, looking, not speaking. I didn't know what I wanted from them. Without having any particular subject matter, I began to write poetry, as a way of giving substance to my feeling of separateness.

Why the poetry, the separateness? I don't know. My adolescence had resembled a long impersonation, a snake dance of attitudes not lacking in excitement or desire, but lacking that fine animal will which knows it is alive. Even as a child, I had loved stories about desert islands—Robinson Crusoe, The Swiss Family Robinson, spaceships wrecked on uninhabited planets—where it had been man against rocks and the muteness of animals, not man against man, or against himself.

Within a year, I left for Paris on a slow Italian boat, as if by this extravagant act I could remake myself as a marginal man, an artist. But there were the surprises. I was not completely prepared for living in a foreign country. Paris disoriented me. It was so gray, so used. The walls of the buildings were streaked and dark; grime created permanent shadows. I was still too young to have a past; I had shed my childhood and my adolescence, like a snake slithering out of its skin. My past was a litter of crusts, pale moundings of time.

Paris jolted me with its deeply lived-in, repeatedly patched and preserved past. The soft patina of the early-nineteenth-century buildings, with small, deeply set windows; the sculpted faces and moldings arrayed over carriage gates or under the arches of the Pont Neuf, crossing the Seine; the blackened portals of Notre Dame, packed with saints and angels, gargoyles, contorted stubs of bodies—it was too much. An overlaying, a crowding of impressions. Every inch of the city bore rubbings of former uses, unlike the spacious, destructible Brooklyn I had been brought up in, made of pragmatic tenements and expedient storefronts, no more than a thin pressing of time subject to wrecking balls and mechanical scoops.

During my first year in Paris, I lived in a small residence hotel on the Rue de Tournon, near the Luxembourg Gardens. I had a long, narrow room, with pink wallpaper and a *porte-fenêtre* that took up all of the exterior wall. There was a stained sink, an armoire with a mirror on it, a skinny bed, a desk and chair; and, facing me out the window, a skyline made of chimney pots and steeples, attics, gray slanting rooftops silhouetted against the sky like a line of script.

I lived in a formidable isolation. For weeks I walked all over the city, whispering my couple of French words in grocery stores and restaurants. As the weeks passed, I forgot what it was like to speak in complete sentences. This was a new kind of solitude. I began to have a fantasy that if I looked into a mirror, I wouldn't see anyone there.

During these weeks, my only human contact was with a group of young Arabs who hung out in a café on the Boulevard Saint Michel. They were immigrants from Morocco or Algeria; most of them were unemployed, their families left behind while they looked for work. One day, I sat down in their café. Somehow they seemed more accessible than the fast-talking French. I mumbled *"Parlez-vous anglais?"* to one of them, and he answered with a friendly twitter and a handshake. He and his friends sounded out slow French syllables for my benefit. They showed me a couple of restaurants with trestle tables and paper tablecloths where I could eat for a few francs. We sat on the curb of the boulevard and looked at photographs of their wives and children, still living in their home villages in the mountains of the Kabylia, in Algeria, or in the Rif Mountains of Morocco. They let me know that they weren't Arabs, but Berbers, mountain people. North Africa had been theirs before the Arabs got there. I barely knew what Algeria was—a crescent of fertile valleys and mountains, lined with pure white beaches, clinging to the northern rim of the Sahara.

Those weeks in Paris were a turning point. I felt stripped of every comfort; my wordlessness was a kind of invisibility that, oddly, made me feel conspicuous: one of Notre Dame's grotesques, with a thick tongue and a ludicrous body. Living less hadn't gotten me very far; I was stupefied by a world gone slightly awry.

And then something happened that was overwhelming, although curiously uneventful. I had no name for it. Little by little I began to make sense out of the French I heard in cafés and restaurants, on the radio, in fleeting conversations. Much of it I still didn't understand, but I began to notice that it was language, expressed by the voices of these people with tight lips who seemed to talk through me with spars and splinters of sound.

I started to spend hours every day reading the newspapers with a dictionary. I carried around a pale blue school pamphlet of Paul Valéry's poems. I still own it, although it is brown with food stains and dirt now. I recited the poems over and over to myself. And as I did, they took on a thickness, a layered life that was the life of language. I acquired a kind of tunnel vision. French words walked in my sleep, masculine, feminine; a sexual throb invaded the little explosions of the consonants, the compressed intonations, particularly the stranglings of the r's, that stamp of true initiation into the street theater and persistent fakery of sounding French.

My solitary life became a form of heroism. I wasn't like those other Americans sitting at the Café de Tournon, across the street from my hotel. All evening they talked English and drank coffee or wine in the pink neon that lit a rectangle of sidewalk in front of the café. I could see them from the opening of my window, where I sat for hours, leaning against a worn wooden rail. I could hear the laughter, the excited voices, the intellectual discussions. Women gathered in the pink light wearing thin dresses, their long hair falling onto their shoulders.

Don't go in there, I warned myself with a determination that seemed to have come from nowhere and given no warning. I found myself wanting desperately to be a foreigner, an alien; I wanted to be walled in by my lucidity. For the first time in my life, I wanted something with all my heart, and what was it? To step across a brink, vanish into a peculiar unsympathetic realm, where I would be a secret visitor, a perfect construction of the will, almost a windup doll, making only the right movements, saying only foreign things to foreign people. America, New York, even my own language, had become like dead skins to me. After a month or so, I started trying to read French novels: Voltaire's *Candide*, then some Balzac, some Flaubert. For a long time there was no enjoyment in it, except maybe the enjoyment of wading in thick space lit by occasional glows of sense. I read with my lips, trying to unravel the clipped sounds, discover where the lengths of sentence hinged on verbs or came to earth solidly on immovable nouns. Often I had to look up almost every word.

Even as I worked, I was aware that I had never thrown myself into something so completely this way before. I longed to expand into whole sentences again. I discovered—it was a trick of physiology—that my accent was perfect. I made those strangled *r*'s as if I had been born to it. The stars which had given me birth on July 14, Bastille Day, twenty-one years before, had decided I would become master of the ultimate disguise. I would become a creature in one of those parallel worlds science-fiction writers love to invent. In one world, I was a poet born in Brooklyn, shy, conservative, but given to irruptions of strange behavior; in another, I was the same man, but French.

The isolation was probably driving me a little crazy. I had become a watcher. I watched little boys in blue uniforms sail their model boats on the pond in the Luxembourg Gardens, and the low tumbling clouds that poured over the treeline across the park. I watched the tired faces of the intellectuals at the Old Navy Café on the Boulevard Saint Germain, around the corner from my hotel. Their weariness seemed to be the expression of terrible knowledge. This was the somber petering out of the existentialist movement. A gloom was concentrated behind the cream-colored wooden front of the café that could not be dispelled by coffee and strong cigarettes, or by the women with adolescent breasts who circulated among the tables.

I watched girls in pert, threadbare coats kissing their friends on two cheeks, or squeezed into a doorway with a lover. I watched the crowds coming up out of the Métro; and the *charbonniers*, their faces gleaming with black dust, delivering sacks of coal from the two-wheeled carts they pushed down the middle of narrow streets. I walked in streets that were dingy and full of smells: the Rue Gît-le-Coeur, the Rue Xavier Privas, the Rue Maître Albert: strips of pure Zola that were grim and damp. The century hadn't yet swept them into its noisy life. They were quiet, morose.

That fall, the Russians invaded Hungary, and Paris seemed to go wild with indignation and fear. Posters went up all over the city: COMMUNIST MURDERERS, FREE HUNGARY. Suddenly I saw what a tiny place Europe was. Paris was only a tank ride from Budapest. This was the continent where armies crashed across borders, and wars were fought in picture-book fields lined with poplars. The last war had ended only eleven years before. Every day, I passed marble plaques bearing the names of young men killed fighting the Nazis. The plaques often had wilted flowers placed on the sidewalk beneath them. They were fresh deaths. In some crowded apartment up too many flights of stairs, they were still mourned: by a mother, a lover, a wife; or else, dutifully, by the local Communist Party cell, commemorating the Party's heroic role in the Resistance.

War belonged to the city's history; the streets reverberated with it. There were angry rallies at the Maubert Mutualité, a neighborhood meeting hall where, only a few years later, I would listen to political speeches and croon the rousing stanzas of the Internationale. Brigades of anti-Communist youths were preparing to fight the Russians in Hungary. They wore black leather and chains, and looked cruelly earnest.

I looked on, feeling dread, but also curiosity for these political passions which were as foreign to me as French itself. I had been brought up in the political consensus of the 1940s. I knew that my mother had once been involved with communism, and during the McCarthy years the spines of certain books were turned to the wall. Politics had seemed treacherous, full of betrayals. But the cold war remained a dim noise that had no bearing on the backyard barbecues and fraternity parties. Even the Rosenberg trial hadn't broken through my visceral distrust of everything public.

But now the passions of French public life disoriented me. The streets roared with demonstrations. Black symbols were painted on walls, with anti-Semitic slogans under them, or YANKEE GO HOME, or some revolutionary outcry I didn't understand.

Toward the end of September I met a girl in a *cave* on the Rue de la Huchette. The *cave* was in a Gothic basement down a flight of stairs. There was a hot musty smell of damp stone walls mingled with cigarette smoke and spilled wine. We danced to loud Dixieland music played by a group of bearded Frenchmen wearing existentialist black sweaters. The girl's name was Nicole. She had dull brown hair falling neatly onto her neck, and unhealthy-looking skin. Between her few words of English and my few words of French, we managed to understand each other. She had just spent a year living in a small village in the Spanish Pyrenees, she told me, because the doctors had found a tubercular spot on her lungs.

Nicole was operatic in the quietest possible way. She was a mouse, winsome and forlorn. We made a pair. She was virtuous and intense, soulful, usually silent. Her eyes expressed quiet hurt. When she laughed, she touched her lips, as if to excuse herself. I found Nicole's reserve incredibly attractive. On our meetings in the Luxembourg Gardens beside the boat pond, or in my shadowy room lying on the bed, barely touching, there was a distance between us. When I tried to undress her, she winced or gave a nervous laugh. And as weeks passed, I understood that Nicole intended to remain chaste. Kisses were all right; so were slow, hesitant talks in the privacy of my room, with our hands touching, and a few wispy caresses. But no sex. I accepted this; I think I liked it. It gave our friendship a forlorn halo, as in an artistic photograph: two people in silhouette on a foggy afternoon. It preserved the abstract quality of my feelings, as if my life were a line drawing.

Nicole lived at home with her parents in a tiny apartment in Montparnasse, with the toilet outside in the hall, and no shower. Her mother was a dental assistant. She usually wore brightly colored dresses with lots of beads and rings, and she had a throaty laugh that seemed to bounce off the walls of the tiny living room. With her mother present, Nicole was even more silent than usual; almost as silent as her stepfather, an old man with a wide, creviced face, who usually sat on the couch holding a crumpled beret in his hands. He was a carpenter, but from the ironic nods of the mother and daughter, I gathered his business didn't prosper.

Nicole and her mother enjoyed teaching me French. They would point at objects, and name them with a precise, slightly pompous tone, as if I were a little simpleminded; and I would talk back at them in my clinking French, swallowing my words, giving them wrong genders. I took on the role of an earnest idiot. Nicole's mother adopted me as her project. While Nicole sat on the couch leafing through *Elle,* her mother made throaty flourishes and fed me foods that bewildered me. I remember Nicole's brooding smile when I was defeated by a leathery green blossom that sat on my plate beside a dish of melted butter. I tried to stick my knife into it. I picked it up and put it down quickly with scalded fingertips. I had never seen an artichoke before, and required instruction.

Nicole's self-contained sadness became a part of my life. We circled around each other mildly. I think she was frightened of me. That was my problem: my invisibility, my living less. But I never saw—never could see—the nomadic glimmers of the homunculus self; the complex loops of the fugitive atom, alone, alone. Nicole probably didn't see it either, at least not in so many words. She simply sensed that I wasn't all there; a foreigner within a foreigner who, despite his relentless good manners, was, probably unbeknownst to himself, fundamentally a wild man.

By now I had a student card, and was able to eat in a student restaurant near my hotel. The meals were served on steel trays: There was usually a watery stew, some vegetables, soup, thin yogurt, and lots of bread. I got into the habit of stuffing my pockets with the bread and munching the crusts late at night while reading in bed.

I had managed to get a job teaching English for a few hours each week in a commercial high school; it was enough to pay the rent and buy restaurant tickets. Now and then I had a real meal at a restaurant in the Rue de Seine, or made a midnight foray across the river to the glass-and-cast-iron sheds of Les Halles, the central produce market, for a bowl of thick onion soup crusted over with cheese. I walked home over the Pont Neuf. The equestrian statue of Henri IV stood in the middle of the bridge, with the empty river behind it. Along one side stood the dark palisade of the Louvre; on the other, the buoyant dome of the Académie Française seemed to float like a bubble. Paris late at night was a dead city. The Métro shut down at one o'clock; the cafés were closed; a faint night light glowed over the zinc counters as I walked past.

All fall I read Pascal's *Pensées*, at first in a Modern Library translation and then, with a feeling of cool daring, in French. As I read the self-mortifying prose and the bleak aphorisms, I was filled with abstract excitement. I longed to be virtuous and pure. On those nights, munching hard bread and hearing an occasional car rumble down the cobbled street outside my window, I could feel the great vacuum—"the silence of those infinite spaces"—and perceive myself standing on a thin line between two infinities: the starlit one out there and the whirling subatomic one within. Pascal

79

was a genius of insecurity; I read him avidly, as one reads a horror story. I followed Pascal in his terrible desire to make man comfortless and exposed. I learned that I was a machine of deliquescing internal parts. When he explained his famous bet, I wanted to bet too: Maybe God exists, maybe He doesn't; but it makes sense to bet that He does, because what do you have to lose? If He exists, you win; if He doesn't, you lose anyway. I tried to bet, I lay awake methodically casting the dice; but I never actually bet. I could strip down, almost gleefully; I could become less; I had a talent for it. But the bet left me cold. I didn't have it in me. The story of the piece of folded paper Pascal carried around with him recording a night of mystical perception (on the paper he had written: "fire fire fire") made me skeptical and a little disrespectful. I suspected it was an illusion, the result of indigestion or a fever.

Meanwhile, I wrote insufferable letters to my parents exhorting them to be moral and good, to have elevated ambitions, to stop being dishonest and merely sociable. When I turned off the light and tried to sleep, I heard my heart beating against the mattress; it was breakable, a clock of death. I shifted until the mattress became silent. Only then could I fall asleep.

My cold excitement matched the weather. December was chilly, and it rained every day. Paris became darker under the lid of clouds. With the cold weather, Nicole seemed to withdraw into herself. She was always cold. Often she seemed to be listening to something, her head slightly bent, as if I were scolding her. We saw each other less and less frequently. I think this was her choice. She was, after all, a middle-class young woman thinking of the future. Her gypsy mother had sniffed me out, while skipping around the apartment to keep me entertained. She was a practical woman, and Nicole's melancholy required measures. It became obvious that I was not going to marry her daughter. I was temporary, a man without a future or with too much future. More like a tropical scavenger who had swung down to earth and was likely to disappear again just as quickly, stealing the fruit in the bowl.

As Nicole became less available, her place in my life was taken by an overpowering desire.

7

ONE day in early December I opened up a paperback novel by François Mauriac, *Thérèse Desqueyroux*, placed my French-English dictionary beside it, and got ready for several hours of the labor that, at times, resembled plowing the ocean: learning French. Every day for months, I had been making a place in my brain and equipping it with syntax, vocabulary, fractions of sentences. I had worked my fat diphthongs into musical vowels. I had collected bits of language, colloquialisms, slang. I had wrestled with subtleties, degrees of intimacy and impersonality in the various forms of personal address: *tu, vous*. My mind was full of voices, lilts of conversation, a babble of French intonations.

I began reading Mauriac: the gloomy pine forests of the Landes in southwestern France; a creaking silence that pierced the heart of his characters; the thin vein of religious exaltation, amid a hunger for self-sacrifice and self-mutilation. The novel was relentless, a kind of hallucination that was deepened by the straining of my attention as I tried to stare meaning into the barely familiar words and sentences.

After a while I found myself drifting into the story. I leafed through my dictionary and underlined words in the text, hardly noticing what I was doing. The novel's dour language enveloped me; I savored and smelled it. It wasn't Mauriac—whom I didn't know anything about—but French. The nasal definiteness of the *passé simple*, turning memory into a sentence of immutability; the needlelike phrases. It dawned on me that I wasn't studying now. I was reading, as if I had crossed a line through a membrane and found myself in a new, unheard-of place full of intense forms that were almost familiar, almost ordinary. Here was the world as I had always known it: the trees and clouds; fathers and daughters; destructive passions and the secrets of souls; but expressed in a syncopated medium, as if I had stumbled on a reality that resembled my own in every way, except for an immaterial glow letting me know that, appearances to the contrary, I was at the opposite end of space.

It took a while for my discovery to take hold: I could read now. French wasn't simply a discipline, it had become a pleasure. A few evenings later, walking down my street, I noticed the rose light of the Café de Tournon spilling onto the sidewalk. The glass front of the café was beaded with moisture from the cold. When the door swung open, voices poured into the gray street. I could make out the blurred figures of men playing chess at the front tables. I had never been inside the Tournon; its clubby atmosphere had intimidated me. But now I crossed the street and went inside. A wall of warm air immobilized me at the door. The room curved around a shining zinc bar. A mural of Paris scenes covered all the walls, its bright colors matching the plastic tabletops and the floor of tiny mosaic squares. Coats were draped over the backs of chairs. People sat amid loops of cigarette smoke. Everyone seemed at home, as if the café were their living room. I noticed an empty table near the back, and sat down. The din of voices stunned me: French, English, German, Scandinavian. A tall black man with a high forehead and closely clipped hair was talking in a singsong lilt to another black man, huge, with a hat clamped over his eyes, and a raincoat which he kept on despite the warmth of the café. The second man muttered a few words, but mostly he was silent, and looked angry. I saw him often at the Tournon in the weeks and months that followed, sitting with his massive legs spread around the table, and his raincoat on. His name was Slim, and he was Nigerian: a former boxer, a former policeman.

One evening I sat near a booth in the back of the café, and heard loud voices behind me. It was Slim, along with the singsong man—a Jamaican named Josh—and a plump, affable black man, an American who laughed a lot and shook hands with everyone who came by. I found out later that the man was Richard Wright, who lived in Paris. The Tournon was his court. That evening, in the booth behind me, I overheard an astounding conversation. Slim was talking in short, angry stabs with his half-English, half-African accent.

"I tell you! You got to hate the white man! Kill the white man! You got to do it!"

It was ritual and rhythmic. Slim was the priest, and the others joined in, or simply grunted. I was overwhelmed. Maybe it is a measure of the schism in American minds in the 1950s, or maybe I had been an unworldly adolescent who couldn't see what he was looking at. There had been plenty of blacks in my high school. But in those days, blacks were invisible in America; even in Brooklyn, where the Coney Island boardwalk near my home rumbled with gang fights between Irish, Jews and blacks. Yet it had never occurred to me that blacks could dislike whites: that I, for whom race was a dim affair without any emotional charge, could be disliked.

Of all the things I have to say about that period in my life, this seems the most unbelievable to me now. I was a Jew who was oblivious of being so. This was only eleven years after the Holocaust. My own family originated in the vanished shtetls of the Ukraine. During my earliest years, my grandparents had experienced a sadness beyond words as the rumors of mass death filtered across the ocean. I can still see the wooden promenade of the boardwalk at Brighton Beach, the scalloped emptiness of the beach beyond, and still farther out, forming a third parallel band, the ocean with its white spindrifts of foam. The old people sat on folding chairs, along the walls of the beachfront apartment houses, and stared. They wore black coats and flowered dresses. They sat all autumn, and far into the winter. And they talked that language of theirs, full of deep quaking tones that seemed to rise out of the ground, and yet also floated in the air like an aria: Yiddish: all those secrets I would never penetrate; the bemused smiles, the yellowing teeth of the very old.

I was a Jew. My people had just been shoveled into mass graves or burned in furnaces. But I had conspired with everyone around me to say nothing, feel nothing. We had labored to preserve the ordinary with a tension which I perceived as lack of feeling, indifference. And I too was indifferent. I was hardly a Jew at all, but simply a youth: conciliatory, not angry, not seeking vengeance or explanations. Living less had become my cover.

Slim's stabs of hate, and the answers: "Yeah," "O.K.," the almost good-natured laughter of the plump American, electrified me. I felt myself becoming hideously visible, yet I was riveted. I wanted to hear more. The world blossomed bizarrely, like one of those Japanese paper flowers that you throw in water. It was all so complicated. Things weren't what they seemed to be, and I was disoriented but somehow deeply pleased.

I started coming to the Tournon every evening. No more Pascal, looking out my window at the lifeless rooftops. No more letters home full of moral astronomy. I sat at the beige Formica tables, and sipped hot wine. I ate long crusty sandwiches of ham and Camembert, and watched the torpid games of chess at the front tables. I made a few café friends—Americans, Swedes, Germans, Romanians—and we talked philosophy or politics. We compared our arduous efforts to learn French. The evenings were long and steamy. Often I sat with a French book, moving my lips like a child struggling with the peculiar substance of written words.

One evening a strange couple came into the café. The man walked leaning forward with a grin that was close to a grimace. His face was covered with shaving nicks; his skin looked old and yellow, and his grin, on second thought, seemed out of focus, almost cruel. He wore a torn black raincoat, and he was incredibly thin and hungry-looking. Because of his jerky movements, everything about him seemed a little humorous. A step behind him came a lovely girl. She was dressed plainly, in a beige smock, and she smiled with a kind of fixed humility. What struck me most about her was her skin; it seemed transparent, almost untouched. There was something freshly created about her, as if she had been manufactured by a master dollmaker.

The girl sat across from him, and they spent the evening without saying anything. She seemed to be watching him, as if to guess some unspoken wish of his before he had it. When he shifted on his chair, I could see her body become tense. After that, I noticed them often at the Tournon; they rarely spoke to anyone and hardly spoke to each other. She trailed after him with a kind of demure confidence. I found her beautiful. For all her careful and almost frightened subservience, she seemed the stronger of the two. His name was Charles, and during all the ten years I lived in France I would see him listing along the streets of the Latin Quarter, with his thin mouth and his shaving sores, his patches of chin hair, his ripped black raincoat. Sometimes his face would take on a gray tinge, like a clochard's; sometimes he would be scrubbed and pink. But always there would be that grin, and his eyes shifting sardonically to watch me pass, as I pretended not to see him, not wanting to acknowledge his mockery and his isolation. The girl's name was Arlette; yes, my Arlette! The arbiter of my fate in the Paris that would be mine. Arlette, whom I would rescue from Charles's physical abuse; rescue from the closet where he would force her to sit for him sometimes, curiously satisfied with her fate.

Arlette seemed imperturbably serious, untouchable. When

Charles's thin yellow figure appeared at the bar, I knew she would be a step behind him, parting the warmth and the noise like a prow. I didn't know her name, had never even heard her voice. But on the evenings when I saw her, with her transparent skin like a fine eighteenth-century doll's, life-size and smiling, the room would seem brighter. Arlette—it was months before I knew her name—had a kind of abstract existence for me. I'm not sure I actually wanted to meet her. Besides, there was Charles, with his dance-of-death grin and his mechanical movements.

For months Arlette was a distant star in my winter of change, my "slippage." You could call it that. For a plasticity had seized hold of me, during the shivering afternoons and the steamy café evenings, as if my solitude in this city of ghostly beauty and steely foreignness, this Braille of crumbling stone and gray eighteenth-century buildings, had decompressed me and loosened me from my own past.

After *Thérèse Desqueyroux,* I read other books with the same feeling of displacement. The words shimmered with an overlay of voices and shifting usages. They began to have histories. There was a conceptual echo behind each word, composed of all the places on dozens of pages where I had read it, half understood it, and then, like a ship sliding along greased skids into the water, had fully grasped its meanings. I hadn't lived in books with such naïve attention since I was nine or ten years old, and had spent months, years, fleeing from one book to another, like a refugee from something intractable and real: family, my shyness, the feeling of a burnt-out zone in which only I lived. Now it was the same.

It was shortly after the New Year. The bakeries were selling a hard, beige cake called the *galette des rois.* In the relentless chill of the bottom of the year, I decided that I was going to read all of French literature, starting at the beginning. It would be like going back to school, and yet it was mad, out of proportion. I felt that I had surreptitiously broken into a building full of unlived-in rooms, corridors and back stairs. I would go from floor to floor, open doors and shut them. I might get lost, never find my way out again.

I started with the *Chanson de Roland,* in a modern French version, puzzling it out line by line. Then I bought a small old volume of François Villon's poetry at a bookstall on the Seine. The paper was brittle and rough. There was a green woodblock print on the cover. The fifteenth-century French was on the left-hand page;

facing it was a modern French version. I would make out chunks of sense in that crusty medieval tongue written with daffy intrusions of odd letters and almost incomprehensible slippages of meaning. Every line was a mouthful; there was a terse lilt and arrogance, a romantic swagger exhaling into elegiac sadness. Villon was a street clown, a ruffian. Somehow by sheer repetition I got him into my teeth and lips. I snapped the brittle edges of pages, broke the dried-out glue of the binding. It was as if I were actually consuming the book; this wasn't only reading, it was cannibalism.

After that came Rabelais, then Montaigne. Book after book, under rainy skies, on streets gleaming with wet; or in the Tournon with its puddle of light and steam, its conversations playing on the surface of my mind. My room was narrow, the light was bad. Gauze curtains blurred the rooftops and chimneys across the street. I took walks in the Luxembourg on the gravel paths. No children pushed boats out onto the pond. It was February. I was between Rabelais and Ronsard; I was puzzling out the erotic acrostics of the *Blasons du Corps Feminin.*

Weeks passed in my feast of language; feast of incredible loneliness too, watching Arlette—still without a name—trail into the Tournon behind Charles, sit across from him and gaze mutely at his gaunt face.

I was a burglar in my solitary castle, a cat-man wrestling with words, naturalizing them with an anxious attention that resembled meditation. I meditated on syntax and grammar; I internalized odors and colors, slants of vision, songs. The language gave itself to me in dozens of voices: it spoke as Descartes and Malesherbes, Racine, Molière; it spoke in flat austere rhythms, or in alexandrines that resembled packages with neat rhymes to seal them shut.

The physical books themselves lived. Molière was red with gold stripes; Racine was glossy yellow. I had to cut Malesherbes's pages with a knife. There was Fontenelle, Voltaire, Diderot, lots of Diderot. Especially Jacques and his dimwitted Master. I rode along those rutted roads of old France, discoursed on fate and the weather. In my room, lit by a forty-watt bulb, feeling disembodied, as if still waiting to be born, I read *Rameau's Nephew,* and felt the flush of his antisocial antics, his cartwheels of self-humiliation and his operatic feats of savagery, self-mockery and obsequiousness.

The labor of reading in a not quite known language gave the words a thickness. Words became substances. Diderot's nephew existed in a tropical depth; he became a zoological monster, a self such as I would never be: caustic and sardonically humble, visible, hilarious. Week by week, I constructed a new past for myself, I cast lines of language backward into imaginary centuries. I transformed myself, gave myself a new mouth, a new walk, new eyes. The books were doing it. I waded methodically up the centuries, spending hours at my narrow desk, or at the Petit Suisse café across from the Luxembourg Gardens, in a warm, noisy backroom where the odor of coffee mingled with the odor of disinfectant. During the day, the café was full of students. There were heaps of coats on the radiators, and books piled up on the tables next to sausage sandwiches and beer or, opened flat, being absorbed by a bearded student in a black sweater, or by a girl almost invisible with exhaustion. I imagined her living in a *chambre de bonne* without any heat or running water. There would be a skylight; some pads on the floor to sleep on; an electric coil for making tea. On some nights, her lover would climb seven flights up the service stairs, carrying a string bag full of *charcuterie*, a baguette, a bottle of thick Algerian wine. There would be a candlelight dinner on the linoleum floor; love-making under an eiderdown quilt, sent from home. All this I saw in her winter face, in her thick sweater pulled down over a long black skirt; in her attentive pencil, bracketing paragraphs, circling words. I too was present in that café backroom full of beginnings. I too was a refugee from chilly rooms and the perennially damp streets of winter.

I browsed at the few bookstalls along the Seine that stayed open in February. They displayed torn leather-bound volumes of Madame de Staël or Saint Simon, or the Napoleon of Las Cases in many tomes, or Michelet's history of France, taking up half a row. There were old yellow Mercure de France books wrapped in cellophane. It was a musty Gallic roll call. The stalls often sold nineteenth-century book illustrations and military medals from World War I. The horse-chestnut trees rose in huge black columns, their branches spindling out against the heavy sky. The river lapped against the stone banks, swollen and muddy; the walk at water level almost flooded. Long, snub-nosed river barges were moored to iron rings set high into the granite wall. The lights were on in their small living quarters, and a plank walk extended from the deck to the walkway, and along the walkway to the stone stairs leading to street level.

One day I was browsing in a bookstore across from Notre Dame when a tall man wearing quarter-inch-thick glasses came in carrying a worn leather briefcase under his arm. He hesitated, as if trying to get his bearings amid the stalls and the sagging shelves that rose to the ceiling. There wasn't much light, and he seemed to be sniffing out the arrangement of the space. He moved with a boyish awkwardness, but his face, especially his mouth—muscular and thin—possessed a peculiar authority. His mouth seemed to have taken over the expressive function of his eyes hidden by the bulbs of optical glass, with small supplementary lenses set into them. Through the thick glasses, his eyes seemed distant and small, almost porcine. The man approached the shelves where I was standing, and inspected a few titles. When he picked out a book, he had to bend his head to within a few inches of it.

I was then at a crossroads. My progress had taken me through the eighteenth century. I had read *Les Liaisons Dangereuses* and Marivaux's plays; I had read Rousseau's *Nouvelle Héloïse,* in two thick yellow volumes of the Classiques Garnier. Now I was trying to decide what to read next, but as I got closer to the present, I found that time had not yet winnowed out the immortals. Who was great, who was only almost great? I looked at a three-volume edition of Maine de Biran's journal. But was Maine de Biran an important enough writer? Or should I read Restif de la Bretonne instead, a half shelfful of small-press editions with brittle pages? Or else Stendhal; of course, Stendhal. Or Chateaubriand, a shelf of dark red tomes, several of them bearing a heavy-handed Romantic title: *Mémoires d'Outre-Tombe*—memoirs from beyond the grave. I turned to the man with the glasses and asked him in careful French if Stendhal was a greater writer than Chateaubriand, and if so, which book by Stendhal I should read.

I had recently begun to talk to strangers as part of my quest for French intonations. I wanted the nasal song and French lilts of actual speech. I wanted the gongs and sighs which were the effects of the language.

The man paused, and then, turning to the wall of books, picked out a cheap, glossy edition of *Le Rouge et le Noir.*

"Try that," he suggested. His voice was bemused and tolerant, his disjointed eyes peering at me from behind his double lenses.

So began my friendship with Raymond, which, twenty-seven years later, still endures. Raymond, more elusive and solitary than

I could ever be, living in his small apartment, piled with books, on the Rue de Sévigné, in the Jewish neighborhood which, a decade later, would be the arena of my disastrous farewell to Paris. When I met Raymond, he was living with a South African woman named Gilian. She had pale, pitted skin, and a mouth that was thin and wide as a guillotine. She was a Trotskyite, she informed me. When she sat stiffly on a kitchen chair in their tiny living room, the world seemed to pass in judgment before her and be found wanting. Raymond would puff soberly on his pipe and nod; but the severity seemed external to him. There was a softness in his awkward body, and his large nodding head. When he laughed, his voice climbed boyishly.

Raymond became my literary mentor. He directed me to Balzac and Flaubert, Baudelaire, Rimbaud. As the century progressed, the books became thinner, more bewildering. Mallarmé, in a meager blue school volume, stopped me in my tracks. The poems dazzled me, they seemed to condense before my eyes into a pure pictograph of words at the limit between matter and nothing: feathers, petals, breaths of wind, glints of light on hair.

But I kept at it, I repeated those barbed abstractions. *La chair est triste hélas, et j'ai lu tous les livres:* the flesh is sad, oh, and I've read all the books. But I'd hardly read any of the books. I had just begun. The empty building with its hallways and its rooms within rooms extended about me. The cosmos was an alphabet without diphthongs: an outpouring of sound that only months before had become knowable sentences, as if a scrambling device had suddenly gone silent, revealing order and sense, albeit bony and undernourished, not sufficiently weighted with use to be a complete language to me.

During the winter and early spring, I ate at the student restaurant on small metal trays heaped with blood sausage or head cheese. I went to the Petit Suisse in the afternoon, but when the weather was warm, I crossed the street and sat on a slatted green chair in the Luxembourg Gardens, beside the dormant flower beds. Already a few girls strolled along the gravel walks. In a few weeks, there would be dozens of them, wearing bright sweaters and corduroy slacks, or dresses that were stunningly simple and probably homemade.

The girls were arrogant in their springtime colors. They were like flowers. They carried bags of books and smoked cigarettes.

And the old ladies in black coats who sat all day in the garden, like the old people of my childhood on the boardwalk at Brighton Beach, shook their heads disapprovingly.

In the evening, I went across the street to the Tournon. But sometimes, at dusk, I felt a nameless impatience. I walked all the way around the high cast-iron grill fence of the Luxembourg observing the dozens of cats that glided or sprawled lazily in the now empty alleys. The sky came down low over the black landscape. The bars of the fence flickered as I walked past, converting the scene into a jerky silent movie. When I reached the Rue Vavin, I turned into it, past the hewn-stone buildings of the very wealthy, past ramshackle artists' studios and streaked working-class tenements. In the late-winter sparkle of store windows and yellow headlights, with small cars rumbling noisily over cobbles, I reached Montparnasse and a dim, serious-looking café, the Select.

All that winter, and for years afterward, I would push open the swinging glass doors of the Select and pick out a small round table on the *terrace*. The café was a space of muted colors. The walls were drab, the banquettes of scratched brown leather. People sat with their coats on, nursing a glass of wine or cognac, or a tall glass of insipid French beer. They had grave faces, sad faces, remote chalky faces, philosophical faces. They were political exiles from Romania or Yugoslavia; painters with discolored fingers; heavy-spirited men from the neighborhood, with newspapers sticking out of their coat pockets and the decline of capitalism on their faces. I never talked to anyone. I wasn't a member of their society. But I loved sitting there; I felt like an onlooker at Plato's school.

Sometimes I met Raymond there. He taught at a commercial high school around the corner. I talked to him about the books I was reading, and about anything else that came to mind. I was like a hermit who can't stop talking once he starts. And Raymond was good to talk to. He wanted to know everything about me: my family, my childhood, the Brooklyn streets and the beach at Coney Island. As I talked to him, I invented myself. I don't mean that I lied; I made myself into a story. I naturalized myself in the language that was still thick on my tongue but available, encrusted in my psyche by months of reading and talking, by the deciphering of store windows and food packages, by listening to the radio and going endlessly to movies.

What I remember most about those evenings with Raymond

was an ache in my jaw from talking too much. When Raymond leaned toward me full of whimsical attention, with his large body and his authoritative mouth, his science-fiction glasses, I wanted to fill in all the blanks, say anything, including things I'd never thought before. Raymond rarely said very much. He puffed leisurely on his pipe, and talked with an indrawn, hesitant voice about matters that seemed more or less secret, having to do mostly with politics. As time passed, I realized that the secret extended to his entire life. I didn't think about it at the time, didn't feel any lack of depth or background. All I wanted was Raymond's bulky presence, his lips tightening around a pipe stem, his curiously feminine receptiveness, while the man himself remained, almost imperceptibly, distant and forbidding.

Only much later did I learn that he had parents and a younger brother; that his "secret" activities were, in fact, preparations for a book which, when he finally wrote and published it, he quietly disapproved of, implying that there was another book, deeper and more important, which he was going to write; a project that would employ all his faculties, express his thought in a large, unique way. Over the years, the project changed. It was a biography of Trotsky, a book on Robespierre; a work on the history of art; a novel about the Vendée uprising during the French Revolution. For a time, the project wasn't a book at all, but the idea of becoming a lay analyst. He underwent Jungian analysis, and recorded his dreams in a thick leather-bound book which he never offered to show me. He puffed on his pipe, fading behind the richly perfumed smoke.

We would meet at the Select, or at the various apartments he lived in over the years, piled with books but essentially bare and temporary. His life seemed to be temporary. He moved in it like a spirit upon the water, and the buoyancy, made of incomplete commitments and partial efforts—an accumulation of small failures—was attractive, almost miraculous. On his pinnacle of secrecy, by turns stern, reflective or playful, Raymond seemed never to get older. He was always on the threshold; life was about to begin. And the years passed, the beginnings receded, replaced by other beginnings, fresher ambitions, which also receded.

He wrote his book, acquired a reputation as an ironical journalist, a mocking commentator on the folly of ideology. But all this was a flimsy business, as far as he was concerned. He didn't like to talk about it. He preferred to gaze severely through his pipe smoke at the peaks that lay ahead, where the real work waited, of which his accomplished work was not even a foreshadowing.

Over the years, Raymond disappeared from my life more than once. I would return from the summer to find that he had moved and left no forwarding address; or that he was living with a woman who became a subtle barrier to our friendship. Raymond had capacities of retreat that left me perpetually off balance. Once three years went by. Then, one day, I found that I wanted to talk to him; not just wanted, needed those silences of his interspersed with hums and grunts; his sympathy, so elusive and solitary, yet so intelligent, so full of tolerance. It took days of phone calls to publishers and magazines, visits to concierges, inquiries with friends.

I found him living in two barren rooms on the Ile Saint Louis, only a few blocks from where I myself was living at the time. His floor was lined with books, his gray wall-to-wall carpet was immaculate, the kitchen bare of personal touches. It was more temporary than Raymond's usual transient nests. The dominant piece of furniture was a stiff-looking armchair positioned near a window. Raymond's eyes had gotten worse. He couldn't see out of one of them. The other had been treated with ice and surgery to heal a detached retina. He'd had a cataract operation which, unfortunately, caused a rise in ocular tension. He now had glaucoma.

Apart from the few hours each day when he could read or write, his life had become a series of maneuvers in relation to light. The transparent shadow several feet from a window was usually best for him, and that is where his reading chair was located. When the sun was too strong, he saw only a milky haze swimming with forms, and could not go out at all. On one occasion, a doctor in prescribing medicine made a mistake that required a major operation, which hospitalized him for three months.

"I understand now what it means to suffer," he said, but so quietly, with his familiar high-strung laugh, that I almost missed it.

There were sheets of paper on his desk covered with his methodical handwriting. There were the usual projects of large scope and thought which Raymond was to undertake once he finished the almost trivial book he was now writing. There was a woman named Jeanne—large and florid, with hazy blond hair—whom I glimpsed on occasion. Raymond's life hadn't changed. Even now, there seemed to be nothing he wasn't interested in, nothing he wasn't willing to take seriously. His paradox was intact: devoted to partial work and partial failures, living in a limited circle of vision—he was almost blind now—he still gave the impression of a man whose arms were opened wide to embrace life. His inaccessibility didn't filter things out, but made them leap the extra distance with a rush; so that, when I was with him, I too felt more alive.

During that first spring of 1957 I saw Raymond often. I felt like a specimen, subject to his reflective scrutiny, absorbing book after book in a frenetic campaign to master all of French culture. My fanaticism was molding me into something new and unreal. By now I spoke French quite well. Often, when I was with Raymond, I would try to hold back, to right the balance between us, but it never worked, and soon I would be talking about my impressions of Paris: the Tournon with its late-evening steaminess; the latest book I was reading—Zola, Jules Laforgue, or the Symbolists, with their poems full of aroma and wind. Raymond, older, physically bigger than I was, presided over my new existence. He was the mentor of my change into a homeless man; not an American anymore, but an outsider who was almost French, almost a descendant of all those books I was reading. They had become my past; but I had no past.

It was bewildering—and exhilarating—to be taken for French by storekeepers. It wasn't only my accent, but the way I moved, my way of walking; my eyes, my shoes, my handwriting. The center had shifted. Brooklyn had become another world. Already, when I spoke English I felt tentative and unfamiliar. I performed for Raymond at the Select in the early dusk or amid the slanting walls and angles of his tiny apartment up five flights of stairs on the Rue de Sévigné.

8

I T was at the beginning of April, one of those days when racing clouds create a pulse of shadow and light over the city. I was coming out of my hotel when I almost bumped into Arlette walking deliberately up the street toward the Luxembourg Gardens.

She started around me and I felt unable to say anything; and then, paralyzed by the challenge, almost wishing she would go away, I managed to blurt, "Hello," and she looked at me questioningly. Her face had that master dollmaker's glow. She seemed amused, even friendly. In that moment of hesitation, I found her incredibly lovely. I saw that she had a book under her arm.

"What are you reading?" I gulped out.

She looked at me again. "I've seen you at the Tournon, haven't I?"

I nodded, and she gave a strange laugh. Charles was in that laugh, full of trills and depths; it was not a happy laugh.

Her book was by Simone Weil. *La Pesanteur et la Grâce.* It was about suffering and redemption, she said, as I accompanied her up the street to the gardens. I felt anxious being so close after months of glimpsing her across the din and the rose lights of the café. The street was cold and wide. We walked in the park for an hour around the pond, and up the monument alley, then down the curved path toward the back, where there were sumptuous lawns and fruit trees, a rich, green privacy. Then she had to go. When I asked her where she lived, she changed the subject. But to my surprise she agreed to drop by my hotel the day after next, and we would go for another walk. Already I had a feeling, which never left me during all the time I knew Arlette, even years later when we were merely occasional friends, living with different lovers, that only the weakest of threads connected us. A strong pull, and Arlette would spin out of reach. Was this my own uncertainty or was Arlette fundamentally distant, a world to herself? I could never decide. But I was fascinated and soon I was obsessed. The next time we met, Arlette showed me some poems she had written. I remember one about a woman walking alone along a railroad track: that was Arlette, solitary, focused on a chilly distance. Or that was part of Arlette.

The other part surprised me a week or two later. She had never mentioned Charles, but I assumed that she was living with him. I wasn't supposed to contact her. Each time we met, we made a date for the next time, or she left a note at my hotel. Charles was the unspoken backdrop of our tenuous friendship. I thought of him, grinning and emaciated; they were a case of beauty and the beast.

Arlette had stopped coming to the Tournon in the evenings now. Once or twice Charles appeared alone, and stood at the bar, looking like a starved bird. Did I imagine that he looked mockingly over to where I was sitting?

Sometimes Arlette and I walked along the Seine embankment near the Pont Neuf. The cobbles were still muddy from the recent high water. River barges clustered two or three deep against the embankment. We could hear dogs barking on board and smell food cooking in the cramped kitchens at the back of the barges. Lines of wash hung over the hatches. Women in peasant dresses leaned out the rear portholes. In the putrid space under the bridges, we passed *clochards* rolled in torn blankets or sitting in a circle drinking cheap wine. They called out to us as we went by: "Hey, young lovers, come on over; have a drink." They wore torn coats smeared with dirt, and brightly colored scarfs, layers of old shirts, shoes without laces that flapped when they walked. Their faces were grizzly masks of hair and dried crumbs. Their hands and ankles were covered with scabs. But they were like overgrown children rolling around on mats of old newspaper and drinking wine out of green bottles.

I don't think I touched Arlette during those weeks, except to shake hands. I was afraid even to brush her coat. At night, before I fell asleep, I could see snatches of her, see her lips move. But when I tried to imagine her stepping out of her clothes, in my narrow room lit by the distant glow of a street lamp, her smile would dissolve; her thin wrists and stately back would vanish. I could not imagine her naked. Late at night, my penis would torment me, but my mind could find only the ghost of a breast, a half-smile. And I would become furious, wanting to tear apart those dollmaker's silences, wanting to fuck her. Then I would come. The darkness would close in again. My sperm would feel cold and sticky. Arlette would shrink into the distance, making small angry movements that mocked me and goaded me.

During those weeks of suspended feeling, I read Gide, Alfred Jarry, Raymond Radiguet; and then, taking a chilly plunge, Paul Valéry. I read about M. Teste sitting furiously in his chair until he dissolved into pure thought, visible only to himself. M. Teste was my hero. I practiced becoming invisible. I lay on my bed trying to empty my mind, or else to fill it with a single thought. I read mysterious poems that seemed to belong to another dimension: "La Jeune Parque," "Le Cimetière Marin."

A few weeks later that summer I would buy a small brown

motorcycle, and head south over the Massif Central. I would cross the *causses*, bleak, empty plateaus with, here and there, a sheepfold and a stone house. I would descend into the low-lying, odorous country of the *garrigues*, and come finally to Sète, a drab fishing town on the Mediterranean. There, on a dry hillside outside town covered with pine trees and brambles, I found the cemetery where Paul Valéry was buried, the actual *cimetière marin*. I sat on his tomb —a rectangle of white marble—and read aloud about a calm roof where the doves walk trembling among the pine trees and the tombs; and the sea, always beginning again. It was a kind of mass: reading scripture over the powdered bones of its creator.

That summer, I visited country churches, cloisters and walled graveyards. I motorcycled across France, Spain, the Alps, and then Italy, wearing yellow goggles, my pack strapped to the rack behind me, with a thousand pages of Proust in a sleek package that had the feel of permanent things, the Pléiade edition, buckled in it.

I spent a week in a tiny Basque village in the Spanish Pyrenees. One day before lunch, I climbed a rough zigzag track outside the town, marked by crude stone crosses. These were the Stations of the Cross, which old women in black peasant clothes climbed once a year on their knees. It wound up an eroded slope, to where an altar stood on the mountaintop, dominated by a stone cross. I took my clothes off, lay down on the altar and dreamed of Arlette. As I lay there half asleep, my nakedness became immense. The little breezes were fingers sliding over my body. Without completely waking up, I masturbated. The sacrilege was thick and real, and I felt cowed by it. God wouldn't have to look very far to punish me. I was waving my penis in His face. I was exposed to the heavens on that block of mountain limestone. I giggled nervously in the enormous silence, happy with the beads of sweat dripping from my stomach, and the harsh wincing light.

You were there, Arlette, in all your forbidding deliberation, like a nun. I could see you clearly unbuttoning your plaid dress and folding it on the chair in my room; I could see you unhook your brassiere, like Jeanne d'Arc preparing for the flames. I could see you in the broiling underspace of my eyes, for you were not a ghost. You had come to me one day early in June. We had been strolling in the Luxembourg, amid the beds of spring flowers. The oak trees and horse-chestnut trees cast green shadows on the gravel paths.

By now I knew that you were living alone in a *chambre de bonne* near the Pantheon. You had left Charles weeks before. After a year of bizarre hurt, a sort of crucifixion, you had decided that no amount of your self-abasement would redeem him from his bilious plight. He was mad, and you weren't going to cure him by cowering in his closet, or sitting with your head bowed while he showered you with obscenities.

Nonetheless, you had kept your distance from me. All your acts seemed to emanate from an immaculate headquarters in your soul. You were poor; you ate lots of bread and blood sausage. Although you were studying at the Sorbonne, I never saw you with a schoolbook. Yet in June you passed your exams with honor. What perverse intelligence! What chilly capacity for rising to the occasion from the depths of your secret sainthood!

This particular June day was no different from a dozen others we had spent together. After walking for a while, we sat beside the Medici Fountain under the trees, hearing the nearby rumble of the Boulevard Saint Michel. For the first time, you talked about yourself. You told me about your father, who had died during the war; your mother, left alone with you and your newborn sister, Claire; your wartime flight to Megève, at the time a village of shepherds with a few high-altitude *pensions.* Your mother married again, a much older man from the village, who was happy only when he was out on the mountains. He didn't talk much. His world was the snowfields and the gleaming peaks rising out of deep shadow, or the remote valleys of the inner mountains in summer. He didn't seem to like you or your sister. He wasn't mean or angry; he simply wasn't there; a thin, slow-moving presence in your unpainted chalet, jammed against a steep hill above the town.

There was a whimsy in your voice as you told me this, as if you were talking about some other family. And as you talked, I noticed a change in you. A softening, a closing of the distance that had made even the inches between us seem vast. The strands of loose hair along your neck were lovely. A self-knowing smile flickered on your face. Suddenly we were very close together on our green metal chairs, watching the linden seeds spiral into the pond and float on the brown water. You took my arm, and we walked along the gravel path to the black iron gate of the park. We crossed the Rue de Médicis between the rows of broad-headed nails marking the pedestrian passage. The cobbles of the street had been smoothed by tens of thousands of tires. Then came the wide sidewalk of the Rue de Tournon, the white facades of a series of small residence hotels; my own hotel, its brown *portes-fenêtres* veiled by gauze curtains. The owner peered impassively out of his *loge* as we went up the stairs.

You stood in the middle of the room, and looked around at my piles of books, my notebooks scattered over the desk, my suitcases stacked in a corner. It was not a very lived-in room, and that seemed to satisfy you, for you glided toward me. We touched, and I began to unbutton your dress. You stopped me, preferring to undress yourself. I trembled as I took my clothes off and, like you, piled them neatly on the table. My body was thin, dark; yours was incredibly white. Your breasts were small. You had the proportions of a statue, and when you held your arms out, I felt I was being called to a ceremony.

I was probably not a very tender lover. I was far too nervous, far too lost in the boundlessness of what was happening. As you moved beneath me your forehead was a little furrowed, as if you were thinking very hard. You were a divinely mental woman. Even the sexual passion that flushed your breasts and neck seemed reflective, almost ghostly.

How much did I ever know about you, Arlette? Not much, I think. That's probably why your memory has taunted me for so many years, your imperturbable smile even when we slid off the bed and had to push ourselves back on, giggling with embarrassment.

A few days later, you showed up at my room with your paper shopping bag filled with underwear, your vaginal foam, some blouses and skirts, your copy of *La Pesanteur et la Grâce*. You were moving in. Now we could wake up together, and share the pleasure of coffee and croissants on the *terrace* of the Tournon across the street. Breakfast was the secret rite of lovers. I had never lived with a woman before, although "living with" is probably not the phrase for our precarious mode of existence. We were parallel. We had to hold on to each other, simply to fit on my narrow bed at night, yet our lives did not merge or maybe even touch.

I may not have been tender but I was hard-working. No sooner had we made love than my charley-horsed penis would rise again, cracking the dried vaginal foam. And Arlette never refused me, although pleasure did not seem to be a major part of it for her. She seemed to be sketching in a bland area, satisfying a lack. The more we fucked, the less Arlette was present to me. She faded, became a distant partner.

I had the feeling my devotion disturbed her, but did not know how else to behave. Yet under it all, I too had become secretly bored, although that only made me more slavish and devoted. At the Tournon, in the evening, I was the one who sat across from her, silently waiting to catch her faintest wish. I was the saint, she was the tormentor. The roles had been reversed.

Our affair lasted only a few weeks. It was mingled with the poems of Paul Valéry—solemn sunlight and birds' wings—and with my acquisition of the three white-covered, plastic-wrapped volumes of Proust's *A la Recherche du Temps Perdu*. The paper was thin, the print stately. The pages developed in a vast, uninterrupted stream. It was less a book than a space full of subtly colored fish and ghostly tangles of coral. My dictionary, thumbed to tatters by now, was only a little help.

Arlette and Proust were the gods (spirits) that crowned my year of change. One was composed of subtlety and reticence; the other of overabundance, great heapings of language. One had a faintly mocking whimsy; the other was always solemn, like a church in a jungle. Arlette made me frantic with her evasive devotion to herself, like a medieval figure of painted wood, aggressively virginal, but inexhaustible too, always seeming to have further depths of self-withholding, of self-abandonment. Proust offered not too little, but too much. He expanded and probed; he cast a verbal halo about every sentiment, every object, like the glow around street lamps on a night of mist. Everywhere, there was a malign gentleness, a remorseless clarity.

I usually read at the *buvette* under the trees in the Luxembourg. I worked to still the wavering sentences, to grasp their elusive physicalness. It was a deliberate, faintly tipsy sort of work. Proust gave himself to me, while Arlette, abandoning her body to me, gave me nothing.

Later that summer I would read Proust in neatly mowed fields at midday lying beside my motorcycle; in youth hostel dormitories; in small-town cafés; and in a meadow atop the Simplon Pass. Always those fluid pages that were, exquisitely, about a brittle and dying social class, a disintegrated young man always on the verge of tears, a France of impoverished grandeur. It was an epic about paralyzed acts, an *Arabian Nights* without any plot or story. And it was astoundingly strange.

I myself had become strange: a Gallic ghost walking the streets of Paris, with my fraudulent but accurate French. On many evenings that June I sat on the rim of the fountain in the middle of the Place Saint Sulpice. The square was empty; the misshapen church rose before me crowned by the two garish towers of which Victor Hugo had written: "When I see the towers of Saint Sulpice, I piss." There was a smell of urine around the splashing Baroque fountain; apparently passers-by still felt the same way. The dark windows of shops selling cheap religious wares lined one side of the square. The cobbled space did not attract many cars or pedestrians.

Proust's former housemaid, Céleste Albaret, ran a little hotel on the Rue des Canettes around the corner from the Place Saint Sulpice. The street was full of basement dives and drab residence hotels. I had gone to visit her one day, and Madame Céleste had been proud to show me her collection of books by and about Proust: gifts from him, from his publishers. The books were enshrined in a glass bookcase in her *loge*, up a flight of winding stairs. A year later, I stayed there for a few weeks, in a room whose only window gave onto the staircase. The hotel had probably been just as cheap and old thirty-five years before, when Proust was living in his cork-lined bedroom on the other side of town, and Céleste, a young country girl tiptoeing around the sumptuous shut-in apartment, had taken care of him, awed by her effeminate employer who rarely left his room, and maybe a little contemptuous of him. Now he was her patron saint. His shrine was a glass-fronted bookcase. His church was a scrubbed concierge's *loge* in a run-down hotel in the Latin Quarter.

By June, Arlette had moved her shopping bag of clothes out of my room, although we still saw each other, as friendly lovers. We agreed that I would visit her in Megève, where she was going to spend the summer with her family. My summer project was to travel around Europe on little roads, visiting places no one saw. I had a vision of tiny fields lined with hedges and plowed by horses; isolated villages where people spoke *patois* instead of French. This was the deep past of fairy tales and folk songs, where farmers walked miles to town, or rode bicycles.

In a curious way, the year had made me a more complicated

person, although not a more experienced one. My existence had turned into a form of theater. I had become French, but not quite: a fiction which, over the years, would deepen and fill out, without ceasing to be fiction. My friends thought this was amazing. In less than a year French had taken me over, bending my very bones to its uses; not a disguise, but another person with rearranged hopes and feelings. This other person accomplished a circus act; he juggled his lips, he tapped into a past that was not his and thereby erased his own past. He no longer smoldered with guilts he had no name for: he was not the son of his father and his mother, the brother of his sister. He had stifled all the unsayable past, which he saw as a distant vision of Brooklyn streets with cracked sidewalks and weeds in the backyards. He remembered himself in that other past as a child without true feelings, a child who had been at home only in books, reading them with a kind of desperation, never wanting them to end.

Once, when I was three or four, I wandered off on the enormous public beach near Coney Island. It was October and the beach was empty. I walked along the water's edge for hours, feeling the little rills flood in over my feet. The ocean was a lace of wave crests rolling toward me. The sun was cool and silvery. A long time afterward, a large man in a blue uniform with gold buttons came across me. He grabbed my hand, and led me across the beach to a public telephone. Was I lost? I didn't think so. I was happy, alone. It turned out that my parents had been looking all over for me; they were afraid I'd drowned. The police were searching the oceanfront.

When the policeman called, my mother was terrified. My father was, well, silent. I suppose I'm like him: evasive and private, a runaway Jew.

All during my childhood, I'd wanted to be unexceptional. I spoke carefully, and never got my clothes dirty. I tried to do well in school, but not to excel. If there is a place where explanations fail me, it is here. I recognize the traces of flight, like footprints around an event that has left no other mark. Flight has since become an appetite for me, a way to get my hands on life, a way to live.

When I was six, my grandparents—elderly city Jews—bought a farm near New Paltz in upstate New York. The farm was sixty acres of woods and hills, with an apple orchard, a cherry orchard and a couple of large fields. There was a white frame house with an earth basement heaped with old farm tools, a butter churn, a bedwarmer, animal traps, bags full of nails. The farm had no electricity. We had to haul water from a well in front of the house. There was an outhouse behind the apple orchard, a couple of oval holes over an acrid-smelling lime pit. We cooked on a wood-burning stove in the kitchen.

My grandfather had been a teamster; he knew plenty about horses, but nothing about cars or tractors, so he bought a horse and buggy, a flat wagon, even a sleigh. Then he bought a cow. It was a crazy idea; but my grandfather was a man who hadn't made much of his immigrant life. He had gone from trade to trade, and managed to fail in all of them, mainly because of his difficult temperament. He was an irritable, physically powerful man: a tall, bald warrior, who quarreled with everyone, especially his own children.

The farm was a tragedy for the family. The harsh solitude of farm life, in a region where there were no other Jews, probably killed my grandmother. My parents, aunts and uncles felt trapped by the responsibility of keeping my grandmother company, and helping my grandfather, a man of sixty-five, to deal with the demands of an unmechanized farm. But my grandfather—a bilious soldier of pure Yiddish stubbornness—was my salvation. He gave me a place that was a pure dream, turning the vacancy in my heart into a country I could explore and love.

I spent summers tracking through the young oak woods or crawling in the tall grass around the house. I climbed a jumble of glacial boulders called Bonneycue Crags, which rose up in the middle of the woods like a ramshackle fairy-tale castle. When I was up there, I could hear the wind growling in the rocks and bending the dwarf pine trees. Behind me stretched a barren spine of boulders and tilted strata, with windblown earth giving hold here and there to a few bald trees. I lay on the edge of the crag, imagining a world without people in it; only a vast horizon, uncut prairies, the American plains before Columbus, or the world before man.

I lived in this fantasy in a dozen ways. Often I would climb through the woods across the road from the farm, owned by the eerily named Smiley Brothers: rise after rise of young oak and pine trees. Boulders deposited by the receding glaciers loomed among the trees, angular and water-darkened, some of them as large as houses. I tried to walk like an Indian, stepping on rocks and roots, but such silence was beyond me. I was the human being in this solitary world; an observer of orange salamanders, and black tadpoles squirming in the brook; a collector of wild strawberries and pine cones. I listened for rattlesnakes or the prolonged slither of a garter snake, and felt a freeze of terror in my lungs.

While my aunts and uncles fought bitterly, my grandfather walked stubbornly to and from his fields. He raised corn on ten acres plowed by a rented tractor. He built a barn to house some chickens. For weeks I knelt with him on the dazzling white pine boards, knocking in nails. The barn rose, plank by plank, with crossbeams and vertical bracing posts, a sloping roof lined with tar paper, wooden roosts for the chickens. I was in awe of my grandfather, who could create this building out of heaps of planks, two-by-fours and nails. He worked slowly, his mouth set in an angry line, as if sealing his lips against the bitterness in his heart.

Once a week I rode to town with him in the wagon to buy chicken feed at Lefebre's grain warehouse. The bags of grain gave off a rich dry perfume and sweated puffs of chaff, as we jolted home. The horse walked philosophically over the iron bridge outside town, and down the rising and falling road to the Four Corners. Then, more slowly, stopping to rest now and then, we climbed the forest road to the farm. My grandfather hummed to himself over the hard-rimmed wheels, slapped lazily at the horse with the leather reins. He spoke to me in garbled English or muttered Yiddish. I felt very small beside him, very much a part of his stern, ungiving personality.

For five years we spent summers, Christmas and Easter at the farm, and once we lived there all fall. My father would arrive from New York on the bus around midnight and walk three miles from town over the dark road, lit only by stars or moonlight.

My father and grandfather loomed large in my childhood, both of them preferring empty spaces to the anxiety of relationships. For a year after my sister's birth, my mother had been sick and the house had a stifling smell of medicine, which I found hard to breathe. I was frightened, probably resentful, but the sickly atmosphere allowed me to go unnoticed on those hot July days when the pine trees looked powdered and metallic, and the weeds in the uncut fields were turning yellow.

I crawled for hours in the tall grass around the house, my clothing covered with wild seeds and burrs. The ground was hard and cracked and hurt my knees. There was a hill overlooking the house, with a grove of tall pine trees on it. I liked to crawl up the hill, and to enter the brown space under the pines. Springy pine needles lay upon the ground. The sky was a splintering of blue, barely seen through the horizontal branches. There was an odor of resin, the deep mattress of needles under my back. Sometimes I brought a book with me. One night, I climbed the hill with my father and a box camera to take pictures of the stars. The open shutter registered snakes of light moving across the black sky.

My father was always bemused and quiet. When we walked in the woods on weekends, he seemed lost and boyish. Being with him was almost like being alone. Both of us were happy to be away from the angry words that often filled the house, my grandfather like a wounded bear, my grandmother, toothless and wonderful, her hair a gray halo around her face.

I can see now that I wanted something from my father, and was angry at not getting it. It happened that I wept without knowing why: from loneliness, I suppose, or because there was no one to save me from my own freedom. I had to people my Robinson Crusoe's world with books, the tenuous ghosts of characters who vanished when I shut the cover on them and went on alone in a subdued panic, searching for another life, another beginning.

A man can spend his whole life looking for his father and not finding him. I don't think my father ever knew what I wanted from him, and I didn't know, either, or more likely I was afraid to ask, preferring to be taciturn and silent. He spoke carefully, as if pronunciation was a shield against the wounds of life, against the streets, and the Irish and Italian gangs that had terrorized him when he was a boy. I see him sitting on the stoop in front of his father's laundry shop in the Williamsburg section of Brooklyn, memorizing Milton, Shakespeare, Wordsworth, A. E. Housman, Thomas Hardy: poets he can still recite uncannily, although he hasn't read any poetry in thirty years.

When we walked in the woods, or climbed the chalky chaos of Bonneycue Crags, he liked to recite to me, and yet not to me. His voice was curiously uncommunicative, and the poems hung in the air between us as things not said.

With distance, the summers have become superimposed. Those timeless summers at my grandparents' farm, where I fled into an empty landscape. That other summer, twenty-seven years ago, motorcycling out of Paris with my backpack and my books, like a traveler into a fairy tale. And still another summer, on the Italian coast near Viareggio, hearing the cicadas in the tall Mediterranean trees outside the house, knowing that everything changed; that the simplicity was gone, the ten years of being a foreigner living at a distance from my sleepy core of longing, the nausea, the fright at too much freedom, living at an uncertain distance from my parents, whom I had preferred to see across an ocean, as originators of another life, not mine. All that was changed and changing.

9

IN the house near Viareggio, Anna, Jane and I formed an incommunicative triangle. We were a family of spare parts holding on to each other apologetically, a little unbelievingly: a mother, a taciturn teenage girl, and a stud. Jane was trying to control her panic at a world that had become harsh and unyielding; a world without a center, without kindness. She was so thin, so pale. She looked eight years old, as if her adolescence had been crammed back inside her. Anna's universe was defined by a bed and some little white pills. It didn't seem to matter where she was: Italy, France. She talked a lot about death. She seemed to savor it as a definitive subject matter. There was a coquetry about it, as she stood swaying against the waves in her black bikini, tossing her thick black hair against the ocean breeze.

"Death is my lover," she said. "He reminds me of David, a little plump and sassy, but kind."

She would look down at the white rills breaking against her body, and smile at some fleshy husband hanging around in the surf, as if he might be the one. Or was I the one?

Amid that vacillating summer, Anna had become my anchor. I had left Paris and my half-empty apartment. In the middle of August, I would drive to Le Havre and board the *France*, for my trip home. I called it home, but it was a foreign, unfriendly place, composed of out-of-date memories and desultory friends whom I had kept up with over the years but hardly knew; a job that was waiting for me; my family exulting at the return of their alien son. My mother would sigh and look anxious. My father would smile to himself, always the immaculate visitor, proud of his incommunicative son, flesh of his flesh, silence of his silence.

Late in the afternoon on one of the first days of August, I sat reading on our little boxed-in porch facing the street. Up and down the street, small Fiats, covered with dusty sand and salt, were parked on the lawns in front of the houses. The street was never busy. The churned, sandy ruts snaked up a hill toward the highway, a mile away. Amid the cicadas, the echoless voices of children, and the occasional strident call of someone's mother, the day was at a still point: hot, aimless, dusted over with grit. I was reading a novel by Simenon, thinking that this landscape could have been one of his: so flagrantly ordinary and uneventful, expressing faded feelings and unstated needs. But it was not like Simenon either. Nothing as definite as murder lurked in these flaccid afternoon shadows. That was Simenon's old-fashioned sleight-of-hand. Give him any dented old hat—a lower-middle-class Italian resort under the pine trees, with radios whining and a beaten-tin sky glimpsed toward a rise in the road a few hundred yards off; a displaced American trying to read, while the uncertainties of the day swirl in his mind: his false wife and false daughter; his dwindling summer, with the day, only a few weeks off, when he will have to face the gulf of the future without any excuses—and out of that hat Simenon would pull a magical dark rabbit: murder, the maximum exclamation point, pure art, like the frame around a picture. But there was no picture here, no murder; only an unraveling tale of impotence, sex and dead friends; and an unsayable fright of the new world that was about to swallow me.

This afternoon, my mind refused to lose itself in my book. I was stuck in this place, hearing the sea wind in the pine boughs. A sticky residue of salt clung to my hair and skin. At the rise of the hill, a small figure came into view, moving alone in the sleepy landscape. At a distance, he hardly seemed to be moving, walking beside the road with a suitcase on his shoulder. My eyes shifted listlessly from my book, to the lawn lapping up to the porch in vinelike strands of thick, brittle leaves, to my dirty blue Simca parked at a tilt on the edge of the lawn; and, on the fringe of my sight, a figure approaching slowly with his jacket slung under his arm. My eyes slid toward the man, not seeing him, yet registering his oddly familiar stride. I leaned forward and looked more carefully: the walk that was almost a swagger; the easygoing shoulders. It was impossible, a fantasy. The man approaching down the street in a kind of eternity was my ex-brother-in-law, Lucien. My mind raced to catch up with my senses. That forgotten lunch of a few months before; the address scribbled on a corner of the tablecloth. It had been a joke, but Lucien had taken it seriously. He was here. As he approached, I noticed his torn shirt and half-ripped-open suitcase. There was a large scratch on his cheek, and a fiery red bruise on his forehead.

I climbed over the porch rail and walked up the street to meet him: the golden boy, with his blond hair falling in a sweaty clump on his forehead, a smile barely visible on his lips.

"Well, I'm here; *comme tu vois.*"

We shook hands in the middle of the street. The sunlight slanted unevenly across Lucien's legs and chest. He squinted while saying hello, and we looked at each other, embarrassed by the strangeness of our meeting.

"What happened to you?"

"I drove down to Nice to see my children yesterday, then continued on here. I must have fallen asleep at the wheel. I ran into a tree about five miles up the highway. The car's wrecked. I walked the rest of the way."

He looked exhausted and nervous, yet as always there was something heroic about him: an edge of tragedy or despair. All at once I was buzzing with anxiety; my sleepy old pain had become fresh and new. Lucien's world-weary body seemed to shut out the light. At the same time, I realized, I was glad he was here. Maybe it would all work out. I would be able to leave, shed my unholy family and drive over those mountains. The thought occurred to me as Lucien stood before me, a tatter of sleeve falling back along his arm as he shifted his suitcase to the other shoulder. Nonetheless I was uneasy, even frightened. The truth was that Anna, Jane and I had worked out a comfortable sort of existence: joyless but predictable and considerate. It had become a cozy hell. But now the golden giant was here, and I could see that he too was scared, although not much showed through his blond detachment and his soft, rich voice.

We went into the house together, and I called Anna.

"This is my ex-brother-in-law, Lucien. He was driving down the highway near here, and had an accident. Do you mind if he stays with us for a few days? He can sleep over there on the couch."

Anna looked small and unsure of herself. She said very little as Lucien told about his accident, but when we were alone in the bedroom, she said, angrily: "I don't like this, Paul. We were doing O.K., weren't we? I don't want anything to change." And then, panicky, almost childish, "We're still going to be able to fuck, won't we?"

There was nothing arch about Anna now. She had built a nest against despair. Any change was full of portents, and she didn't want it. All she wanted was me, her partner in refuge, her pliable fantasy-husband.

With Lucien present, the house seemed smaller. We bumped into each other and the furniture. Jane reached for deeper layers of resignation and indifference. She was hardly present at dinner, stabbing at her sausage and spaghetti. That evening, we were all uncomfortable. Lucien's physicalness challenged me. Even his car accident seemed to give him an edge. His pain wasn't nebulous and interior; it was gorged on destruction, it was dangerous. Lucien's bruised forehead shone bravely as he talked in fumbled English with Anna, whose French was opaque and mysterious, understood only by herself.

The next morning we went to the beach. We spread our blanket on a ridge of sand near the water, and Jane and I lay down, while Anna and Lucien went swimming separately. But after a while, they stood together looking out at the ocean. Anna was small, and deeply tanned; Lucien was tall, his white skin rippled like a fine cloth that might tear, his neck and his arms red. When they came back to the blanket, they were friends, and I sensed that the lines of connection in my little family were shifting. Anna and I had talked about driving back to Paris in a few weeks, or I might drop them off in Milan, where they could fly to Greece. Now, without anything being said, there was a change.

Lucien tried to keep out of my way. We had never been able to talk, and we didn't succeed much better now. It occurred to me that he wasn't very articulate: he hesitated, reached for his words; that rich voice had a flaw. His physical panache had always carried the day for him.

That evening I asked Anna how she liked Lucien.

"He's a nice man, and he's very beautiful. This morning, on the beach, we talked about death. The ocean was a beautiful nothing rolling up and clinging to me. He understood that."

What does he understand? I wondered. Because I didn't understand a thing. About anxiety, helplessness, I understood. I understood that whatever I did, I was tunneling into life or I was crushed by it, or, rarely, carried upward into something spacious and bright. But I didn't understand death at all. Life gripped me with a kind of frenzy. Lucien's flirtations with suicide mystified me. When Anna talked about the dark one she languished for, the smoky seducer, warm lush nothing of death, I saw it as bizarre, a dance without any music. I didn't follow. I lacked the imagination. But Anna and Lucien shared it. They heard the music. I saw them standing up to their knees in the water, saw the froth breaking against them. Their backs were to me, and they were talking about death, while all I saw was a blue-white sheen glancing from the water, a pale horizon line where sky and sea touched. It was a glorious trap, relentless and hungry; life, always life.

With Lucien there, I felt liberated and defeated at the same time. The anxiety stifled me, yet I was singing, I was happy.

"What would you think about staying here with Lucien?" I asked Anna that night after we had made love, feeling the sand on the sheets underneath us. She didn't say anything.

As I spoke, I was filled with the absurd expediency of our relationship. I knew there would be no problem. Anna had been clinging to a ghost, not to me. It would be a small adjustment; I would leave, Lucien would replace me, and the ghost would go on. I would pack in the morning, and leave after breakfast. I planned to drive over the coastal mountains, and head for Siena. I had always loved Siena's rose-brick buildings and its Piazza del Campo like a sloping seashell. I had spent weeks there over the years, admiring Duccio's sultry Madonnas, the striped cathedral on a hill resembling a Gothic zebra, the concerts of chamber music at the Accadèmia Chiggi. Then I would drive to Venice for a proper farewell, without Anna's oversized presence. After Venice, I would head west all night over the monotonous autostrada, then the road twisting across the Alps. Maybe I would have breakfast on the beach at Cannes, before the long drive up to Paris.

The family would go on. Anna and Lucien; Jane so lonely she couldn't feel it, sitting on the beach, or in the drab furnished living room of the house, without speaking, her face expressionless and childlike; waiting, always waiting. I imagined Anna and Lucien topping each other's death fantasies in a zany competition: Anna, all hard edges; Lucien ambling in a vast isolation. They would fuck and talk about death, and swim in the ocean.

The next morning we had breakfast and I packed my suitcase. Lucien acted as if it had all been worked out beforehand. This is what he had come for: to help me out, to spring me loose from my unholy responsibility. The unholiness was right up his alley. It seemed incredible that he had built his summer around an address scribbled on a tablecloth. His behavior was on a level with his little suicides. It was the punch line of a desperate tale, as in the story of a man who is the life of a party, and then goes home and shoots his brains out. Behind Lucien's easygoing mask was a life stretched thin.

After the summer—Anna's siren song may have had something to do with it—he joined a left-wing splinter party, and started talking in tiresome slogans about world revolution and scientific socialism. He became a union organizer, a militant hard-liner. The golden boy had been buried on the Greek beaches where he had ended up with Anna and Jane, continuing the morbid charade I had begun. He wouldn't be Rimbaud any more, but Robespierre.

Anna and I hugged on the doorstep. It was a brotherly embrace. Already I was the one too many in the house, and it was natural for me to be going. Anna was affectionate, grateful but distant. Lucien hung behind in the living room. I wasn't only leaving, I was being expelled; anxiety was blowing me out of the house. Jane waved from the window as I got into the car and chugged carefully up the sandy street. The low-slung car scraped over the ruts. There was a lot of traffic on the coastal highway, and I had to wait before turning south. A mile later, I turned inland onto a hairpin road that climbed past the chalky fields and the marble quarries. Flocks of goats scrambled on the high slopes and the ocean in the distance resembled a wide blue wrapping around the gnawed shoreline.

I was alone. The car still had the sticky smell of ocean air. I had ten days to get to Paris, and then to Le Havre. Ten last days of summer. Ten last days of the only life I had ever really known.

PART TWO

I

WAS brought up as a child of silence. Silence about the Holocaust, and then, during the cold war, silence about politics. The enormous killing of the war seemed to have no content in my neighborhood of brick tenements and aging three-family houses. It was an empty catastrophe for the old people who had fled Poland and Russia forty years before, looking for the better life they may have found on these wide streets lined with crushed little houses and columns of smoke rising from the incinerators—an irony that no one may have noticed. Now, a little shrunk, a little sad, they meditated on this immense twentieth-century pogrom that seemed to blot out even God and the past. They themselves had spent forty years forgetting the past. But now it wasn't merely forgotten, it was plowed under, erased; written not in words, but in thick oily smoke on an unblinking sky. But they never talked about the Holocaust. In my house, it was present as a silent bewilderment, and a struggle to be cheerful. I remember it, I suppose, as a lack of light in the various apartments we lived in, or as a sagging in my grandmother's face. To be a Jew, when I was a boy, was to be unhappy, unspeaking; it was to live within an invisible limit. My neighborhood was a mental ghetto created, in part, by the history which hadn't happened to it, hadn't produced tears and mourning, but only a wily, angry distrust of gentiles, who were devious and powerful and a source of catastrophe.

Later, the silence expanded. By the late 1940s, the McCarthy years had begun. Friends of my parents were losing their teaching jobs in the public schools because they had belonged to Communist groups before the war. Books disappeared from bookcases, or were turned with their titles to the wall: Marx's *Capital,* Lenin, Engels, books on unionism. The blank books stared at me from the shelves.

There were other silences too. My father was not an expressive man. He spent his time playing handball and sleeping most of the day when he was on the night shift at the post office. He read poems to me, corrected my grammar, muttered angrily when I picked my nose or looked bored while he played his precious albums of classical music. Classical music is still for me those dusty torn albums, the dreary black discs, the careful sounds that were supposed to make me better, even if I didn't want to be better.

My childhood resembles a silent movie: I see the actors, watch their lips move, but I don't hear what they say; as if there were a space that had to be crossed, so easy for those grown-up legs and those vast arms. But somehow no one seemed to think of it, or, more likely, I myself made the space inviolable. Who could believe I had such power?

I remember playing with my little group of friends at the Brighton Beach Baths, whose private beach fronted the ocean a few blocks from our house. We were three or four years old, and we roamed over the beach all day. The brown sand was as vast as an ocean; and the green beach buildings with their peeling paint, the smell of hot dogs and sauerkraut in the enormous round cafeteria with its dozens of doors, the clayey brown of the paddle-ball courts and the thunk of the hard black ball on the handball courts that smelled of wintergreen oil and sweaty gloves, where my father ran after low-angled shots and returned them with a jerky movement of his whole arm: all this formed all the world I knew.

Around the age of five or six, my friends vanished, and I was alone. It seemed to happen all at once. One friend moved away. Two others also moved, only a few blocks, but to a more expensive part of the neighborhood. Their parents were getting richer. The boom of the war years was on, but my father paid no attention. He went on working in the backroom of the post office, where banks of pigeonholes bore the names of towns, and he sorted out the mail, his intelligence compressed to a work of empty routine that contained no possibility for hurt or disappointment. So my parents and my friends' parents lost touch, and I lost my friends.

There was something else too; something that my little boy's smile was incapable of expressing; something I have forgotten so deeply that even now, remembering it, I am still forgetting. I was six when my sister was born. It was April; the beach was still empty and almost wintry. Seaweed was piled up along the waterfront in a tangle of black tendrils and slimy green strands. Tiny crabs burrowed into the sand and made bubbles. I felt lost in all that chilly silence, hearing the crash and whisper of waves that broke onto the sand and scurried back, to be stumbled over by the next wave coming in. That is one memory. In another, I am sitting against the wall of a building around the corner from our apartment. My nose is bleeding, and someone has stopped to help me. He leans over with his handkerchief, and presses it against my nose and upper lip. He is saying something reassuring, but I'm not frightened. Maybe the man's confidence has calmed me, or maybe I'm terrified in my own way: quiet, waxen, like a tide that has withdrawn into its depth, or a small creature flattened against the floor of its burrow.

Those remembered scenes are curiously innocent and precarious—so clear, so intense—because they hover over a vacancy. Where is my sister? Where is my mother's changing body, the rush to the hospital, and my sister in her padded bassinet, like a ruddy obscene doll with a crack between her legs? Where am I? Nothing is left.

It may be that a man is best defined by what he first forgets. That he is sculpted by what he forgets, not by what he remembers. If recollection forms his visible identity, the bones are of oblivion.

Years ago, when I was still living in Paris, I remember being struck by how clearly I could picture virtually every phase of my life there, starting literally with the first hours in the late summer of 1956, when I arrived at a hotel on the Rue de Tournon. Soon virtually every street over a vast area of the Left Bank, and parts of the Right Bank too, contained a multitude of impressions one on top of the other, like emotional transparencies, a trick photography of the mind. Noticing the sign over a shoestore on the Rue de Rennes, I could remember sitting across the street from it in a café, feeling dazed and a little scared because some friends had just been arrested for giving aid to the Algerian rebels. I could remember every time I had walked, mused and ached in sight of it. This was also true of certain Métro platforms, the fronts of buildings, the Luxembourg Gardens, the promenade along the Seine. I seemed to have lost the faculty of forgetting.

For ten years the memories interpenetrated and resurfaced, they acquired perspective. After all, I had lived so many different lives, each with its own boundaries and landmarks. I had been a clumsy American youth, a leftist militant and a Marxist, a husband; later a street person, smoking hashish in North African cafés, trying to pull the strands of my intelligence together to become a writer. I had made friends, and lost friends. I had done everything but forget.

Maybe that's why those years seem all of a piece to me now. At the same time, all that remembering has given them a curious feeling of unreality, to the point of imagining, at times, that those ten years never existed. How could anything so clear and whole be said to exist, when experience tells us that reality swims out of sight all around us, that even the clearest memory hints at something uncontrolled, maybe even monstrous, which keeps to the shadows, so that our experience always seems to be the loose end of some frayed connection that is out of our ken?

My sister's birth is one of those frayed connections. Neither she nor my mother's pregnancy exists for me in memory. Already, as a small child, I had lived with my foot half out the door, a vacant, elsewhere sort of boy, whose only fullness of feeling came when he was alone, on the beach with the irrepressible waves, looking out at a low tongue of land speckled with houses that reached around like an arm, as if to keep the ocean from escaping: the peninsula of Rockaway, almost another continent, despite the heavy arches of the Marine Parkway Bridge linking it to the mainland.

Another memory. One night, when I was around nine or ten years old, I got out of bed and went down to the basement. The cement floor was covered with a layer of coal dust that was soft and fine to my naked feet. The furnace loomed in a corner, cold and black; it was summer. I took my pajamas off, and felt the cool night air all over my body. My penis rose like a small, thin bone, and the darkness wheeled about me slowly, peacefully, and a wild contentment ran down my legs. After a few minutes, I put my pajamas back on, and went to bed. Such were my moments of true living: cosmic, blank, almost impersonal. But my sister's birth I have forgotten. She doesn't exist for me until she is two or three years old. In her place, there is nothing; a loss of friends, a lovelessness like a gas subtly thinning out.

My psychoanalyst tells me I must have experienced an anger so destructive that I had to suppress it, and suppress the rest of my feelings too. I had to become a ghost, cut off from friends, as in the

Gnostic story of the lost boy cast into the world. But what the psychoanalyst couldn't know was that my friendlessness was mysteriously rich, full of rooms to explore and sudden perspectives. In my strangled unspeaking way, I was happy. As if I myself had chosen not to have friends, and instead to lose myself in books, to puzzle out the constellations on a clear night, or to lie on a concrete slab near the ocean listening to a portable radio and feeling the humid heat of summer; or to spend all day walking in the woods on my grandparents' farm. My life became its own refuge. I learned how to be alone even when there were people around. I went to school, studied, raised my hand in class, made "friends." But nothing could take the place of the friends I had lost years before, when my sister was born, and I became an orphan.

A few months ago, I went back to visit my old neighborhood, not far from Coney Island. It was a cold, rainy March morning and the chill coming through my shoes was like a pane of distance between me and the streets with their rows of brick tenements, their fruit stands and delicatessens, which had endured for thirty years with a kind of seedy persistence, giving me the impression— so strong it became unpleasant—that I had entered into a tale about a thin, dark-skinned boy with large ears who once had lived on those streets. All morning I teetered on the edge of the tale, sometimes in it, and sometimes, with a peculiar wrench, outside it, reviewing all the ordinary details that, for some reason, composed the tale. Why those? Why were they saved?

For example, why this sunless courtyard lined with garbage cans and closed off by a spiked gate, where I played make-believe adventure games that broke down into shrieking arguments, a sort of talmudic tournament, about who was allowed to do what? Why the weather-softened board fence behind the house where my grandparents lived, with its odor of old linoleum and decay, of old bricks and cockroaches? Incredibly, the same odor pours out of the hallways and basements of the neighborhood even now.

As I walked around the old streets, I tried to remember what it was I had fled thirty years ago. Why had this place become the symbol of not living to me, so that I had to get out or die? College, the writing of poetry, a decade in Paris, finally even the French language, communism, Third World revolt. I couldn't get far enough away, because I couldn't become someone else.

I suppose I've been a wandering Jew of sorts, a creature willing to gnaw its leg off to escape from any trap; yet, curiously enough, the obsession of having a home has stuck to me through everything. Even now I can't seem to go anywhere even for a few days without arranging in my mind how to come back to it anytime I want. Part of my pleasure lies in this echo of returns I'm always constructing. I caught myself doing this once in the middle of the Sahara Desert, in a place I was not likely ever to see again or recognize if I saw it, and I was dumbfounded. I realized that I had been acting all my life as if everything that happened to me was endlessly repeatable —and all because I couldn't bear having a past. The past diminished and scared me, because it was comprised so much of that which would never be possible again. I suppose that's why traveling to a new place, even making a new friend, has always unsettled me. Here is something else to repeat, a new orbit to trace, with its threat that sooner or later it will disappear and be lost, that entropy will take hold.

Yet even as I write this, intrigued to have told a truth I didn't know I possessed, I can see how incomplete, even misleading, it is. For despite what I say about home and repetition—all true—the fact remains that I have walked out of my life repeatedly, without looking back. Worlds crawling with connections have abruptly ceased to exist for me. Later, when I run across someone I had known in one of these earlier existences—a college roommate, or a best friend from childhood, even a woman I had loved deliriously —I feel like a traveler wearing a space suit which my friends recognize oddly as my face, walk, flesh, persistent physical traits and voice, intimate scars. This space suit enables me to survive in an alien atmosphere, to breathe reminiscence and eat memory with no harmful effects.

I remember standing on a height overlooking Honfleur and the estuary of the Seine a number of years ago. The coastal land was so low and flat that it seemed to melt into the water. Europe ended here, and my life in Europe was ending too, after ten years. In a few hours I would drive to Le Havre, board the *France,* and it would be over. As I looked out over the hazy water, I kept saying to myself: Here is the end of Europe, the end of the world. Yet somehow I couldn't grasp the drama of this extraordinary moment, the end of the strangest decade of my life, maybe because I was still lost in the middle of it, or maybe because there wasn't any drama. So I decided to remember the lack, and post that memory to myself at a later date: a man near the edge of a cliff, with the rooftops of Honfleur below him, a vanishing coastline, water so smooth it looks solid extending to the horizon. At his back, France, dozens of friends, the knowledge of being a person with definite interests; a foreigner, which is to say free but also, unavoidably, solitary; hundreds of books, buildings, faces steeped in familiarity; more than anything else, perhaps, a number of songs he had hummed or heard, suffusing the whole with an atmosphere he would always recognize painfully, like a surf breaking over him. He had turned his back on all this, not defiantly, but simply, as if obeying a law of nature—for example, the law stating the impenetrability of matter: Two stones can't occupy the same space at the same time, and he, going home, couldn't also be in France. Momentarily, therefore, he occupied a nowhere without regrets or nostalgia, without drama, as if the nowhere were inside him too.

Years later that memory reached its destination when I visited Paris again, stunned by the recognitions leaping at me from the gray-white buildings, the storefronts and cafés: neighborhoods I had internalized without knowing it, along with their inhabitants, the former friends whom I located again and who, incredibly, were glad to see me. I was choking on repetition, frightened by it, filled with a wild gluttony for more of it. It was the same feeling that had possessed me earlier in the spring, in Brooklyn: the feeling of a torrential return; layers of the past smashing together, like a car flattened by a gigantic press in a wrecking yard.

Everything I had walked out on in my life—all those chapters my right hand had crossed out without letting my left hand know about it, every suppressed panic and cowardice, the acts of selfishness, the vulnerability, the smells and colors that belonged to them —was becoming frantically alive again.

For thirty years, Paris and Brighton Beach had been the odd couple in my life. They had never really been on speaking terms. In fact, they had deplored each other. During all the years I lived in Paris, I had almost daily flashes of the poolroom one flight up on Brighton Beach Avenue, with its backroom—more tremendous to me than the local shul—where the bad ceremony of poker was performed all day and night. (I wonder what the Jewish equivalent of a black mass is.) I was an inept poker player, and pool was a beautiful, masculine, maddeningly delicate, maybe criminal activity that frightened me. Paris was my revenge on the pool hall. "If my friends could see me now," I would think to myself mechanically, *in French*.

It was my revenge on so much else too, but what? I tried to remember as I walked up Thirteenth Street to Oceanview Avenue, and down Twelfth Street to Brighton Beach Avenue. I tried to remember as I stood in front of P.S. 225, looking up at the school, with only a few scattered classrooms lit up in the gray day. The school was mostly empty now, kept going by the children of recent Russian and Israeli immigrants. I tried to remember on the stoop of my grandparents' house on Thirteenth Street, in front of buildings where best friends I hardly remembered used to live. For all I knew, their parents still lived there. Or maybe they themselves still lived there, forty-seven-year-old strangers I wouldn't recognize. I tried to remember, but I couldn't. The flight, the revenge, were my life; but they were traces of a vanished need.

I walked around the old wet streets; along the boardwalk, with the empty beach and the ocean on one side, and the decrepit, sadly gay beach tenements on the other; I passed boarded-up knish stores; the pinochle club where my grandfather used to play, already open for the season, with a few bare bulbs lit inside and a group of old men with their coats on, sitting around a table where they had been playing for a century or two, would never stop playing. I felt grateful that this shell of a neighborhood had endured long enough for me to pay my respects. But nowhere could I find the clue that would explain to me why I needed so badly to get out that I'd gone halfway round the world, a distance of 180 moral degrees, where Paris would cure me of Brighton Beach.

Cure me of what? Of my grandfather's tall bald brooding, his face of a Gothic prince? Of my grandmother's gray Afro and her exquisite tenderness, her Friday baking, her bemused, unconditional love for me; the handkerchief on her head when she lit the candles on Friday nights; her cracked English riding on a flow of deep, incomprehensible Yiddish? Cure me of my father reading Shakespeare, Wordsworth and Milton to me when I was six, my father who still speaks with freakish elegance (freakish for Brighton Beach); of my mother, athletic and beautiful as a movie star in the few old photographs I've seen of her, who even then was transmitting to me her legacy of anxiety, her tendency to talk too much when she was nervous.

After that morning in Brighton Beach, I drove to my parents' apartment a mile or so away in Sheepshead Bay to have lunch, and found out something that I have been mulling over ever since. Apparently I had gotten my childhood all wrong. We had lived with my grandparents on Thirteenth Street for only a few months, and in the tenement with the sunless courtyard for scarcely half a year after that. Nothing had happened during those months, but it had been a wild and savage nothing. My sister had been born, and the memories of this period had become charged with displaced feeling.

Is time a river, or a slowly moving wind? Can I feel it on my face, or see it rippling over the sidewalk like heat? Or is time simply a theory, useful because it explains so much: the aging of bodies, the upthrusting of the grass, or else that bundle of vacated rooms and amazing basements known as memory. But if time is only a theory, then why do I hear its muffled tick inside me all the time? Why do all the sights and sounds of the world—women's faces, the human voice, like a suite of rooms with the same wonderful lover undressing in each of them—resemble a permanent springtime that is nonetheless passing, like God's parade, or the cosmic procession Walt Whitman wrote about, tapping his foot to the music and thrilling to the drum?

For me, time is Paris and Brighton Beach. Time is the failure of love; for that, I suppose, is what my sister's nonbirth represents for me.

I have a feeling that for weeks after she was born, I watched my mother's pinched face and stooped walk, finding her oppressively brave, nauseatingly secretive. I crept around the three-room apartment on the first floor of the tenement with the sunless courtyard, knowing what had really happened on that day in April in 1941: that I was the one who had been born—shoved into life; that is to say, shoved aside.

Needless to say, this scene is a fiction; not even a cover memory; I don't remember any of it. But whereas Plato wanted us to distrust our lies, Freud taught us to honor them as traps for the truth.

At the age of six, I became an orphan of sorts—that is, an adult, a reader of books. Brighton Beach became fixed in my mind as the place where I lost my friends, the place where time began.

Since then I have often had the fantasy of a large family with lots of aunts and uncles, swarms of cousins. A family so large that when they get together and have a few drinks, they spill out of the apartment into the hallway shouting at each other and talking about baseball. I know such families exist on another planet, along with my sister, my parents, happy after a huge meal, swimming in the yellow light of the dining room, in the smell of esoteric dishes that were steaming on the table. This other planet is in my mind, and maybe I will visit it sometime, have visited it in the past, and visit it even now from time to time. How hard it is to keep from glancing away again, and suddenly looking back: on my actual sister, now a grown woman with children of her own; on my parents, on the swarms of real cousins; on the aunts and uncles who are beginning to die, their places taken by a new race of elders, by me.

2

I wasn't a very political adolescent. I had grown up surrounded by unexplained cautions, by ellipses, and all these silences had sealed off the public world, so that I didn't really believe in it, didn't know it was there. I could look out from my insular world at the ocean, a blue plain that sometimes heaved wildly in a storm; or I could escape into the green and stone wilderness of my grandparents' farm. Later I could read. Even school stretched too far from my private center to be wholly invested with belief. But politics, war, social injustice, public issues of any sort, were flimsy fictions, and they were subtly dangerous. My mother avoided talking about them when I was present, as if to spare me some contagion. Once, when I was practicing the piano, a neighbor shouted across the alley that if I didn't stop making a racket, she was going to tell everyone that my mother was a Communist. I asked my mother if it was true, and she said no, but that she had belonged to leftist political groups when she was a girl, during the Depression. I was surprised to learn that my grandmother, who had recently died, had been a socialist in Poland half a century before. I remembered my grandmother lighting candles on Friday night, or sitting in the synagogue on the high holy days. She was "religious," as opposed to my parents, who weren't. But religion had been a late nostalgia, probably caused by the war: suddenly, my grandmother had wanted to remember. No, my mother wasn't a Communist. Mostly, she was afraid. She spent years waiting for a note from the principal of the school she taught at, denouncing her for her former political affiliations, but the note never came.

I looked up communism in an encyclopedia, and my general impression, as I remember, was that it sounded pretty sensible: a scientific society, the abolishing of all injustice. I filed it in my thought as a remote speculation, unconnected to real acts or passions.

My world was a small, sharply lit territory, surrounded by mist, as in Chinese landscape paintings, where the details of ordinary living vanish into a misty space, above which, distant and jagged, rise the inaccessible peaks of mountains; there was nothing in the space between. And the space between for me too was empty. There was something dreamlike about all this; for when there is no public world, the inner world becomes overloaded, frozen. Having less, one has even less, and then still less.

During my college years, McCarthyism was afoot in the land, creating not only fear and angry patriotism, but claustrophobia. At Columbia, where I went to college, desks were set out in front of the buildings, where students talked quietly about the atom bomb, and Students for Democratic Action. Later, there were petitions for the Rosenbergs. I didn't sign any of them, partly because I had absorbed my mother's furtive fears, but also because I didn't really believe any of this was happening. Who were Julius and Ethel Rosenberg? Did they exist? Yes, but in the mist. And my little overloaded life went on. The first anxious love affairs, fraternity life, the discovery of books and ideas, the thrill of not living at home, of being independent. Yet under it all, I began to know that, in some deeper sense, without a public world there is also no private world; there is no world.

After my first year in Paris, I had gone back to New York to go to graduate school. The year-old Frenchman in me became silent, unused; and the result was a feeling of homelessness. I felt unhinged: a man and his double, and yet apparently only himself. As a graduate student, I started reading books about seventeenth-century English poetry, English history, the sociology of English literature. The university library fulfilled a curious fantasy: its narrow corridors lined with books, the cubicles at the far end, a pool of light on an oak desk. As a boy I had dreamed of such a place, far away from the confusions of friendship and family, where people passed only in the distance, too busy to notice me. Was I thinking of my father sitting a few blocks away at his pigeonholes in the backroom of the General Post Office downtown? I saw his life not as sad but as curiously joyous; what he bottled up in that hard, kindly face of his was a stubborn pleasure, a refuge that he kept intact, even from me.

But the library wasn't refuge enough, nor were the rooms I lived in on Waverly Place, and then in the empty neighborhood down toward Canal Street. The city seemed raw and wild to me as never before. I felt that I had stepped through a portal into a world where things happened. Somehow, when I wasn't looking, my life had begun, and my unraveling emotions lay about me at night, while I listened to the fallible thump of my heart mingling with police sirens.

I piled up thick black books on my little desk at home. I laid them in disorderly heaps on the shelves of my cubicle at the library. I dreamed of entering into them, like an angel with a scythe, reaping the spiritual grain. T. S. Eliot's essays on Milton and the Metaphysical poets; Milton himself transposing me into the peculiar gnawed shapes and trail markers of his blind eloquence; Douglas Bush's reassuring compendiums of literary knowledge; Basil Willey's utilitarian house of ideas securely mortised and tenoned into a structure as high as a watchtower; and above all Arthur Lovejoy's Great Chain of Being rising gently in a soft light, like geological strata beyond time, beyond the thudding and shrieking of the streets with their blackened bricks, their spider-cracked windows, their streams of indifferent ugliness. But the books didn't work. The desk, the room, the cubicle deep in the stacks, were porous; somehow, there was too much of me. I had cracked the chrysalis of my father's cubbyhole life, and felt alone and helpless.

Within months, I knew that I wanted to go back to France. I wanted to walk on those dowdy streets, and sit in the Tournon, where all of living was a matter of conversation. I wanted to stand on the Place Saint Sulpice with its slowly trickling Baroque fountain sounding like Victor Hugo's piss, and Madame Céleste around the corner, buxom and coy in her black dress, showing strangers her bookcase filled with signed volumes of Proust.

New York was too big, too raw. It was like me: banged up and bruised, full of comfortless wisdom. Suddenly I had grown up and I didn't understand what I was seeing. That year, the Rosenbergs were executed, and I didn't notice. I noticed West Broadway choked with throbbing trucks, and the cast-iron warehouses that held no romance for me. In my apartment, in the evening, I heard rats scampering in the walls, and spent half an hour hunting for holes to stuff yet again with newspaper. I was afraid to go out of my bedroom at night, and often urinated out the window onto West Broadway. Mine was the only apartment within blocks. During the day, there were trucks, street peddlers and swarms of workers. The stores played music from buzzing loudspeakers, and were lit up by red and blue neon advertisements. At night the neighborhood emptied out and became an immobile fantasy, like my dysfunctioning self.

I wrote jagged poems that tried to capture these broken bits of self. It was surrealism without the exuberance, disruption without the dream of a golden future. That winter I sat for a few days in an orgone box in a friend's loft on Spring Street, and didn't feel any shower of cosmic rays. Saint Sebastian never longed for arrows as I did for the rays. But I left the lead-lined box, a disenfranchised mystic. Did the Yankees win the pennant yet again that year? Was Mickey Mantle still hitting tape-measure home runs while leaping against the outfield walls and damaging his knees? Was Gene Kelly dancing, and Eisenhower playing golf? Were Roy Cohn and Alger Hiss trading evil intentions across thick, barred walls? I don't know. I was somewhere else. Even my books couldn't help me. Even Thomas Traherne, the gentle seventeenth-century mystic, whose *Centuries of Meditation* was the subject of my thesis, could offer only a comic relief to my thin and broken identity.

Traherne was the perfect subject for a man in a hurry. He had been a lost writer. His cheerful masterpiece had sunk into the well of vanished books, until Edmund Gosse came across it in an antiquarian bookstall in London at the end of the nineteenth century. English literature had done without him for two hundred years. He hadn't influenced anyone; hardly anyone, since, had remarked his existence. He was still almost lost, and as such represented a remarkably compact subject matter: a pure book, a book without a halo; a book trailing a small bibliography; a book such as could be mastered and written about quickly. No one came before him, no one came after him. Thomas Traherne became my ticket back to France. That anomalous, smiling country preacher kept me busy for two weeks in January. Desperation can make a man single-minded. I wrote for hours every day. I proved a variety of points in grammatical prose. I fed the pages to a typist.

Thomas Traherne inhabited my whispering rooms on Canal Street. He sang to the rats scampering in my walls. When I pissed out the window, he laughed like a golden child and looked with loving curiosity at the worn-out asphalt of West Broadway, the bar down the block winking red and blue, the stray cars that stopped at the lonely red light on the corner. Thomas Traherne was the godfather of my impermanence. He assured me that I would be able to depart in June with a degree in my pocket; that the god of prodigals favored me, and maybe even smiled on me. His love of life matched my crumpled nerves. He soothed me, by speeding me on my way.

3

FLEW to France in early June, on one of those numbing twenty-hour flights. It was just for the summer, I told everyone, and I believed it. My canvas suitcase held a few shirts, some light slacks, a volume of Proust, my stained blue pamphlet of Paul Valéry's poems. I had written to Madame Céleste, asking her to hold a room for me at her hotel on the Rue des Canettes. The scrubbed gray stairs with polished wood balls at the head of the banisters, the smell of disinfectant, the dim little room with a window that swung out onto the stairs, were seedy and welcoming. I was home again, and I knew it. New York had expelled me; I was a reject, an American who didn't fit. It was hard to understand. In all the vast grid of the city, with layer upon layer of apartments, office build-ings, downtown cafés; on the rebellious streets of Greenwich Village, or in the dire districts to the east where marginal individuals hung on amid the unfriendly squalor of aging Jews, Italians, Poles and Hungarians—wherever I looked, there was no place for me. New York was full, it squeezed me out. And I left. Not for good, only for the summer, or maybe for a little longer. I would perfect my French; it wouldn't be time lost. Lost from what? A career? I had the sense of a thread that might break, and leave me hanging.

A few days after arriving, I was walking on the Boulevard Saint Germain, not far from my hotel, when I noticed a face amid the round tables crowded onto the sidewalk in front of the Old Navy Café. That ineffable reserve, that willed pallor: I would know it anywhere. It was Arlette, like a ship's prow parting the casual conversations, and the snarling motorbikes and the cars growling five abreast down the Boulevard Saint Germain. She was sitting with another woman, who could have been her exact opposite: large, physical, with blond hair hanging loosely over her shoulders and a look of intense concentration on her face. She laughed and tossed her head in response to something Arlette was saying. As she did so, she seemed to explode with sheer overabundance, of nerves, of blood. There was something quietly berserk about her.

I came over to their table, and Arlette smiled quizzically at the appearance of her lover of another year, *l'américain* who had sputtered over the mountain roads on his motorcycle to see her the summer before in Megève. I hadn't thought about Arlette all year. She had been an unresolved memory that I had left behind in Paris, not meaning to return. In New York, my laboriously acquired French double had been submerged by the panic of suddenly growing up and trying to find a place for myself in the world of careers, the world that had a future.

Arlette introduced me to her friend. Her name was Michèle, and she was a painter. When she talked, she chewed her cigarette and leaned back in her chair with a defiance that would have been masculine except for a sexual softness in her face, and her nervous hands. Her laugh ended in a high, explosive sigh. She and Arlette were very much wrapped up each other. They had their jokes, their complicity. Arlette seemed to bask in Michèle's extravagance. There was a whimsical distance in Arlette's voice when she spoke to me that let me know immediately where I stood: The past was past. Our little affair of the previous spring had been an incident.

She was beyond it—beyond me—now; although where she was would have been hard to say. She seemed to have her own chilly space that amused her. Michèle too seemed amused. I told them about my year in New York, and my plans for the summer, my idea of somehow staying on. I didn't know how I was going to do it, if I did do it, yet after a few days in Paris I knew I had no place to go back to. It was precarious and exalting to be nowhere, almost to be no one. I felt stirred by Michèle's casual intensity. When she leaned forward, her long hair fell over the V of her tight red sweater. Her mouth and her hands seemed light, almost floating. After a while, Arlette said she had to go. When she stood up, I had the impression that she was handing me on to Michèle. For the past half hour, she had said very little; she had been remote, approving, an impresario. And now Michèle and I were alone.

I walked her home. Behind a high iron fence at the corner of the Boulevard Saint Michel the black stone ruins of the Hôtel de Cluny stood in a pool of menhir-like stillness. The wide sidewalk was full of slim girls and defiantly shabby boys. A sultry light reflected from the rows of *portes-fenêtres* along their narrow balconies, silvered the young leaves of the horse-chestnut trees. Michèle and I walked in that liberating light. What did we talk about? Did I tell her about my studies and my poetry; about Madame Céleste in her hotel on the Rue des Canettes, and the profound, almost frightening release which these streets provided: the sizzling of *pommes frites* in little stalls in front of the cafés, the smell of blood sausage drifting from an all-night restaurant near the Odéon, and the light, yes, the light showering from a sky that was low and wild, with its billow of soft pastels. Did Michèle laugh with her high, soft sigh as she told me about her painting; about the village in the Alps where she spent the war years; about her mother, who still lived there; and about her marriage, because, yes, she had been married. In her rage to be independent, she had run away from home when she was seventeen and married a journalist. She wasn't a girl, she was a woman; she had weight, she had a past that ran deeper than her years. Or did I learn these things later, when she began to open to me like a Chinese scroll, endlessly complex and vast, its layerings of life heaped vertically from lakeside to flowering hills, to wild, snowy peaks, all eerily precise and still. Memory has erased whatever was said that day, and left only a glimpse of two people walking, two people erecting a kingdom. A creeping light had isolated us. We were lone inhabitants of ourselves, faces moving in a fabulous transparency.

As we walked up the Rue de la Montagne Sainte Geneviève and then along the Rue Descartes, we entered a neighborhood I had never seen before. Here were deeply gray, tilted buildings that seemed to swim up out of the city's past and stand blinking in the light. This was Michèle's neighborhood. The groceries, bakeries and butcher shops were tiny; lines of customers trailed onto the narrow sidewalks and into the streets. The stores were painted red, beige and green. The Rue Descartes ran into a square with a couple of low trees in the center. The buildings on the square were even older and more crumbling. Old store signs were painted on the walls, but the stores were gone, or they were different stores. The faded signs gave the square a crumbling festiveness. Half a dozen *clochards* lay on a raised island in the middle of the square. They clowned and fought among themselves, and drank from those bottomless green bottles. One of them got up and stumbled about in his smeared shirt and sagging pants which slipped down while he danced. He grabbed at them, while a friend tried to pull them down, and they roared with thick laughter, their voices raw and full of mucus.

The square, the Place de la Contrescarpe, was the center of a tiny working-class neighborhood wedged between the Panthéon and the solid bourgeois buildings of the Rue Monge. It was an island in time; a place where the old working-class lore was still alive. The language spoken here wasn't French, but a whimsical Paris slang known as *parigot*. I heard it whanging past my ear, full of twangs and swallows.

We walked down another street and turned into an alley that ran between walls stuccoed with gray cement; a dingy vein running deep behind the street, to a courtyard filled with plane trees and parked cars, and surrounded by a ragged series of buildings: a low barracks-like apartment house; an elegant nineteenth-century *hôtel particulier,* with white slatted shutters at all the windows; and, occupying the favored place, a misbegotten concrete wafer, full of cracks and angles, one of the last buildings that had been put up before the war, in that era of concrete architecture, monuments to modernism and the ambient fascist aesthetic.

This was where Michèle lived. We got into the wheezing elevator—a box of glass and polished wood about the size of a coffin—

and crept up six flights. The apartment was tiny: a living room, two small bedrooms, a tiny kitchen. It had been her parents' apartment before the war, and had only recently been recovered from a homeless family that had taken it over after the war, after the Nazi officers who had requisitioned it had left. Michèle lived here with her two brothers. As the oldest, she had the living room, a large brown room with a low bed against one wall, and an easel placed near an open window. The easel was occupied by a canvas covered with slashes of color. The paint was thick, almost sculpted. A square palette lay on a stool beside it, pitted and streaked with dark reds and yellows; blue swirls like eyes rose from it. The colors were a moonscape, or a tropical seascape, deep and rich with the energy of the brush. The palette lay like an exposed inner world; beside it, the canvas seemed almost chaste.

Michèle's room rushed out the windows. The two double *portes-fenêtres* stood open, and Paris, in a vast hazy bowl, opened beyond it. The bright dome of the Sacré Coeur glowed on the northern rim. Notre Dame sat heavily in the middle distance, like a heraldic animal. The great clock tower of the Gare de Lyon was off to the right. Here was all of Paris: the silver slopes of the rooftops, the chimneys, the valleys and the heights; the faintly traced streets. A fretwork of angles and cubes, like a gigantic cuneiform text gone haywire. The beauty of the scene was overwhelming. It was like a glimpse of eternity.

I think I fell in love with everything all at once. Michèle, and her neighborhood, and the view from the window, and the jabs of color on her palette. On a low table between the windows was a photograph of a man's face turned theatrically in profile, with a bandanna around his neck. The photograph was blurred, and the paper was old. The man had sharp features, and a deeply creased forehead. There was something chilly and profoundly moral about him. Over the years, that face would haunt me. It would become a silent chorus, a refrain, peering at me out of its heavy wooden frame, or not at me but beyond me, as Michèle, so often, would fight her way beyond me in a fine moral rage.

"That's my father," Michèle said. "It's the only photograph I have of him. He was killed during the war, in the Resistance. My parents were both in the Resistance. I hardly saw them during the war. Then he was killed. He was an aide to Colonel Fabien. They were killed together."

Michèle's face had become guarded and quiet. The year before, I had often walked past the bronze stick figures of the monument to the Resistance, surrounded by closely cropped lawn, in the Luxembourg Gardens, and read the words of the dirgelike hymn inscribed at the base:

ami quand tu tombes
un ami sort de l'ombre

Michèle's room was frozen to its past. Michèle too seemed frozen. Her voice was level and unexpressive as she stood in the hazy brightness, with all of Paris pouring in the window, and her father, blurred and silent, on the table, staring in the photograph toward something gray and speckled, maybe a mountaintop.

For years, our lives would be shadowed by legends of the Resistance. A friend of Michèle's, an old factory worker, whose wife ran a fabric shop down the street, had been captured by the Nazis, tortured, and sent to a prison camp. He spoke in a hoarse, wheezing voice, or what was left of a voice after the camps. He limped up the steep street on a crooked leg, the result of beatings he had received. He was a martyr, and his wife, plump and bright, sitting all day in a rocking chair inside her cluttered store window, was the goodly mother of the class struggle. There was also Gilda, a friend of Michèle's mother, full of boisterous student mannerisms, although she was almost fifty. Gilda had been a terrorist. In 1943, she had walked up to a German Gestapo officer in the Gare de Lyon and shot him in the head. There were other people too, whom Michèle pointed out to me on the street, smaller than life, wearing clothes that didn't fit, smiling with a gold tooth, lugging a string bag full of *charcuterie* and bread along the tiny sidewalk. They were soldiers of an old army, survivors of a time when souls had been made and broken without niceties. Michèle still had a foot in that time. Her father was the dead but terrible witness to an unfinished task. These were things I would learn only gradually. But today, in the splendid afternoon glow, on the heights of the Montagne Sainte Geneviève, there was Michèle, and she was enough, her beauty deepened by the perspective from her window, and by the silent seriousness of her dead father peering from his wooden frame; by the teenage marriage that had made a woman out of her, and by her passionate laughter, as if she were spilling over softly, unstoppably.

When, several days later, we made love for the first time on the wide hard mattress in her luminous room, I was overwhelmed. Michèle's physicalness was so powerful. When I entered her, she seemed to rush over me like a soft river; then she bit my chin, and I went wild. I felt lost, exalted, and frightened all at once. That was what it was always like with Michèle. She was passionate, distrustful, angry; she laughed like a torrent. Our love was charged with ironies that I didn't yet grasp. Only later would I understand the profound rebelliousness of this woman; her instinct for disruption; her pride, like a violent force lashing out willfully, often indiscriminately. And the plea that no one saw, and that I rarely understood, amid our tropical rages and our defensiveness: the plea to be accepted to the depths of her being; to be embraced quietly, even religiously; embraced, no doubt, by someone who no longer was; someone who glared out of his wooden frame in an aging speckled blur.

A week after we met, I brought my suitcase up to Michèle's apartment, and bought a knapsack. I put some shirts and pants, a few books, a notebook, into it. Early one morning we walked down the creaking circular staircase into the first light of day. The streets were empty; it was too early for people going to work. The Métro was still shut down. Our feet scraped cheerfully as we walked up the Rue du Cardinal Lemoine, and then down the decrepit Rue Mouffetard, with its faded residence hotels, its narrow cafés, already lit for the day, with a couple of men in *bleu de travail* tossing down a few glasses of white wine before heading for work; its boarded-up lots; the grubby Vietnamese restaurant, *Le Bar des Isles*, where we would often eat in the years to come.

In the lower part of the street, the market was already in full swing. Steel shutters clanked up, dollies clattered over the cobbles, vendors shouted to one another as they set up their stalls: the fish stalls packed with crushed ice, the vegetable stalls, the cheap hardware, and the cheese, and the fruit heaped in pyramids of red, orange and green. The market was alive with color and coarse street poetry. Voices twanged from side to side of the descending street.

Michèle and I were heading for the Porte d'Italie, where we planned to hitch a ride, preferably in a truck, heading south. We were going to Provence, to Les Baux, a little ruined city on a cliff near Arles, with a spicy Provençal breeze whining among the stones, and a sky that was always taut and blue and lightly glowing.

I remember the chalky stone walls rambling over the rocky pinnacle of Les Baux, like bloodless hedges. All the air of the summer blew in hot pipings across that small desolation; air from the hazy hills below, with their patches of green combed into taut braids of well-dressed vines; air from the shimmering silver to the south, the Mediterranean, barely visible from an outcrop of smooth limestone on the cliff's very edge, where Michèle and I would lie at sunset, hidden from view, and sniff the sky, and feel the warmth of the vast baked stones rise into the gathering dusk. Sometimes we would pull our clothes off and make love, sandwiched between the earth's heat and the ebbing air; air that arrived like a heat blast from Africa, beyond the almost visible sea.

We stayed at a youth hostel which occupied the lower floors of a ruined palace. We ate baguettes and cheese, bought at a tiny shop wedged among the ruins, and drank powdered coffee. In the morning, when too many visitors were roaming about the ruins, we climbed down a path into the valley and crossed the brittle scrub to a little rise of red earth, in the crooked shade of a couple of pine trees. Michèle took along a pad and some gouache, and she spent the morning sketching the wild valley with its bright-somber vegetation. She caught a few mournfully crippled trees, and the earth like a raw slab, red and creviced. She caught the palings of light, and the vineyards with their sumptuous green rows. While she painted, I wrote or read, and sometimes, looking up, we felt the sweat trickling from our faces, down our chests, and we would get undressed again and, on the harsh, red earth, swept clear of spines and sharp stones, make love again. We brought summer into our bodies in this basin of wild earth surrounded by hills and by the limestone cliffs of Les Baux. There was a desert silence, brittle, dried out. It was only June, and already the sap had been burned back into the earth; the trees stood in the brightness like parched fingers.

I felt the wonder of Michèle's ruddy face, her mouth gnawing at itself as she bent over her pad, daubing colors in a fury of browns, yellows and oranges that floated like hieroglyphics, a cele-bration of pure heat. Her landscapes resembled living bodies. Whatever she put her hand to became erotic; but an eroticism without sentiment, without love. It was cosmic, a swell of breasts and legs; but look again, and there were the crooked trees, the harsh red slopes, the rows of vines, and the gray-white limestone, almost blinding in the desiccated light. Van Gogh had painted his mad landscapes only a few miles from here. They looked as if he had clawed the paint onto them with his fingers. Michèle had her own madness that played in her wide hips and her strong white thighs; in her breasts that swung over her pad, large-nippled and powerful.

From the beginning, we argued a lot. Ideas were a passion for her, and she became enraged if I didn't take her ideas seriously: ideas about Chinese painting and Gothic churches, the monastic life, about Picasso, whom she loved. Her mind was full of harsh assertions and angry ideals. She struggled to make things clear. About one idea, however, she was silent, almost gentle. We never argued about it, maybe because it so intimidated me that I lost my footing. Michèle was a Communist. Her mother was a Communist too. Her father had been a Communist. Michèle told me that he had been betrayed to the Nazis by anti-Communists in the Resistance, an episode in the quiet civil war that had raged in France for two centuries like a disease of the spirit, full of subtle skirmishes and treacheries.

Michèle went to cell meetings, and read the Communist newspaper, *L'Humanité*, for which her ex-husband had been a reporter. The people she talked to on the street in her neighborhood—the old factory worker, the lawyer who wore dark suits that were too large for him, the students with uncombed hair, the young dentist who walked with a slight stoop and smiled fixedly—they were Communists too. On the Sundays before we hitchhiked south, I had seen them standing on the Place de la Contrescarpe selling *L'Humanité Dimanche* and *France Nouvelle*, or passing around a petition to get the American army out of France. But their presence hadn't really registered. Such enthusiasm of belief was almost unimaginable to me. Michèle's world confounded the political images that had colonized my imagination: images of humorless men who lived only for the revolution, horribly self-denying, and filled with scorn for private enjoyment. Communism, as I had soaked it up from the frightened newspapers of the McCarthy period, was metaphysical as much as political; it was like an acid, or a disease; nothing was safe from it. It was the only evil people could imagine in the amnesiac America of the 1950s. Without it, wealth and happiness would rise like bread in a great pan. Communism belonged to the great darkness. How I reconciled these feelings, largely unconscious, with those from my own family history, I don't know. The latter were nourished by Paul Robeson's voice booming out "Ballad for Americans" when I was a child on the scratchy black records that stood anonymously amid those of Beethoven, Mozart and Tchaikovsky on the family record shelf. All that combative virtue, brightened by my mother's bouncings and tearful smiles. My political thinking was that primitive. Despite my years at college cramming the classics of Western political thought, Plato and Machiavelli and More, Rousseau, Marx and Engels were only vaguely embroidered on my consciousness.

But here was Michèle, smelling of woman's flesh, a painter, tearing the crusty baguette with her teeth and slicing off chunks of Cantal cheese with a penknife. Her politics glimmered in her hungry laughter, but they were not her. She was a "dedicated Communist," as the phrase went, but she was also a wily woman simmering with needs; a lover of churches; a hungerer after gargoyles and church grotesques; sighing berserkly in the crude country monasteries we visited. Why did all this overwhelm me? Why was it so much to take in that I glossed over it, except for a sense of having slipped out of my depth, into a world of incredible surprise? Michèle was more complex, more elusive, but also more real than any woman I had known. She imprinted herself on my nerves; left her mark upon me from moment to moment.

When I had arrived in Paris only three weeks before, I felt as if I was moving into my future. Now I was losing all the ties that had bound me. The thin imagery of my past was being swept away, its place taken by a hot Mediterranean valley, and the wreck of an ancient town perched on a high cliff: a jumble of walls, odorous herbs, and the raw creaking of cicadas. And by Michèle, who swept me up with her quivering nerves, her sudden expansions of feeling. I was cut loose; a sweating body on a red patch of ground, naked except for my smudged undershorts, chewing cheese and brittle bread and sucking half-mouthfuls of weak wine from a clear bottle without a label.

One morning, on our way down into the valley, we picked up a local newspaper, *La Dépêche de Provence*, at the little grocery, along with our provisions of bread and cheese, a couple of yogurts, and a half bottle of pinkish wine. Some large photographs took up half the front page: American Marines were storming onto a beach, and then walking in double file along an out-of-focus street, their guns held high. We sat on our rise of red earth and read the article together. The beach was in Lebanon; the street was a main artery in Beirut. What were the Marines doing there? I didn't know, and what did it matter? In those eerily peaceful years between Asian wars, a raid by the Marines onto a remote Middle Eastern beach didn't seem very important. But Michèle devoured the article with sober glee. In her huskily clear voice, as if sunlight had licked down into a nasty place, she asked:

"Qu'est-ce qu'ils y font, ces marines? De quoi se mêlent-ils?" What business do those Marines have in Lebanon?

This was her gentle question. But her tone almost thundered with revealed truth: as if she knew—and she did know—perfectly well what the Marines were doing in Lebanon; knew it with all the glare and harshness of obvious truth. She didn't say anything more, but her question clanged in my mind. I didn't know the answer. There was a wincing light under my eyelids, as if I were getting a headache. I was supposed to know, but I didn't. There were things that had always existed for me in a mist: wars, atom bombs, sputniks. They existed not in the real world but in the newspaper, which shuffled them together day after day in a kind of confused murmur, like a bedtime story to a sleepy child.

But this morning I listened differently. Michèle brought to bear a disturbing moral gravity that emanated from her father's photograph in her bedroom overlooking all of Paris; from that legendary death, and from the faces I had seen, the Communist friends on the Place de la Contrescarpe, the dentist, the old worker, the lawyer, his chest still wheezing from his years of imprisonment by the Nazis.

Suddenly the map of the world seemed to contract ominously. I knew what those Marines were doing in Lebanon—knew it deafeningly and terribly. They were soldiers of American power, swinging a big stick while my country's smiling President spoke softly. The ideas spurted like gleaming jets, the product of a sort of moral engineering. Capitalism. Suddenly the word had a cracked ring of indignation, while Communism sounded single-minded, self-confident, just—a banner of the disinherited. I saw the faces of the *charbonniers,* black with coal dust, heard the twanging speech of the Rue Mouffetard, where the people "spoke Communist" and were comrades. It was so complete, so without transition, as if in

136

that moment I had blown away the misty in-between space that had made politics unreal to me. Or rather, as if I had been transfixed by Michèle's swinging breasts and her high, sighing laugh, full of defiance and revolution.

Thirty years later, Lebanon is in the news again, and the ideas have gotten lost. A boy in a plaid shirt and jeans runs into the middle of the street with a shoulder-carried rocket launcher. He plants his feet like a pitcher on the pitcher's mound, leans forward with his fat, half-aimed tube and touches a button. The rocket clacks, and a whoosh of flame shoots out both ends of the tube. The boy trots back along the street to smoke a cigarette and have a Coke, before pitching another rocket down the wrecked, empty street, into a building almost out of sight, with its furniture exposed, like guts, behind its gashed walls.

Michèle was squeezing tubes of gouache onto the grainy cardboard she used as a palette. She wore a thin pink blouse, with rings of damp under the arms, and a pair of red shorts. Her legs were shapely but strong, almost fleshy. I sat against a scaly pine trunk, the newspaper half crumpled between my legs, feeling all the power of the staggering perspective that had burst upon me. All at once, I was only half an American. There had been a cleansing, an elimination, and now I had no home; unless this glaring valley was my home; or Michèle—whose angry concentration had already forgotten me, as she daubed and brushed at her white pad of paper —was my home. Or the gray city we had walked through at dawn a few days before; the cocky workers tipping up glasses of white wine under the speckled neon of cheap cafés; and the Communists, whom I saw now as moral warriors, with their faces that understood: the students and the factory workers, the stooped-over young dentist, and the Savonarola profile of the lawyer who seemed to see everything through eyes that were reticent but inexorable in judgment.

We left Les Baux a few days later and hitchhiked across the bristling hills of upper Provence. I was going on to Italy. Michèle would head north to the Alps to spend a month at a hotel her mother had started up in the family's ancestral house in a small resort town near Geneva. In August, I would come north to meet her there, and we would return to Paris together. Already neither of us was looking back. Yet Michèle seemed angry when we got down from a rattling truck full of Cavaillon melons. I think she wondered if she would ever see me again or if I was simply another vagabond American fleeing south. Michèle was like that: passionate and impulsive, but with residues of distrust that could make her icy and frightened, and then her rages would hit me like a freezing rain.

We were embarrassed to kiss on the roadside next to the hurtling cars and motorcycles. As I watched Michèle trudge around a looping road onto the Lyons highway, I felt a mysterious weight of repudiation. I would keep on toward Nice, and then Italy. But I wasn't fleeing south. Between Michèle and me was something harsh, almost unpleasant; a fascination, a darkness of feeling. She was going to have more of me than she knew. As Michèle disappeared down the hill shimmering with heat, I knew that a part of me would be marking time until we met again, at the place she had circled for me on the map, in a green crease running south toward a roadless mass of brown—the high Alps of Savoie.

4

I SAW Italy differently that summer. In the perched hill towns of Tuscany, I noticed red storefronts painted with a hammer and sickle, tucked in a corner of the main squares. A couple of men in faded work shirts and baggy pants with suspenders and canvas espadrilles would sit on straight chairs leaning back against the storefront. With a sort of bifocal vision, I saw them as unsmiling Communists, almost criminals, but also as grandfatherly men without guile who, somehow, had seen things as they are.

One day I stopped off for a few hours in a roadside village south of Rome. The streets were crowded with red balloons and sizzling brochettes of lamb and sausage. Red banners hung from the balconies, and huge photographs of Lenin and Togliatti stood on wooden supports scattered along the main street. It was a local "Festa de *L'Unità*," Italy's Communist newspaper. People wandered up and down the street, stopping to shoot with small, echoless clacks in the shooting galleries, eating cotton candy and candied apples. Several stands displayed colored posters advertising the happiness and justice in the USSR: there were smiling women on huge tractors; robust men dwarfed by the gushing water of hydroelectric plants. Work was beautiful, the photographs were saying, the USSR was all Technicolor, gleaming sputniks and smiling athletes. The coloring was blurred and old-fashioned; the paper was too glossy, too heavy. In the scratchy poverty of the unpaved streets, and the pink and brown stucco peeling in irregular patches from the houses, the posters and magazines seemed exaggerated, almost insolent, like the splashy colored images of saints pinned to the walls of country churches: images of a better life, of the best imaginable life.

The town was perched on the edge of a volcanic lake, and the *festa* sprawled along a promenade overlooking the steep, perfectly round crater, with a lens of winking silver at the bottom. Between the empty valley that fell away beyond the granite balustrade, and the loudspeakers blaring the Internationale, I felt that I was walking between two fantasies. One was of a shipwrecked world, stark green pine forests, a silent gleam of water, harsh and hot under the Mediterranean sun. The other was exotic and shocking; it startled me to look at the brown faces of the farmers come in from the surrounding country to spend the day, and the plump shopkeepers, the young girls scampering up and down the fairground. They were all Communists. They had understood. But what had they understood? The deceptions of an exploitative class weaving a smoke dance of wealth and temptation? Or maybe something deeper, more secret: happiness, sheer physical exuberance. I saw life in their clumsy hands and their phlegmy laughter. Their speech was rich and garbled, like rabbis mumbling over a book, telling God something that was only between them; they rocked back and forth as if they couldn't contain themselves and were about to start jumping around like a herd of goats.

As I walked timidly around the irregular town square draped with red banners and striped canvas awnings flapping in the hot breeze over candy stands and great wheels of cheese, I felt profoundly moved and also scared. Once again, I had been swept further than I meant to go. I was an American. The Bolshevik with a knife between his teeth was still oddly real to me. But here I was tiptoeing among them. What if these people knew who I was? I wanted to cry out: I'm not your enemy. But I wasn't sure; maybe I was their enemy. I would continue to see the *festa* and the posters of smiling children with clenched fists and red hammers and sickles, like dream windows, on the walls of buildings wherever I went in Italy that summer: in the pink streets of Siena; in Arezzo, where Piero della Francesca's women moved in frozen prospects of awe and faded fresco tints; in nameless crossroad villages, surrounded by olive groves and thickly glowing fields of wheat and barley. Wherever I went, the old beauty of Italy was accompanied by this jarring exuberance, this explosion, this breaking free.

I too had broken free. I had broken out of my small life into the epic of the world; I had overleapt the misty space and stood on a large stage accompanied by brothers who called themselves comrades. I liked the sound of that, but I didn't dare say it. I felt as if I were peering through a window, shuffling my feet with the excitement of what I saw, but an outsider. For I was confused. Michèle had given communism a face of emotion and human complexity that wasn't accounted for by the frightened silences of my mother trying to shield me from the infection of politics. Russia had been completely bad, but now I saw that maybe Russia was good. Truth and falsehood seemed drunk that summer, as they teetered and changed places with a shuffle that left me dizzy.

There wasn't much politics in all this. I was more like a man trying to keep his feet in an earthquake. I hadn't yet started reading the uniform editions of books on Michèle's shelf in Paris, books that belonged to her mother: half a shelf of Lenin's *Complete Works* in that spidery Moscow print, on glossy long-lasting paper; another half-shelf of Stalin's *Complete Works* in red covers; Plekhanov, Engels, Marx; Georges Sadoul's *Histoire de la Révolution Française;* Roger Garaudy's dialogues with Catholics; Maurice Thorez's collected speeches, full of thundering vowels and of "objective" certainties that had been concealed by the shimmer of bourgeois deception. Terms like "dialectical materialism," "bourgeois subjectivism," "the masses," "scientific socialism," hadn't yet acquired the pure explanatory power of Church Latin, or the wise mumbling of Hebrew in the mouths of rabbis on those high holy days, dominated by old men swaying with knowledge, in the stale synagogues of Brighton Beach when I was a boy. I hadn't yet acquired the habit of buying *L'Humanité,* the *Herald Tribune* and *Le Monde* every day, so as to keep my finger on the decaying pulse of capitalism. I hadn't begun to follow the stock market as the world's busiest negative investor. When the market plunged, my heart sang. When a major corporation stumbled, I saw it as a crack in the dike; capitalism's "internal contradictions" were at work.

In that summer of 1958, sitting on the mica-covered sea rocks below the stone fortress at Lerici, my politics were a shimmer of sunlight and Mediterranean foam. The youth hostel on the upper level of the fortress was run by an eccentric old woman with long tresses of bleached blond hair knotted together by the sea air. She usually wore a housedress half unbuttoned over her bony chest, and cackled in Italian at the collection of half-naked youths who strewed themselves over the ten-foot-thick battlements overlooking the bay of La Spezia, with its shifting tints of blue—so peaceful, so unchanging, it was hard to imagine the squall of wind that had drowned Shelley, almost within view, more than a century ago. Bony old Maria was half crazy, we whispered among ourselves. Every once in a while, she literally swept us all out of the stone dormitories with a mangy broom, beating our heels until we scattered down the passageway onto the grassy path that angled back and forth down the cliff. For a night or two we would sleep under a fig tree beside the path, until Maria relented and we could return to the hotel. She would be sitting outside her tiny room, on the stone deck of the fortress, her frail arms busy around her face as she tried to comb out her mess of hair.

A boy from the village told us that Maria was a Communist. During the Mussolini years, she had been an anti-Fascist militant. Then when the Germans came, she became a colonel in the Resistance, hiding out in the scrub wasteland, the *maquis,* beyond the town. Her crazy antics took on an aura of solemnity for me. I wished I could talk to her, tell her I knew what she was and loved her for it, a solitary, slightly mad old lady, who embodied all the heroism and all the stubborn vision I longed to imagine that summer. I saw communism as a form of eccentric courage; a lucidity at the fringes of sanity.

In August, I hitchhiked across the Simplon Pass into Switzerland, and then around Lake Léman to Geneva. The orderly stone city stretched along the lakefront. A plume of white water jetted high into the air in the middle of the harbor. Geneva was intensely scrubbed and well behaved. The cafés and ice-cream parlors seemed to whisper, and even the traffic had a diminished growl. I felt like a secret agent tiptoeing through this city that resembled a bank vault turned inside out. Thin, deeply tanned, my hair curled by the salt of the Mediterranean, wearing floppy sandals, I padded along the broad street, with trolley cars rattling down the middle, leading into France.

The French border police took one look at me and hustled me into a windowless room next to the road, where they pushed me against the wall and looked as if they were getting ready to hit me with a couple of nightsticks. Looking into those fat pink faces spitting French at me, I was too panicky to understand what they were saying.

"Sale bicot, montre-moi tes papiers. Papiers, papiers! Oui! Ta carte d'identité! Bougnoule, porc, raton!"

It dawned on me that these white cops, in their thick blue uniforms, with their funny hats, like toy soldiers, thought I was an Arab. I was their nigger, and they were going to toss me, with a few bruises and broken ribs, back into Switzerland, where the police were too dumb or too rich to care about niggers like me. In a daze, I fumbled at the zipper pocket on my backpack, and tumbled out my international health card, my traveler's checks, my aspirins, my ballpoint pen, my needle and thread, a cellophane bag full of hard candies, and my defeated-looking, rubbed and dirty, flexible green passport. The policeman thumbed it open, and looked from me to the sallow photograph with the embossed seal bitten into it: a thin-faced, large-eyed boy. I felt an irrational fright, as if, by mistake, the photograph in the passport would be of someone else. But it was me. They saw it, and grinned with porcine camaraderie. It was all right. They weren't embarrassed or apologetic as they helped me on with my backpack and tapped me playfully on the shoulder.

"Ça va! Laisse-le passer!"

I had been frightened, and then so relieved I didn't really try to understand what had happened. If they had taken me for an Arab, why were they going to beat me up? I remembered the Arabs who had befriended me in Paris the year before. There were plenty of them in France, working as temporary laborers, without families. They swept the streets and worked on building sites, or at the worst jobs in factories, or in the coal mines in the north. Or they picked the sugar beet crops, and did other seasonal labor when they could find it. Since arriving in France, a month and a half before, I had heard about an uprising in Algeria. There was fighting. French army posts were being attacked. I didn't know much about it, but as I climbed into the bus leading from the Swiss border to the French town of Annemasse, and as I sat, an hour later, in a tiny wood-burning train that groaned up a wild Alpine valley, I understood that it wasn't a good idea for me to have dark skin, black curling hair and a long nose, and to walk around wearing baggy unwashed trousers, with cheap sandals on my feet.

In the years to come I would remember that green cinder-block room without windows, a scarred table, a chair, a filthy concrete floor; the huge policemen with their nightsticks like stubby brown baseball bats, their flushed angry faces; and me bounced against the cinder-block wall, wearing only a thin shirt that wouldn't cushion any blows. If they had used those clubs, no one would have heard me screaming. The dead walls would have sealed in my terror. That sickly green room was full of dead cries, dazed heads with curly black hair and sharp noses, bird-chested men who had done nothing but be Arabs, *"ratons,"* *"bougnoules,"* *"sales bicots."* I would think of that room, and know that there were rooms just like it in the neighborhood police stations I walked past every day in Paris, where no sound was ever heard, but broken men emerged, to be hustled to prisons or thrown out onto the sidewalk at three in the morning with a kick in the ribs, their hair matted with blood.

There was a war on by then. The Arabs wanted the French to get out of Algeria, and they were fighting with old rifles, hand grenades, even knives, against the entire French army. They were fighting in France too. They organized migrant Arab laborers, and rolled homemade bombs through the swinging doors of police stations, and they killed; they killed each other, they killed cops, and they were killed in a creeping street war that made ordinary life in Paris nightmarish. I would have my part in that war. I would become an Arab by choice; a part of the violent machine that shook the streets of Paris, and all of France, in the early 1960s.

But now, in August of 1958, slumped on the hard wooden bench of the tiny train that was taking me to Michèle, at the upper end of the Alpine valley, as the shadow of the mountains slid across the narrow fields and the sky turned a wild, deep blue and then black, but speckled with such a blazing quantity of stars it seemed lit up and festive—on that exhausted evening, rattling up the winding valley toward a place where the valley pinched together and a pencil on my map circled a town named Samoëns, I felt exposed, almost afraid the police would drag me off the train at the next stop. Or maybe I was afraid the darkness itself would erase me, that I would be removed from the record for some error that made me instantly knowable as a nigger, a Jew, an Arab, a capitalist, an American. The contradictions didn't trouble me. Gradually I fell into a doze, as the train swayed on its narrow track up the valley, and a faint odor of wood smoke drifted throughout the compartment from the wood-burning furnace of the locomotive.

An hour or so later the train stopped next to a bare platform. Several boxy hotels were scattered along an empty street. The town looked abandoned, except for the weak glow of a few street lights and squares of yellow light in the windows of some houses. As I walked down the road, I could make out the wide sloping roofs of the Alpine chalets wrapped around by narrow balconies. After a hundred yards or so, on the other side of a crossroads, I saw a low, gently sloping roof, a stuccoed house partly masked by a high hedge. I recognized it from Michèle's description. I swung the heavy iron knocker; after a minute the thick wooden door swung open, and she was there, her hungry smile and her strong body, her blond hair gleaming in the vestibule light. She sighed that high explosive sigh of hers and her eyes seemed to expand and capture me, as if we had never been separated.

We hugged in the open doorway; then Michèle brought me inside to meet her mother in a small sitting room next to the front door. There was a narrow studio bed covered with cushions, a phonograph playing chamber music, a yellow light gleaming from the pinewood beams and wall panels. Two black-and-white dogs with long floppy ears and wagging tails that shook their whole bodies were draped across the bed. Julianne had been reading; she stood up and shook my hand. She had strong hands and was solidly built. Her alert gray eyes seemed to live independently of her wide, deeply seamed face: a strong, silent woman, who said she was glad to meet me—"*enchantée,*" she said, but didn't sound very enchanted by it. Her eyes took me in slowly. I wasn't very reassuring. Along a single shelf, behind her tightly arranged hair, I saw the black and red bindings of books with the names of Stalin and Lenin embossed on the spines.

I looked at Julianne, and saw sixteen years of being wedded to a photograph. I tried to imagine her beside the young man in the photograph in Michèle's room in Paris. I saw it here too on a low writing desk, beside another photograph of the same man, sitting beside a matronly girl in a light flowered dress, wearing walking shoes. The scene was a mountaintop: a blur of grass at their feet and a faint white line of higher peaks in the background. At first glance, Julianne hardly seemed younger in the photograph; then, looking more closely, I noticed smoother skin, a shapelier body; but the same manly poise, the same sense of waiting. For what? For the present to be worthy of her past? For the sacrifice of sixteen years to bear fruit? And one didn't know if it was her children she waited for or the revolution. Possibly her children didn't know, either.

I ate some leftovers in the empty dining room, beside a bay window opening onto an inky mass of trees and bushes silhouetted against the stars. Half a glass of wine made me heavy-headed, almost dizzy. I told Michèle what had happened at the border, the police taking me for an Arab. She looked serious but unsurprised. Then she snorted ironically, as if a new thought had occurred to her.

"You, an Arab: *Quelle blague!* They must have fallen over when they saw your passport."

I felt vaguely offended. To Michèle, I was gilt-edged, fully shielded. Americans didn't live in the same world as other people. Ordinary dangers didn't touch them. Men in crew cuts with beer bellies, with oversized shoes and pants, were always coming to their rescue from some embassy or other. Those Marines walking with their rifles raised down a street in Beirut were my birthright. I could never shake them off. But Michèle was wrong. Those Marines had nothing to do with me. This afternoon in the room with a couple of racist cops, I had felt unprotected. Yet there had been that small book with its green cover that said that no matter how oddly French I sounded, no matter how bronze-dark, curly-haired, long-nosed and suspiciously bird-chested I was, I was an American; not an Arab or a Greek or a Sicilian laborer; not a Yugoslavian migrant or a Turk. It disturbed me to know that but, not wanting to acknowledge it, I was reassured. There were things I couldn't change; invisible pins that kept the world in place, even as I flew in strange air.

We slept in the attic of the hotel, under a canopy of pine beams. During the ski season, the attic served as a dormitory; empty beds were lined up under the eaves, along both sides of the large space. Michèle and I pushed two beds together. The attic smelled of warm wood. It creaked as the huge beams, with cross-stays and conical wooden pegs, contracted in the evening air. Silently we took off our clothes. Michèle's body shone whitely in the woody light. I felt alive and thankful. We touched each other almost timidly. And then Michèle swam beneath me. Her face became wild and full. I screwed my eyes shut, and had an image of a thrashing horse, the play of hooves, the long muscles of the back slippery with sweat. The horse gave a low sigh that exploded into a cry. I hardly felt myself come amid the thrashing of my whole body.

The next day we took a ski lift to the top of the mountain above Samoëns. As we rose along the mountainside, we seemed to be walking on the tips of the high grass speckled with flowers that swayed beneath us. The warm August air was streaked with veins of cold flowing down from the high peaks. We spent all day climbing the bald slopes of the high country. To the south, we could see the white dome of Mont Blanc. Nearer to us, summits of bare rock crested to the horizon. Tiny purple and white flowers dotted the hills, which Michèle called *montagnes à vache*, cow hills, meaning that as Alps go, they hardly counted. But I felt close to the lid of heaven all that day. I tried to tell Michèle about Italy, the storefronts painted with red hammers and sickles, the Festa de *L'Unità*, and the people who had seen through all the deceptions. There was a truth in those lean faces, faces close to the earth, fierce, simple, full of toil. I groped excitedly, stumbling over my words. What was I trying to say?

"It was like a vision. I felt so close to everyone, but I was afraid they'd find out I was an American. I talked French to people, even when they didn't understand. I couldn't get the English words out of my throat. Not that I wanted to fool anyone. I just didn't want to be an American. I didn't want to be their enemy."

"*C'est très romantique, tout ça,*" Michèle said, quietly disapproving. She didn't trust me on this subject, yet I felt that she was pleased. It made her nervous that her lover, with his French lips and French shrugs, should be an American. Not so long ago, she had been shouting "Yankee Go Home" amid a sea of demonstrators mobilized by the Communist Party. She had chalked slogans on gray buildings of another century, accusing the American commander, General Ridgway, of being an assassin. Beside such clairvoyant rage, my vision of a world of comrades wasn't very substantial. And she was right. What did I know about politics and revolution? Had I ever personally known the working classes—those men with rough hands and a twang of Paris in their speech, the women exhausted from childbearing, their faces old beyond their years—who lived in small half-furnished rooms on the sloping streets of Belleville or in the red suburb of Saint Denis; lived in residence hotels, whole families to a room, heated by a coal burner or a kerosene stove? There were black company towns in northern France, where the coal miners lived: rows of crumbling brick cottages on ruined streets, coal dust etching the lines of their skin and the walls of their houses. Had I seen the housing projects —they were called *HLM*—that sprouted like evil mushrooms around the northern rim of Paris, once a region of tar-paper huts and crazy gardens that had been called the *zone,* and was now compressed into a huddle of gray cement buildings with staircases winding up the outside and cracks already splayed across walls that had been built only a few years before? No gardens, no landscaping; gray boxes in a square of concrete or asphalt, or simply mud and dust, where the gruff resentment of workers—*les ouvriers*—many of them physically small from generations of undereating, could be safely contained.

No, that summer my politics were light; a fairy tale of repudiation. I didn't know any more about *les ouvriers* than I did about Pittsburgh, and the smoke twisting over the fire pits of the foundries; or Harlem, and its decaying brownstones, its tenements still adorned by the friezework of Italian stonecutters, a white trimming on hovels of helplessness and exclusion. I had gone to college on the edge of Harlem, but had seen it only as a checkerboard of tar-paper roofs from the top of Morningside Drive.

But now, as I climbed the stony ridges of the cow hills above Samoëns, everything had changed. I had repudiated my past, I had become a Communist, or almost one. In fact, I was soaring in a space uncluttered by ideas or exact notions of any sort. Before long I would learn things I had never known. From my room in a hotel around the corner from Michèle's house, I would look out on gardens the size of small rooms, where a few tomatoes and lettuces, and a crooked lattice of peas, grew amid rotten tires and shacks of gray wood that reminded me of the storage shacks behind my family's apartment in Brighton Beach when I was a boy. It was a minimal landscape, a clutter of small hopes, crowded behind the residence hotels and crumbling tenements, where very poor families tried to earn a few francs with some vegetables, or a few chickens and rabbits. I would climb the staircase of the hotel smelling of rats and decayed wood; the walls were a yard thick and sweating with the damp of centuries. At every floor, an odor of hot oil and horse steak, turnips, potatoes and thin soup, would seep under the doors. In the narrow rooms with a cracked window at one end and a discolored sink jutting from the wall, families were cooking on kerosene stoves.

From these punched-in buildings small men in blue work clothes would go to work before dawn and come home after dark, six days a week. There was a shifting, drifting relation between them and a band of *clochards* on the Place de la Contrescarpe. The latter twanged their thick Parisian slang, and nattered with the neighborhood people who often brought them a bit of bread and cheese or a leftover dish of turnips and greens. Occasionally, one of the workingmen in the neighborhood would sit on the curb of the circular island in the middle of the square, and take a swallow from the nameless green bottle that was never empty. The next day he would still be there, and soon, his overalls blackened with dirt, his face bristling, his shoes swollen with wet, the laces untied, he would melt in among them. Or else, conversely, one morning a new face would be pushing the *charbonnier*'s two-wheeled cart up and down the busy street, shouting good-humoredly for everyone to move their asses, serious work was being done here. On a closer look, the new face would be familiar: pasty and white, a weak jaw; hurt, busy eyes. Of course! He'd been sitting for months on the hot-air grating on the square, roaring with his phlegmy voice, and sucking on that fabulous bottle. But today he'd gotten himself shaved. Someone had given him a threadbare set of overalls, and an old pair of shoes. He'd persuaded the owner of the café down the block, which sold coal and firewood, to take him on. And now he'd moved up a subtle rung to the shifting base of the working class, probably sleeping in the back of the café at night; until, a few months later, his bunch of jolly drunken friends on the square, with their chest pains and their rotten teeth, their ulcerated legs and their perennial diarrhea, would call to him, and he would come back.

No, I hadn't seen much as yet, but that morning on the shaved hills above Samoëns, I felt formidably alive, as Michèle and I clambered up the rocky slopes creased by the spring melt, and then, more precariously, went jumping on our heels into steep valleys beyond the ski slopes. It was a world of chilly angles and treeless plateaus. Toward late afternoon, we came to the edge of a horseshoe valley high in the mountains, with an unpainted shack far far down in the middle of it and a few dozen cows scattered across the hummocky bottom of the valley. We made our way down the steep side of the valley and walked over to the shack, which grew into a vast, flimsy barn as we approached. A man came out to look us over. He was unshaven, and wore a grimy oversized shirt and overalls. He looked at us out of his animal silence, as if trying to identify our species; and then he gave a hoarse laugh, and came to shake hands with Michèle. He was a cowherd; he spent the summer in this isolated valley, where he and a few young boys made wheels of *tomme* cheese from the milk of the cows. He and Michèle had gone to grade school together during the war. The man spoke a garbled French I could hardly understand. It was as if he had forgotten how to talk in this isolated valley, where the days and the nights blurred together for months on end. He invited us into the barn, and we each had a tin cup of milk with lumps of cream floating on the surface. The barn had no windows, and the space inside was a mahogany darkness. Here and there, slats of solid sun fell upon the floor. The wheels of cheese were piled on wooden racks, like automobile tires. In about a month, the cows and the cheeses and the men would start their trek into the valley, far below. But for now they were shipwrecked on a barren world. The silence and the rich smell of the fermenting milk were over-powering.

Michèle had her roots here. Her directness, her wild distrust, belonged to these rocky remotenesses where she had roamed as a girl during the war, while her father and mother packed their bags and left on unannounced trips to nowhere, always nowhere. They returned, also unannounced, and never talked about where they had been—to Michèle, the trips had been empty, pure loss—their faces drained by the strain of anonymity, as they slipped past German soldiers and the more treacherous soldiers of the French *Milice*, who seemed to be able to smell out Resistance fighters by some power of antipathy and fear. Her father didn't return from one of these trips; and her mother developed a mask of grief and became almost cold from the power of her will. She would carry on. Julianne, the country girl, the lover of classical music, who all her life had known the mountain shadow that closed off the day in midafternoon, the brash chuckle of the torrent across the valley, the wincing brightness of the snow glazed with ice; Julianne, daughter of old Catholics, one of whose ancestors had carried on a polemical correspondence with that arch-atheist and philosopher Voltaire, according to a leather-bound history of Samoëns, printed on thick glossy pages and written almost a century ago by a local priest; Julianne would keep her husband's death alive, not by mourning for him but by living his sacrifice over again. She too was a Communist. She too would keep aloof from a society mired in privacy by practicing a sort of Calvinism: she would refuse to have a private life; she would be a silent soldier of revolution. She compressed her feelings until her children felt emotionally starved and Michèle, as an adolescent, dreamed only of leaving home; leaving this intractable mother who couldn't get the simplest feelings past the mask of her faith.

Michèle adored her mother and fought her; between them was a pleading rage that never lapsed. Maybe I was a pawn in their silent war. Michèle could never outdo her mother's faithfulness to the photograph on the table. She could never fit her life into the heroic mold of a "Communist warrior." She had to fail, and she did so in a rage of resentment and self-accusation, an inner chaos that expressed itself as an appetite for more life. Her paintings were fierce and dark; not portraits of ideological war, but a deeply lived inner war against form, against singing tomorrows and gushing hydroelectric plants; against comfort and happy endings. And now she had brought into her mother's home a peculiarly troubling man who had the instincts of a Frenchman but who was not what he seemed. I think Michèle was attracted by my paradox. I was a transgression, an outrage; I was suspect. My very presence mocked the family myth. There was a destructive urge in Michèle that erupted unpredictably. She clung fiercely to her past, and to the keen face in the photograph of her father, whose first name I don't remember—I think she never told me; it was enough that he peered from his heavy wooden frame year after year, a spirit of high purpose, but also a judge at whose feet our tangled lives struggled helplessly. But she also needed to violate the myth, to punish her mother; and also, perhaps, to punish me for being her accomplice. And the irony was that I was fascinated by the family myth. I felt awe and compassion for stony Julianne, who often seemed girlish and unworldly behind her quiet willfulness. During all the years Michèle and I lived together, from our angry beginnings to our improbable marriage five years later, to that cold afternoon only a few months after our marriage when, already separated, I had begun my solitary life and, as a first act of solitude, sat with Julianne in a café on the Rue Soufflot: she asking me, like an old-fashioned matriarch, to give an account of myself; I tearfully unable to, but feeling a grudging love for this intensely solitary, untalkative woman—during all these years, Julianne would be a sort of Alp in my life: sharp, cold, beautiful, fine, and implacable when Michèle threw herself against her with embraces that were almost assaults and assaults that were almost embraces.

Michèle and I said goodbye to the cowherd outside his flimsy barn. It was almost evening, and we hurried down a twisting footpath through a forest of thin mountain oaks, stumbling in the dried-out ruts of old wagons. The mountainside grew dark, and the sky began to shine with a metallic glow. The dusty green of the August trees turned gray and then black. A single star hung over the valley, which had become a black river prickled with lights. A patch of lights shone off to the left, where the town was. By the time we reached the paved road, we were exhausted and famished. Julianne was waiting for us when we reached the hotel. The stringy tones of Vivaldi came from the open door of her room. She sat with us in the kitchen, while Michèle dished out whatever was left in the pots on the stove. The kitchen was hot and cozy; a lot of living was done in it: meals, cards after dinner with a neighbor, cleaning the snails we caught in roadside ditches or the mushrooms that grew on the wooded slopes of the valley. This was Julianne's kingdom. There was a conviviality, a motherliness, in the cluttered shelves, the heaps of shining pots, and the great square coal stove that gave off a soft shimmering heat, and made you want to drink weak wine and spoon out cherries in brandy from a large crockery jar. In a way, the kitchen was Julianne's secret; it brought out her tenderness and care, her human side.

5

Michèle and I spent ten days in Samoëns. We hiked up and down the valley with Julianne's floppy-eared dogs, and ate large meals in the woody dining room of the hotel, among a scattering of guests. In the evening we sat in the kitchen with Julianne, listening to Mozart or Bach drift across the hallway, playing cards or talking. We talked about the uprising in Algeria; the Arabs' struggle for independence, and the hysteria of the *pieds-noirs*, the European colonists, who held frenzied demonstrations in Algiers's central square and talked about killing Arabs. They seemed crazy to me. I couldn't understand the destructiveness, the unembarrassed desire to kill.

In the morning, we would buy the previous day's edition of *Le Monde* and *L'Humanité*, and I began my political education. I constructed a kind of demonology from the newspapers and added to it over the next year or two. Jacques Soustelle, General Salan, General Massu, de Gaulle, Malraux the minister of culture, Camus the morally paralyzed *pied-noir*. There was a literary demonology too: Bernanos, Montherlant, Giono, Drieu la Rochelle. Whether they had been collaborators during the war or simply old-line Catholics, nationalists, anti-Communists, they were impure; reading them was an act of treachery. On the side of the good were Vercors, Vaillant, Aragon, Sartre, oddly enough Genêt, the Communist novelist André Stil, Picasso. For some reason, Céline wasn't a demon. He had been a collaborator and an anti-Semite; now he was a spiteful old man who lived behind a chain fence with an attack dog, spitting out his verbal mania in thick, hysterical slang. But somehow he was forgiven. Maybe we saw him as a sort of shaman, a possessed man who scoured heaven and hell out of some destructive or self-destructive compulsion, but who was bizarrely innocent of the ravings of his unconscious. We saw Céline as a twentieth-century Marquis de Sade who tried out all the permutations of transgression and assault but, in his soul's fortress, was a philosopher not a criminal; maybe even a kind man. After all, he was a doctor, he treated poor people for nothing.

The Communist newspaper, *L'Humanité*, described a world without shadings or hesitation. There were no complex motives, no confusions; only Fascists on one side, and *progressistes* on the other. It was all epic, a struggle between good and evil. The actors were garishly painted puppets. Class warfare required simplification, and I found it exhilarating. Here was a bold picture, where before there had been mist. As I read the newspapers, puzzling over the acronyms of political parties and names of important people I'd never heard of, I gathered that France was in a crisis. The Fourth Republic had become a comic opera of rising and falling governments. People were humiliated by the fighting in Algeria; it was as if a handful of retarded children were managing to hold an army of grownups at bay. In the background was a name: General de Gaulle, a shadowy warrior, the hero of the Resistance, but somehow not a hero to Michèle and her mother. He too was a Fascist, they said. His people had probably killed Michèle's father. The newspaper photographs showed a tall, slightly pear-shaped man with a big nose, and a large flaccid mouth. He wore a uniform, and lived in stubborn reclusion in a small town in northeastern France.

For ten years, de Gaulle would be the emperor of my dreams. That very summer, he would drive from Colombey-les-Deux-Eglises, where he had brooded and kept his own counsel since shortly after the war, to Paris, in a procession of buglike black Citroën DS's, an ugly car, shaped like the influential men who sank into its comfortable seats and sped in the hum of superior engineering to some official destination. France had called him, and he had come. France would always be a woman to him. *Ma femme,* as Walt Whitman had written incongruously of America. He lived in mystic communion with Jeanne d'Arc, Richelieu and Napoleon. Here was the authoritarian France. The France that wept sentimentally at the spectacle of power. The France that had a heroic destiny, embodied in its famous anthem. The France of magisterial professors and vast utterances, the France for which Versailles had been built and Haussmann had plowed up Old Paris to create his solemn boulevards. With a whimper of frustration, the National Assembly had called upon de Gaulle to create a new government. And this slow-moving, large-mouthed man had agreed.

None of this meant much to me until a month or so later, when I came face to face with de Gaulle one October day across a surface of weaving heads on the Place de la République, in Paris. On the far side of the square a podium rose brightly in a drapery of red, white and blue. The French colors stood out with a circus gaiety against buildings streaked with black from a century's wear, and the more recent corrosion of automobile exhaust. The government had announced an official demonstration. The people of Paris were invited to cheer the General's labor of national reconstruction. He had already spoken grandly to a hostile crowd of *pieds-noirs* in the central square of Algiers, many of them armed and ready to assassinate him. In his skeletal voice, he had said: *"Je vous ai compris!"* I understand you, I know what you want. And in the end they had cheered him wildly. The cheers nourished him. And now France —that lady—was about to cheer him on again.

But Michèle and I had come to the République with a different purpose. The Communists had announced a counterdemonstration for the same time and the same place. From Belleville, Billancourt and Montrouge, from Clignancourt and the northern suburbs, from Saint Denis—from the factories and the cheerless streets with narrow cafés and wash hanging out to dry—came crowds of men in blue work clothes, and women in loosely hanging dresses. They held handwritten banners and cardboard signs announcing the factory they worked in, their union. The official demonstration near the podium had been carefully winnowed, and we stood far at the back, at the meeting of two large avenues. The podium dwarfed the tiny figures that bobbed on top of it and the shifting, muttering mass before it. It was a cool, bright afternoon. All around me people seemed relaxed and quiet; they smoked and told stories in that twanging language of theirs. Yet I could feel a quiet wariness. Behind me the crowd stretched out of sight, and more people kept pressing in from the side streets. A group pushing into the square had been singing the Internationale, and now their voices soared in the heavily laden air. Other voices joined in. The sound multiplied and spread up and down the avenue, took on depth and confidence as tens of thousands of voices chanted: *"c'est la lutte finale."* I shouted the few snatches of words I could make out. It was a cry of confidence in the future, a promise of justice and comradeship. I joined in and felt the breath of history blowing upon me. I was one of them, full of angry song. I wished I knew all the words, the melody was so virile, so lovely. Far across the square, a tiny figure stood with his arms raised in a clumsy V, and a counterhymn started up far ahead of us, close to the podium: *la Marseillaise;* once a song of murder and revolt, now it had become plump and pious, a national anthem, not a passionate cry. The Internationale swamped the timid *Marseillaise.* It was a civil war by song, while the General, his arms raised, seemed to embrace his lady, while waiting to whisper words in her ear and undress her in the grand empty rooms of the Elysée Palace.

Michèle and I held hands and sang; and the men and women all around us sang; the trim mustaches and the goatees; the straggle-haired woman with discolored teeth and a cheap dress standing next to me sang, and the lady in high heels wearing a tight skirt and a white cashmere sweater. All sang: *"c'est la lutte finale,"* the final struggle is upon us. Shimmers of sunlight glanced from the windows of the apartment houses where faces, half veiled by the reflected light, peered down disapprovingly.

All at once, from narrow streets on both sides of the square, a line of police vans knifed through the crowd, their motors snarling and roaring. They sealed off the front of the square, near the podium, from the back. Without any warning, the vans had cut the demonstration in two. The General was out of sight. We could hear his voice booming beyond the police vans, but couldn't make out what he was saying. Behind the dam of black hulks, we shouted angrily. We milled about on the broad avenues feeding the square. The Internationale rose sporadically, and sank again. Soon the crowd had settled down to our own party. The jokes and the cigarettes, the young women distributing tracts denouncing the Algerian war and de Gaulle's *"Je vous ai compris!"* Other tracts cried up the bankruptcy of democracy and offered "scientific" analyses of the "internal contradictions" of capitalism and the law of "absolute pauperization."

The crowd filled the street and the sidewalks as far as the eye could see. The side streets were still pouring in, carrying banners painted with red letters. We all pushed closer together, still festive and relaxed, de Gaulle all but forgotten now. It was a happy day, not a political demonstration anymore but a celebration of the power of numbers. The black vans, their motors shut off, loomed ahead of us, one behind the other, like a line of circus elephants. Then, far off, I heard a low rumble and the street shook. I thought it was a passing subway train. But the crowd fell silent, a woman muttered, *"Mon Dieu, qu'est-ce qui se passe?"* My God, what's happening? The rustling became heavy and thick. Michèle grabbed my hand and said, "Let's not get separated," as she pulled me toward a nearby side street. The crowd seemed to sway in upon us. Then everyone was running and shouting. A man stumbled past with blood running down his face. The whole avenue stampeded. A block or so away, I saw a line of black-helmeted police advancing slowly toward us, their long clubs rising and falling, rising and falling, like reapers at some insane harvest. The rustling was the sound of the clubs on flesh, thwack, thwack, sickening, methodical; a harvest of bruises, fractures, concussions, blood. The sound became louder now, and the shouts built into a wail coming from thousands of throats.

As we pushed ahead between the parked cars, I heard a screech of panic in my ear: my own voice. Michèle seemed to have a plan. She pushed closer to the sidewalk. "Come on," she shouted, and we rolled and fell over the parked cars. She pressed a brass button and the massive brown door of the building clicked open in front of us. We tumbled into the hallway, and shoved the door shut behind us. It was black and ghostly quiet inside. The cries of the street were faint. A smell of garbage fouled the air. We groped our way back, not wanting to turn on the *minuterie*. The darkness felt like an armor. At the rear of the hallway was a space underneath the stairs, and a few half-empty garbage cans. From behind the cans came whispers and the sound of breathing; other people had had the same idea. We pushed our way in, and crouched in a huddle of breath and sour sweat. A few more times, the front door clicked open, casting a brief slant of light across the shabby hallway. The street became loud, and then soft, as the door clicked shut again. More people jammed in behind the garbage cans under the stairs. And we waited. Silently breathing. Not talking. After a while, the street seemed to quiet down. By this time, I think it had dawned on all of us that we had taken a possibly foolish risk. What if a couple of cops clicked that door open and ran inside, cursing and screaming, with their clubs and their hard black boots. We were trapped, helpless, we couldn't even run. So we waited, afraid to make a sound. There must have been almost a dozen of us crouching in that slanting space. Someone was going to have to take a look. A faint light seeped under the front door. Michèle pushed quietly between the garbage cans, and went up to it. She stood listening for a while, then pulled the bolt; the door swung in, leaving a bright vertical slit she could look out through.

"Come on, Paul, take a look. I think it's clear now."

I came up and looked. The street in front of the door was empty. Everywhere shoes were scattered over the pavement: moccasins, espadrilles, high-heeled shoes, loafers. In their panic, people had run out of their shoes. The street resembled a prairie after a shoot, everywhere the dead birds lying, huddled and pitiful; hieroglyphics of helplessness and fear. Opening the slit further, I saw policemen standing around talking. Their clubs dangled from their wrists on leather thongs. They were holding their helmets under their arms and smoking. They looked huge and black, yet their faces seemed so ordinary: pink skin, thin trimmed mustaches; they laughed and leaned wearily against the cars. A few demonstrators walked past them gingerly, as if holding their breath, but the cops didn't seem to notice. The screams of rage, the sickening thunk of clubs on retreating bodies, were over. Somehow it seemed even more horrible that they didn't even hate us. They weren't monsters who couldn't help themselves. They were simply nothing. When some lieutenant blew a whistle, they stopped and brushed off their uniforms, and stood around relaxing. If the whistle blew again, they would clamp on their helmets, throw us to the ground, and club us and kick us. They would throw a woman against the side of a building and watch her slide slowly to the ground. They would knock a man down onto the street, and kick him in the ribs, and run on waving those long black clubs like insect feelers. No, they didn't hate us. They weren't our enemies. They manufactured order; it was called crowd control. And they were good at it. Even now, huddled behind the bright slit of the partly opened door, we were terrified.

After a few minutes, a man shouldered past Michèle and me, and pulled the door all the way open. He stepped onto the sidewalk, muttering over his shoulder:

"*Ça va, j'y vais.*"

He was elderly and heavyset, with a graying mustache and faded overalls. He looked a little like Stalin, standing warily, half-hidden by a Citroën panel truck. Then, taking a breath, he walked past the clump of policemen, not looking back. His broad, heavy back seemed to say they were all alike, the police: dumb and predictable Judases who had sold their poverty for a uniform and some shiny buttons. I saw the history of our century in that defiant, slowly lumbering figure: how many demonstrations, how many thwacks on his stubborn flesh, how many years in a factory somewhere turning a lever or tightening a screw, but still unbroken, believing that everything was going to change, that the final struggle was coming. Those bosses would have to knuckle under; the workers would take charge, and they would do it better.

One by one, the rest of us stepped over the doorsill onto the narrow sidewalk. The street was in shadow now. The sky was a blue strip between old buildings, their fronts slanting a bit, their windows set into a soft gray stucco. The police were still standing around. They didn't even look as we walked quietly past them; we might have been invisible. Michèle and I didn't talk. We walked slowly at first, then faster; the street angled slightly, and after half a block we were out of sight. Groups of demonstrators wandered around the side streets like stragglers from a routed army. Once a man climbed onto a car and started shouting obscenities at the police, at de Gaulle. People looked up at him curiously and shrugged, muttering *"provocateur,"* while the man gnashed his teeth and shouted bizarrely into the muted afternoon.

We made our way home through the quiet streets of the 3rd and 4th arrondissements. Deep alleys plunged between the houses, some of the alleys partly roofed over with glass-and-metal sheds. It was a neighborhood of small factories and artisans' shops. We passed storefronts heaped with leather scraps or cheap jewelry. The alleys were filled with tiny industries of all sorts, where they made pocketbooks, clothes, furniture, plumbing fixtures, tubing, hats, mirrors. The buildings were run-down, the facades partly cracked, the stucco crumbled, the shutters hanging loose, their paint encrusted with layers of grime. The streets were barely wide enough for a car to pass. And everywhere the whining, clicking and hammering of work emerging from the open doors of the dimly lit shops.

We were already far from the excitement and fright of the demonstration only a few blocks away: the thwacking of the nightsticks, the General's booming voice on the other side of the black vans garbled by distance. These were neighborhoods that had barely made it into the twentieth century. The tiny groceries

wafted the smell of olives and fresh fruit into the street. The bakeries sold the long, thin breads the French loved, but also great
wheels of *pain de campagne,* and a few cheap pastries: flans, bread
puddings, *chaussons,* and a few croissants. There was no violence
here; only a sleepy, very poor sort of living. But not a defeated one.
The men walked down the middle of the narrow streets with a wiry
pride. There was a brash good cheer in the bare little cafés where
people stood at the bar nodding at some private joke, or leaning
solemnly over a small thick glass of *marc.* Across all the abysms of
class, poverty and wealth, I seemed to see a dazzling fact: man was
wholly man wherever he was. He could be poor; he could fumble
in thick, broken sentences; he could live in grim little rooms, and
barely know how to read or write; he could work in factories that
hurt his ears and his nerves, and bring home just enough money
to eat and buy an occasional pair of shoes. There was still room for
joking over a glass of wine and flirting, for hurt and expectation;
there was room for the human face, with its strangely fluid expression that seemed to exhibit the entire soul in a glimpse. A man was
always all there, always complete. Years later, I would see this
again in a desiccated valley a few miles north of Bombay, in India.
People lived in straw shacks with dirt floors, and they had nothing:
a few rags of clothing, some tin pots, dried turds to cook with. They
were dark and incredibly thin, with large black eyes, and shining,
very fine hair. They were called *ardivarsi,* and they were despised
and marginal, aborigines, jungle folk. But they seemed luminous.
Because they had nothing, their humanness was elementary and
profound, like sunlight playing on their dirt floors, their torn
smocks and pants. There, as on those gray streets walking home
from the demonstration, I felt close to these people I would never
know: the man bent over a lathe in a metal-working shop; or the
humpbacked old woman walking toward us across the street, wearing a black coat and a flowered kerchief on her head; or the thin
blond man standing at the bar in a café, his hair greased stiff and
one huge yellow tooth staring from his slightly drunken smile. We
were "comrades." The walls of my private world were crumbling.
There was so much fullness, so much connection. "Comrades."

When Michèle and I came back to Paris that fall, I moved into
a cheap hotel on the Rue Mouffetard, the Hôtel du Midi. It was a
crushed, crooked building that seemed to be held erect mainly by

the equally crushed and crooked buildings on either side of it. The concierge lived in a tiny room one flight up a dingy staircase. The maroon paint of the stairwell was smudged by shoulders and the walls were gouged and scratched. The concierge's door was always slightly ajar. From her dark vantage, she watched the early-morning traffic heading for work; she watched the children in faded dresses and pants who raced out to school or to buy bread, talking in hushed voices, as if too much noise might bring the ancient hotel down around their ears. The concierge had a panel of tiny light bulbs fastened to her wall. Whenever someone turned on the electricity in his room, a bulb lit up on the concierge's panel. Electricity was used sparingly in the poor man's France. The lights on the stairs clicked on for about half a minute when you came in: time for a fast climb, with the key already aimed at the lock. If the concierge felt that you were keeping the lights on too long or playing the radio too late she unscrewed your bulb. I got used to finishing my nighttime reading by flashlight, in my hard, grainy bed on the fifth floor, in a corner next to the sink, beside my opened suitcase which served as storage for whatever I couldn't hang on nails on the back of the door.

The Rue Mouffetard was narrow and always busy, with trucks brushing the walls as they inched downhill toward the market, wives in lanky country dresses, wiry men in blue work uniforms heading up to the Café des Cinq Billards, for a flute of white wine. A block or so farther down, the hotels were even cheaper, and were inhabited mostly by Arabs. The Arabs stood around all day wearing gray jackets and unpressed pants; they talked in closed groups that seemed to turn their backs on the life of the street. They were very thin, with sharp brown faces and fast, nervous hands. Their language was a chaos of clicks, swallows and little explosive snorts. Already they were considered suspicious, outsiders, watched by unspeaking policemen who stood across the street or sat in black-and-white police cars around the corner. The war in Algeria was spreading. Very quickly, the Arabs had become enemies, as I had learned that summer. Their idle, nervous talk as they stood on the street in front of the cafés made people angry. They were supposed to be quick with a knife and devious, those *ratons*, those *bougnoules*. You couldn't trust them. They smelled bad, and they lied and stole. They were lazy. There was an ugly undertone on the street, and sometimes fights broke out on weekends. But usually there was no trouble. Only a sense of danger, of the unknown.

By midwinter, I was pretty much living with Michèle in her room with Paris at the window, and the easel—surrounded by massive palettes sculpted with color—dominating the beige space; I lived with the photograph on the dresser, the intense profile which stood as an inaccessible, almost nameless witness to the moral perplexities of his children, who had never known him but who had planted him relentlessly in their hearts. I went back and forth across the Place de la Contrescarpe, with its *clochards*, the yellow Café de la Chope, the lank trees standing like tired old men, slightly bent, clothed in dusty green patches.

Michèle painted all morning. She stalked around the room, angrily poking at her palette, slashing lines of color onto the canvas. Her concentration was powerful; it filled the room with tension. Often she made pencil sketches that were a tangle of lines resolving into faces or anguished bodies. In the afternoon, we sat at the Café de la Chope and read the newspaper, or any of the several journals I was beginning to pore through, as if looking for the key to existence: the *Economist*, *L'Observateur*, *Les Temps Modernes*, the *Monthly Review*, the *National Guardian*, which I bought at an American bookshop across the river from Notre Dame. I read Engels on the family, Marx's *Capital*, the *Communist Manifesto*, the *1848 Revolution*. I read Stalin on dialectical materialism and Lenin on the imperialistic phase of late capitalism. I read to gather news of the apocalypse, *la lutte finale*, that was sending shivers of premonition through all those mysterious centers of power, the stock exchanges, the boardrooms of international corporations, the offices of malign colonial administrators whom I imagined sitting behind desks of precious wood, deciding who will live, who will die. My ignorance was vast, and was never really dispelled. I felt that I had stood the world on its head. The revolution was in my mind, and it was wild; a sort of nightmare that did good.

It is difficult to reconstruct my enthusiasm during those months. In a way, politics was the least of it. Politics was a language for the shucking of myself. I had become my own alien. Years later, when I met the Polish novelist Witold Gombrowicz, we used to take walks together in the weedy park of the Abbaye of Royaumont, north of Paris, and then sit in a long salon while the Gothic windows went black with evening and the fireplace, empty in summer, loomed as a silent mouth above our heads. One evening, in the dark room scented with furniture wax and old ashes, Gombrowicz's voice, tender and acerbic, reached out to me, and said: "Paul, I'm going to tell you something. It seems to me that you are a modern-day wandering Jew, someone who doesn't have a home, and doesn't want one. You speak French so well, it is uncanny, even unhealthy. Did you ever think of that?"

In that vaulted stone room I tried to think of it, tried to imagine my way out of French, out of the homelessness that had possessed me and become my life. For it was true. My actual home had become a shadow of a place, drained of substance like something barely seen in a snowstorm. I had no anchor.

When there was a rally at the Maubert Mutualité, we went and sang the Internationale. The rallies were like secular masses. Maurice Thorez strode to the podium, and the room rose breathlessly, in a thunder of applause. A minute, two minutes, three, as if to stop were a failure of hope. More minutes of bruised hands, shuffling feet, faces that hurt from smiling. When Thorez spoke, his voice was rasping and definite; it could be soft and then swell to assertions that lifted us from our seats. Revolution hung upon the air, it was in our lungs, while, mysterious and little-known, the mother of the revolution gave her blessing: the USSR, the place from which justice had begun to propagate like an evolutionary wave. The USSR was our great friend; miracles were being accomplished there: factories, dams, tractors, education. We saw it in the wide toothy smiles of the workers in those heavily glossy photographs, who were happy at their job because their government was the "scientific" reflection of their needs. All of Russia was aloft with the sputniks that had made America tremble; all of Russia was in the wheat harvests and in the folk songs and folk dances that expressed national joy, as if the revolution had been fifty years of partying in the streets.

Only two years before, in 1956, Nikita Khrushchev had told the Twentieth Party Congress about the sordid horrors of Stalinism, the paranoia of the man with the square, fatherly face and the brushlike mustache. The god had fallen. All over Russia, the camps had opened; tens of thousands of political prisoners had come home, witnesses to hundreds of thousands more who had died while doing slave labor or from malnutrition, despair and humiliation. All that had been spoken. But somehow no one was listening; I wasn't listening. The vision was too powerful.

Already in the autumn of 1958, with the war in Algeria stirring, and the General's villainous voice booming over the radio, I had gone beyond myself. If I wasn't technically a Communist, it was only because the Party wouldn't have me: I was an American, possibly a spy. I accepted the distrustful looks of Michèle's neighborhood friends. The lawyer who was secretary of the local cell froze me with his deep-set eyes whenever we met on the street. We would shake hands, and his tall bent body, like a bird of prey, would loom over me. He bore the marks of the camps in his cough and his pale, glassy skin. I was in awe of him. His silent, inquisitorial eyes seemed to ferret out impurities I didn't know I possessed. Maybe I was a spy, maybe I was a bad influence on Michèle. But maybe she was a bad influence on me too. Or maybe the two of us were trying to move out from under the shadows we didn't create or even understand.

During those months, and then years, Michèle and I grew together. We became both antagonists and lovers. There was not much tenderness between us, and there never would be, until years after we had stopped living with each other. Only then did we discover that, new husbands and wives aside, we had become welded to each other, that we had exchanged substance in a mysterious and painful ceremony made of a thousand ordinary things. Now, when we made love, we collapsed into our dark places. When I was with her, I always felt on the edge of fright, always ready to flee behind a nervous mask that, when it came, infuriated Michèle. Already during those first months of passion and confusion, Michèle and I were molding each other, hewing each other out of raw feelings, raw distrust, and a sexual stirring that seemed to be the vulnerable side of my ideological fervor.

I remember an evening sitting on the rug in Michèle's room with her brothers and a few friends. We drank a lot of tea in those days; thick smoky tea heavily sweetened with slabs of crystallized honey from a farmer's hive near Samoëns. The tea was bitter and tannic. We sat in the darkening light of early evening and talked about politics; and the talk too was bitter, relentless, as if we were driving history forward with our words and our purity of thought.

"The kulaks were objectively counterrevolutionary; they had to be neutralized. The USSR was surrounded by enemies. Stalin

163

saw all that. He understood that building socialism in a single country was an act of war. History required extreme measures."

The speaker was a curly-haired, chubby friend of Michèle's youngest brother. He spoke seriously, almost pedagogically, and none of us argued with him. History carried weight in that breezy room, where the past glowed whitely in its tracery of evening lights spread out beyond the window. Who were the kulaks? A few million grits in the machinery of time. We were a roomful of Robespierres; we lopped off heads with a word, wiped out millions with a phrase. It was all so clear. Shadings of opinion were cowardly. Doubt was a social disease. Someone who didn't agree with you was "objectively" a Fascist, a person whose hand you couldn't afford to shake. Class warfare was the only reality we believed in, the powerless against the powerful; the ugly, hurt and tired against the beautiful people; poverty against wealth; the masses against the government, except in the special case of the government that wasn't really a government, because it spoke, by mystical transference, with the people's voice: the government of the USSR.

For a year or two, we were all Stalinists, and it was a purely mental attitude: a passion for history that wasn't concerned with actual history, with things that happened, but with the vast, solemn security of time. But was it only mental? A few years later, the chubby curly-haired friend of Michèle's younger brother, who had dispatched the kulaks one harmless evening over tea, was drafted and sent to Algeria. He became an army photographer; his job was to photograph dead Arabs. He went in with the troops and took pictures. With time, he built up a remarkable collection: hundreds of bodies laid out flat, or crumpled on the edge of holes in the ground, or half screened by bushes, or burst into pieces by hand grenades or high-caliber bullets. He became a lover of death, an aficionado. He carried a submachine gun too; some of the dead were his, he said, grinning.

What amazes me now is how we could accept a world that was so completely without surprise or compassion. Social justice had become a murderous ideal, a form of blind, biological destiny; it was governed by laws of numbers that were intricate and vast; the individual was like a molecule of gas, undetectable, a form of nothing, but grandly weighty and predictable in large numbers. The terms of Marxist thought were like great stones lined up in alleys, pointing to the rising sun. There was no need for delicacy or observation. The truth leapt up at you when words such as "dialectical materialism," "infrastructure," "alienation," "imperialism," "scientific socialism" and "surplus value" were applied to it.

One evening each week, Michèle went to a cell meeting, in the millinery shop at the bottom of the Rue du Cardinal Lemoine, where a couple of gray buildings leaned wearily against the massive white ramparts of the Ecole Polytechnique. The curtains of the shop were drawn, but a fringe of light showed at the bottom, and a discreet mutter of voices reached the street. Only the gentlest sort of revolution could be cooking in that crowded hat shop, presided over by the lumpy figure of Jean and his fluttering wife, Renée, with her girlish heavy body, and her high fluting voice. Along with Michèle came the lawyer Roger, the butcher from the square, a bookstore owner and a couple of students. Mostly they planned petition campaigns, and decided whose turn it was to sell *L'Humanité Dimanche* in front of the Café de la Chope that week. There were ideological discussions, sessions of close reading from Marx's *Capital* or some text by Lenin or Plekhanov. Once that winter, the local section (made up of a number of neighborhood cells) held a celebration in a small meeting place on the Rue Tournefort, around the corner. Michèle made sure I was invited. She asked me to bring my guitar, and I sang a couple of American work songs. Even Roger, the local Robespierre, applauded the *camarade américain.*

Very quickly the little triangle of streets around the Place de la Contrescarpe became my home. Their worn cobbles, their tilted buildings with gray scuffed facades, seemed to have been only barely coaxed into a present of tiny cars parked along one curb and low-watt light bulbs that shone frugally from the shops in the early evening. This was now my neighborhood, chosen by me, made mine by small daily acts of shopping and chatting and sitting for hours at "La Chope" each morning, reading or writing. But mostly it was made mine by the *camaraderie* of the revolution, which spoke brutally but acted with a neighborly gentleness that took me in and made me happy. Capitalism was crumbling; friendship was flourishing; a savage fullness of feeling possessed Michèle and me, and it too belonged to the revolution.

For in France in 1958, the revolution still lived. All the normal complications of life seemed secondary because something enormous and gentle, although maybe bloody at first, was about to happen. Almost everyone I knew believed it, and the belief made marriages more spacious, apartments less confining, work more bearable, anxiety trivial, bad acts of all sorts ephemeral—the moral sweepings of a bad society. The revolution was in Gilda's aggressive laughter, as it had been in her girlish courage when she shot the Nazi officer in the Gare de Lyon; it was in the humorless directives that showered down from the Comité Central to the section, to its neighborhood cells, adjusting our convictions and our actions, our moral visions, our interpretation of history, as it positioned us perfectly to see the approaching sunrise, provided that our eyes were kept trained on the proper segment of the darkness. Without the revolution, very little of those years in France makes sense. It is like watching people who seem to be moving strangely until we hear the music and realize that they are dancing, although as we think of it later, the movements are no less strange.

This neighborly statelessness of mine lasted for a year or two. It was the far arc of my flight from home, and yet it was so friendly, so comradely. Home had never been like this: the little triangle of streets behind the Pantheon had become the wandering Jew's republic. A hungering soul, I had no idea of that at the time; see it only in retrospect, twenty-five years later. Ideology had coaxed me awake, not to any great ideas (I had trouble with great ideas in college) but to something more furtive and nameless, disheveled, timid, casual and wide open. My sense of belonging was made up of the ammoniac smell of old Camembert, or better of Livarot cheese, which I learned to chew slowly, so that it barely slid over my taste buds, cut by thick Algerian wines. It was the smell of the horse-meat butchers in the building up the block. It was the acrid smell of Michèle's vagina, when it was wet and full of my come, a smell that frightened me, with its suggestion of marshes and peat bogs that were insatiable and ominously soft. It was the smell of thick coffee, and bitter black tea when we were sitting on the floor of our room discussing Lukacs. It was the smell of the perfume worn by Michèle's younger brother Lucien, which clung to the walls of our little hallway, lingering in the bathroom, full of arrogant eroticism, and Lucien swinging past us, his magnificent blond head falling into statuesque poses, as if by some genius of the blood.

I belonged also to the gray stucco walls, leaning in, as if to catch their breaths, and to the white flood of light crowning Montmartre and the vast bowl of the city spread out at our window. The sky was low and alive, an active blue, with clouds like weightless boulders hurled over us. The light wrote in shadow script on the buildings and the horse-chestnut trees along the river, on the alleys of plane trees in the Luxembourg where I went to read Hegel, Fichte and Kant, to the tunes of sparrows and pigeons, and children with high-pitched voices, more careful than American children as they pushed model boats out onto the pond and wiped the gravel off their navy-blue school uniforms, complete with caps and worn canvas book bags.

I was living a secret life; a life of the nose and fingers, and of the eyes that peeled glimpses from what they saw, and stored them, in ineradicable flashes that erupt, even now, as part of my own long essence. In those first months, I took in enough to make a new past for myself; I took in Paris, like a gas, breathing it, tasting it. All of this immediacy possibly had as a side effect my belief, now, in history. Suddenly time was on my side; humanity was on my side.

It was a queer sort of communism; and whenever I stuttered a few words of it to Michèle, she snorted with a kind of cold outrage; and I knew what she meant, it was after all peculiarly shameful that my father hadn't been killed by Nazis as hers had; that I had spent the war playing games on the beach and digging a pathetic victory garden on an empty lot. At most I had spent a few hours, in ten-minute stretches, sitting under my desk at school, for air raid practice. My war had been imaginary; some headlines, some maps in the newspapers, a few place names, the Battle of the Bulge, Salerno, Normandy. And that noisy day in 1945, when the streets were full of grownups weeping and laughing, and men in white Coast Guard uniforms from a nearby base sang at the top of their lungs.

I was virtually unborn compared to Michèle and her brothers and her Communist comrades. My opinion carried no weight. My moral fervor was unshod, unreal; it was a form of poetry. I acknowledged that. I sought for the real, and never seemed to find it. I was innocent; Michele and all of France were congenitally and fatally one up on me. That's what it meant to be an American; even a lapsed American, who spoke French and put his shoulder to the wheel of world revolution.

Therefore I kept my happiness to myself and mostly from myself; for it too seemed oddly shameful, not part of the program. I made myself study Marxist economic theory, and tried to understand why the working classes were becoming morally impoverished despite rising wages, four-week vacations, and a car in every garage: pauperization, it turned out, was a complex state, and I glimpsed a depth of meaning my Marxist texts surely didn't intend. Scarcity played an ironic music in human affairs. The rich were possibly poor, if their obscene needs were taken into account. The poor man who sloughed off the bloated shell of his needs became robust and healthy, like the Russian farmer on his immense tractor. Surely none of this was intended by the dazzled articles of *Les Cahiers du Communisme*, which specialized in "objective" socialist analysis. Such hopefulness was a product of my overexcited mind, a spinoff of my rioting senses, a bourgeois deviation. I was a closet "idealist," a renegade in the making.

And yet how faithful I was, how serious, how methodical even, reading three newspapers a day, my three weeklies, my *Monthly Review*, my *National Guardian*, my complete set of Marx's theoretical works, my Hegel, my Proudhon, my Bakunin, my Rosa Luxemburg, my Tagliotti, my Roger Garaudy. I was unusally well informed. Every morning I took the temperature of worldly capitalism. Wherever I looked, I saw surplus values, and alienation; I saw people made crazy by "society"; I saw that man was good, but had everywhere become lopsided and incomplete, through no fault of his own. There was no good and no evil; only the pathos of hurt men, only the state like a perennial bad dream with its complex inventions of power. The revolution would change that, but meanwhile I was changed.

6

FOR a while I earned my living playing the piano for a fellow named Al Dorsey, who booked shows into the American armed forces bases around France. Every weekend, we drove to Saint Germain-en-Laye, Orléans or Chambord to entertain the troops. The soldiers were usually cooped up on remote bases behind fences, and spent their time beating each other's brains out and getting drunk. Dorsey was black, a plump, smiling, fast-talking New Yorker who mc'd his own shows, and always managed to stir up trouble with his smooth, educated voice that seemed surprised at the obscenities it was obliged to utter. The audiences were mostly white boys from the South, with a handful of black brothers guffawing at Al's dumb jokes. White and black alike were usually drunk, depressed and vaguely angry, and Al kept them simmering. Al gave us survival instructions, in case there was trouble, when we set up in some plasterboard enlisted men's club surrounded by parking lots: keep your mouth shut and locate the nearest door that works; if there's a brawl or a race riot, get out that door and keep out of sight. Dorsey kept us all on our toes. The weekends had a taste of dumb danger that never really materialized, although the roomfuls of crew-cut boys, usually only teenagers, with muscular builds and pink faces alternately roaring with laughter and shouting obscenities at Al, at each other, at the army, at the fucking cosmos that had thrown them down here in this wilderness of boredom and loneliness (fuck communism! fuck anything but home and mother!), held the feeling of danger bottled up like a homemade bomb.

I wasn't much of a piano player, but I could sight read a bit and fake progressions of chords if they were obvious enough, and I could thump convincing rhythms that kept everyone reasonably happy. I played from sheets of music covered with food and drink stains. Our acts were strictly second-rate, performed by a marvelous bunch of drifters and terminal eccentrics. There was Yogi Clemendaus, who wasn't "material," as he put it. Sitting and sleeping in his fur hat, he sipped weak beer and read comic books, and he fasted sometimes for weeks at a time—to keep his body well oiled, he said. At the shows, he unhinged his various joints while standing on one leg to my accompaniment of Hollywood-style music. After a time, he added a limbo dance to his act; he would slither under the bar while shrugging and shaking his brown, incredibly thin chest in rhythm to the piano.

One weekend, a new musician joined us: Slim, the huge Nigerian I used to see at the Tournon during my first months in Paris. I remembered him sitting there with his legs sprawled around a table and a dangerous scowl on his face. But Slim wasn't like that at all, it turned out. He arrived at Al Dorsey's apartment, near the Gare de Lyon, with a set of African tribal drums, his shoulders taking up the whole hallway and a humorous porkpie hat tilted on his forehead. He recognized me right away. With a wild chuckle in his voice, he said, "Hey, man, you used to sit at the Tournon. I used to see you there! You play the piano? For this man?" He pointed over at Al; then he laughed with his thin African voice, warm and friendly. We played together all that year. Slim slapped and thumped his drums with complex enthusiasm. Beneath his hands, they had flights of hysteria and little hiccuping conversations. At some point, he would give a tribal yell and rip his shirt off; with his back to the audience, and his arms flung up in a gesture of power, he rippled his shoulder muscles, and laughed. Slim was a very funny man. We would stop en route for a drink in some gray provincial town, pushing open the door into a café that smelled of disinfectant. Under strands of old flypaper, Slim surrounded his bowl of café au lait, like the genie escaped from the bottle: blacker than black, and vast, with dazzling teeth, and a gentle, humorous way that it was impossible not to like.

But my buddy on those long weekends of driving to army bases through the winter fog and sleeping in flimsy hotels in small, lost towns was Joe Breitbart, the strongman. He must have been around sixty, and had spent most of his life traveling with small circuses. When he wasn't traveling he performed in a crummy nightclub in Montmartre.

He drove an old Renault 4, shaped like a beetle. I was usually assigned to ride with him, being the only person small enough to fit into the car once his bulging body had lowered itself inside. Every Friday, Joe arrived with his string bag full of food prepared by his wife: a carton of chicken soup, pâté, pieces of chicken wrapped in wax paper, a container of tripe and sautéed vegetables that Joe ate cold. The cups of weak camomile tea that he drank reflected his nature: kindly and old-fashioned, a grandmother with muscles. He took me under his wing. If I had a cold, he would share his chicken soup with me, saying, "Eat, eat; it'll do you good." Joe, the Alsatian showman, was pure Brighton Beach. I loved his act. While I banged away at "Stardust" or "Georgia on My Mind," he tore packs of cards in half using his thumb and forefinger; lopped off the heads of teaspoons with a blow of one finger; did an old-fashioned accordion shuffle while holding up a half-dozen soldiers on iron rods. It was awesome to see this wide, short, soft-looking old man, with wisps of hair curling over his bald head and a motherly solicitude in his eyes, almost apologetically perform his acts of maniacal strength. He would lay a fifty-dollar bill on the piano and pick up a fat iron bar. He would look at the bar as if concentrating on his forces, and then, with a heave of his shoulders and a show of his expanding arms, he would bend the bar half a foot or so. In thickly accented English—like my grandmother's, I thought—he announced that anyone who could budge the bar even an inch could collect the fifty dollars. The soldiers lined up, the physical-education specialists and weightlifters and brawlers with beer bellies. All that red American beef; all those rows of white teeth and bristly scalps yearning for the fifty-dollar bill on the piano. Their eyes bulged, their faces got redder; they tried it standing up or kneeling or in other contorted, bizarre positions. You could smell the animal juices, the sweat, the sour beer breaths. But they couldn't budge the bar. Then Joe picked it up again almost casually, and while still shuffling his feet and searching for his grip, as if by accident, he bent it into a U. The audience went wild, while Joe grinned a little sadly, as if such strength was beyond his mental control. Feats of strength were his lot, he seemed to be saying, but were not his love, which was more in the direction of gentleness, of chicken soup and camomile tea. Good old Joe! He took care of me, in his embarrassed, concerned way, put-putting across France in his tin car which he could lift out of a ditch with one hand.

After a year or so, de Gaulle pulled France out of NATO and began to close down the American bases. Dorsey made plans to take his show to Spain and Italy, even Turkey, but that was more than I was ready for. I was exhausted by the schizophrenic way of life that had taken me every week from my neighborhood Communist friends, my sessions with Marx and Lenin, and quiet side trips into Trotsky, to those mini-Oklahomas and Tennessees, wrapped in mire, deep in the French provinces. I felt like a spy taking notes on the American dream of empire, and found it made up of noise, muscles, racism and oceans of weak beer. So I said goodbye to Al, that smooth perfumed dude, and to Joe, to Slim, and the cute unicyclist in her white bathing suit, and the just-divorced dark crooner, who sang sad songs in French and then, with an irresistible accent, in English. My career in show business was over.

Raymond got me a job teaching American civilization in the commercial business school he worked at. Every week for fifteen hours, I told a bunch of dull teenage boys about the New York subway systems and the system of checks and balances, about states' rights and civil rights. I also had to explain to them how to play the game of baseball, and discovered that baseball was something you were either born to or not, like rhythm or perfect pitch: it couldn't be taught. Baseball was a purely American folk art, along with jazz and gospel singing. It was also a living ghost for me —just about all I could remember and love of my homeland.

Those boys in their dirty tweed jackets, tittering and shifting in their seats, were a glimpse into another France: the unbelieving class of shopkeepers and accountants and middle-level bureaucrats, whose sons had limped through the lower grades and now were shunted onto this private track of business schooling, sufficiently low-grade to ensure boredom but garnished with the prestige of the Paris Chambre de Commerce, which ran the school. The school emanated meanness of spirit. The boys were bad in a bottled up, harmless way. But it was a living.

Raymond had ended up here because of his eyes, but also, probably, because of his secretive, feminine rebelliousness that wouldn't give in to normal ambitions; he wouldn't humble himself to the iron routine of an *agrégation,* or the required patronizing relationship with a thesis director, who, for ten or twenty years, would dole out approval and disapproval while you perfected your knowledge of some untouched but unbearably minor pocket of learning worth fifteen hundred pages of exposition. Raymond was like a beacon at the school. With unspoken authority, he cast a spell on the dreamy boys, as if he had spied in each one the perishable glimmer of freshness and nourished it with his sympathy. Raymond came alive with young people, of which, I realized, I was one, only six or seven years older than my students.

Occasionally I would spend the afternoon with Raymond; we would visit the Musée d'Art Moderne or the Musée Guimet, with its displaced Buddhas sealed into a silence from which they stared with curiously feminine smiles and droopy lids. Or we would drink thick red wine in the apartment where he lived five stories up under the eaves with his friend Marguerite, on the Rue Dauphine. As always, my throat would ache from talking too much. Raymond, by means of the nods and soft *hms* that conveyed his Olympian curiosity and his powerfully receptive nature, would seem to pull the words from me, and then pass them through loops of pipe smoke, blue, in the white light of the rooftops. At the museum, he would surround a statue or painting, move in close, with a shy hungry look, and take it in in small patches, like an appraiser moving his magnifying glass over every square inch of the work. Then, by some feat of visual memory, Raymond would rebuild the whole from his discrete blocks of vision. Maybe his semiblindness contributed to his aura of wisdom, but he saw far and deep; I sensed a power in him, and relied on it.

Now especially I deferred to him as to a standard of pure thoughtfulness. His Marxist credentials were reassuringly clear; although, in fact, I knew little of his activities. I had the impression that he frequented a neighborhood cell somewhere; perhaps one of those legendary cells where intellectuals and artists met to forge rigorous lines of thought. I could barely imagine such meetings, elevated but gruff and proletarian; over in the 5th arrondissement, on a quiet cross street somewhere—was it the Rue Vésale, the Rue de Lille?—where Aragon, Tristan Tzara and Picasso, the aging warriors of the new, met to discuss party matters and express their fidelity to the overthrow of old ideas, of outmoded and strangulating structures of social existence. Maybe Raymond came across them, or even met with them. The character of his Marxism was unknown to me and, in fact, I didn't know at the time that he had finally drifted across his fine but implacable line and had stopped going to cell meetings. Unreached in his private spiral of pipe smoke, he didn't tell me, but continued to clear his throat and lean back boyishly, stretching out his soft bulky body while I talked about time, history, and the organization of human needs; about the inexorable decline of capitalism, as the colonies shook loose from their bloodsucking masters and Lenin's imperialist phase of capitalism came to an end.

As for Raymond, he had handed back his Party card, exhausted finally by the pressure of political clichés and the drugged simplemindedness of ideology as a view of life. His deepest commitment, amounting to a biological drive, as I finally understood, was to the purity and supple truthfulness of language. He experienced banality as a form of terrorism; deliberate slogan-making twisted his nerves into painful kinks and gave him hives. Even after he had drifted out of the high-handed spectrum of French political life, out of society itself almost, snapping friendships, rejecting left and right alike as forms of public lunacy—even then, perched on his solitary island, he listened with boyish seriousness to my ideological monologues. Occasionally he interposed an idea, and then I heard a nervous urgency in his voice, as if his words were stumbling after his thoughts and not keeping up.

"Marxism stands, finally, on a theory of human needs," he said, "but is there such a theory? Where do we begin? With Freud? But who reads Freud in France today—half of his writing isn't even in print—and who reads Hegel? Maybe the Americans and the Germans have something we can learn; all the French have is a form of social irritability they call communism; and a dead heritage, as dead as the eccentric aristocrats of the nineteenth century who conspired in their moldering chateaus to bring back into being a dead heritage, although it twitches and dances, called the Revolution. We invented it, we created the floor plan for it, now it's our national treasure. Marx even solidified it in *The 18th Brumaire.* De Gaulle and the Revolution; the hard fathers, and the helpless sons, with their tantrums and, even more, their collective nihilism. That's France for you."

The apartment of Michèle's family, on the Rue du Cardinal Lemoine, simmered with emotions. Lucien, the younger brother, glided in and out like a perfumed cat. We had the impression that he was registered at the Sorbonne for a degree in psychology, but in the atmosphere of rivalries and differences that reigned among us, we didn't ask each other too many questions. His wife, a dark beautiful girl, already at twenty-two simpered and complained about her health—she had a shelf full of pills and colored liquids —not from mean-spiritedness, I think, but because her beautiful husband rarely emerged from his erotic dreaminess even when it made use of her.

Michèle's other brother, Gilles, spoke in a thick Parisian slang. He was an actor; he sneered and yelled, as if every day were a new melodrama. Gilles and Lucien were both afraid of Michèle: She had powers of feminine disdain that made them choke with frustration while she wept with rage and failed tenderness. But that only sharpened their teeth where I was concerned. I was free game; Gilles made a specialty of mimicking me whenever I made a mistake in French. He became my baleful shadow, prying his little blade into every crack in my foreignness. He never let me forget what, in fact, I was happy to remember. I was not of this place, this cramped bowl of unlovingness, intense and wild, like the nest of gargoyles, suspended by an angle of vision, which glared at our windows. Paris was not my home; I was subtly distant; I kept appointments with elsewhere, although, in fact, I had none to keep and lived the spiky life of our three-room circus as best I could.

In the fall, Julianne usually came to stay with us for a few weeks. The brothers and Michèle pretended detachment and perfunctory hospitality, but the anxiety, the secrets, the competitions, were like a heat in which we sweltered. Julianne walked around Paris in a touching daze; she was stiff, more preoccupied than any provincial (she had lived in Paris most of her life), because the city crushed her sacrifice and mocked it. In Paris, the past was past. The marble plaques, with their wilted flowers, commemorating fallen heroes of the Resistance were small and silent in the crazy life of the city which manufactured its present out of whirring motorbikes and the sexual semaphore of strangers in tight pants and unbuttoned blouses, and the mélange of smells and voices multiplied by the high houses. Amid all this, Julianne was silent and repudiating; her children courted her while seeming not to and she seemed not to notice it.

The apartment was too small even in normal times, when our psyches brushed past each other in fresh irritations. But with Julianne sharing Michèle's room and giving lively dinner parties for her old friends; with Gilles snoring and Lucien whispering quizzical insults; with Michèle suffering the subtle martyrdom of her mother's silences, I felt expelled into the streets. I spent more of my time at La Chope, or in a tiny bistro a few blocks away, sitting next to the coal stove to keep warm, while I read Lévi-Strauss's *La Pensée Sauvage* and Michel Foucault's *Histoire de la Folie à l'Age Classique*, or Pierre Richard's *Mallarmé*. The stirrings of a new intellectual passion were upon me, as I shook off the Revolution and looked around for some new total view that would outwit ordinary living, as if my secret effort was, somehow, to be smarter than life. There was a nice irony between the new cant of "structuralism," "deconstructionism," "semiotics," Lacanian psycholinguistics, and the destructive work of the private acids brewing in our minds in the apartment on the Rue du Cardinal Lemoine.

7

REALITY was taking a brutal form in 1960 and '61; and the noise of it made our ideological fervor seem small. The Algerian war was not going away. The French had sent a large army to North Africa; they had built electrified fences to seal off the borders with Tunisia and Morocco; they had launched counterterrorist campaigns; they had used napalm. They won all the battles; but the Algerians had turned into a fluid army, slipping through the brutal scrubland of the Kabylia mountains. They were the resistance fighters, the maquisards, and they awakened a troubled response in the French, who were half remembering their own national epic of resistance to overwhelming force. In 1960, the FLN brought the war to France. They started shooting at police stations; they assassinated political opponents; they sent representatives to collect dues from Algerian workers in France and convoyed suitcases full of money across the mountains to Switzerland, where they fed numbered bank accounts.

Paris had become a city at war. The police built concrete bunkers on the sidewalks in front of the police stations and stationed men with submachine guns in them. The newspapers were full of stories about Algerians found dead in the street, with suspected police bullets in them. The white-and-black squad car with the honking horn was a terror vehicle in the squalid streets around the Rue Mouffetard, or across from Notre Dame, on the Rue de Bièvre and the Rue Maître Albert, where Algerian workers lived six and eight to a room and others slept in parked cars in shifts. The shabby cafés and couscous restaurants were filled with dark nervous boys who worked ten hours a day on construction sites, or as unskilled labor in the factories. These were closed neighborhoods to Frenchmen. They had a reputation for danger—hissing voices full of insults; knives and guns; rapes.

As is usually the case in a society at war, the menace of the local Algerians was mostly imagined. They were a timid, careful people who froze whenever a police car crept up the street, the stubby barrel of a submachine gun visible through the glancing light of the windshield. They were also sullen, resentful, besieged, lonely. I watched them sipping sweet tea in dark cafés, buying spices in hole-in-the-wall groceries that stayed open until after midnight, cooking on a camp stove in their overcrowded rooms. I was particularly aware of the Arabs because they were a different sort of alien; in their case, their foreignness was stamped on their faces. They couldn't go underground, couldn't scrub the foreignness off, the way I had, to become laundered Frenchmen. The police would drive up in big square trucks painted deep blue, cordon off the sidewalk of the Boulevard Saint Michel or the Rue des Ecoles, and then winnow out the narrow brown faces with long teeth and curly hair, men wearing loose old trousers and seedy gabardine coats. Sometimes they asked to see their *cartes d'identité*, sometimes they simply rounded them up and whacked them with night sticks as they stumbled into the back of the trucks. In the trucks they were beaten and humiliated; I could imagine what that was like from my experience in the bilious green room at the Swiss border, with the fat pink cops and their long sticks. After a night at an empty caserne in the Bois de Vincennes, most of them would be released; some would be arrested and sent to the prison at Fresnes; others disappeared. Nobody kept a strict account—after all, they were only Arabs. The police saw themselves on the front lines defending France against body snatchers, vampires; it wasn't a war, it was a horror movie.

But gradually the war invaded our lives. It put the finishing touches on our disaffection with the Communists, who took an embarrassed, nationalistic stance when speaking about the war: Why did those Arabs want to be independent anyway? France was a good friend, enlightened, revolutionary in its heart. Be patient, my Algerian friends. Let history take its course. There was an unspoken fact behind their shiftings: French workers didn't have much use for those *ratons* who smelled bad and lied and stuck knives in people for a bet. The Party didn't want to get too far ahead of "the masses."

The war was also in its way a civil war; the political tensions were uncontrolled, and a sense of corruption, even evil, was in the air. We came to see the police as a state within the state—a lawless one, torturing suspects, some of whom died. There was a subtle racial line drawn that none of us wanted to accept: On the whole, we were safe; they didn't murder white people, although in the backs of the dark blue trucks we might be roughed up, a few whacks with rubber hoses that leave no marks, a little twisting of the head and cracking of ribs; boots in the stomach—samplings of terror, before the door of the truck would open on a dark street in some nowhere suburb amid sad lampposts, parked cars, a ribbon of pavement; no lights in the houses, and the white man would be rolled out in the middle of the pavement, while the truck rumbled off in the arrogance of grinding gears. There might be a half inch in the paper a few days later; or an article deploring the arrogance of the police, exercising a form of state terrorism. Sometimes the government would seize the newspaper and try to force it into bankruptcy, without even bringing legal charges. We had the sense of a government out of control, a moral rot that was frightening. Everywhere, black buses full of CRS, Gardes Républicains or some other paramilitary police force would have their lights out, waiting; you could see the cigarettes winking inside. During the day the men played cards behind the windows newly covered with a grill; in the evening they sat in military silence hour after hour. I could imagine their boredom; they were mostly ex-peasants or ex-soldiers, ex-legionnaires; some were *pieds-noirs*. Sometimes the Latin Quarter would be full of buses, lined up along a side street. These streets full of students were enemy territory too; to the police these smart university kids, wearing colored scarves, sandals and arrogant bushy beards, were perverts, Arab-lovers, enemies of the nation.

The long black police buses were something Jean Cocteau might have dreamed up. At the height of a demonstration, the streets would be thick with cops thankful to get a chance to break some heads; the demonstrators were almost always outnumbered. The state preferred a few cracked heads and a brooding edgy atmosphere to actual opposition. Submachine guns were everywhere. You saw them in front of police stations and public buildings, their muzzles slanting in the air; you saw them cradled in the laps of cops sitting in police cars; or hanging from the shoulder of a cop standing guard on a back street where Arabs lived. The cop was the only new, shiny thing on these streets; a product of technology, like a new car, out of place amid the bloated patches of stucco falling off the walls, and the subtle stinks of age and moisture breathing out of shabby doors leading to courtyards it was better not to look into.

One day while I was shopping on the Rue Mouffetard I heard

a sharp snap. In the street up ahead a group of Arabs were standing in front of a café. A man walked casually into the Rue du Pot-de-Fer. Another man lay half on the sidewalk and half in the street, curled up and still, and very alone. Suddenly everyone scattered. I ran down the street and then stopped. I didn't want to be the first person to reach him. I could feel the grip of something cold in my stomach that possessed me whenever I was present at a street fight; the spectacle of physical anger always pierced me with guilty interest and sympathy.

But there was no anger here; nothing berserk and crazy. In the magnifying silence, a man lay dead. Killed by someone he had been standing next to and maybe even talking to. Someone who without personal motive had reached into his pocket for a revolver and shot him. Then he walked, not ran, into a nearby street. The newspapers called it a *règlement de comptes,* an act of discipline or revenge by one Algerian faction against another. I never got it straight: left against right; militant against collaborationist; Marxist against Islamic royalist; the FLN against a rabid reformer? The murder was neat and undramatic: the man could have been sleeping, or drunk. He didn't bleed much and the blood was so thick and dark it looked like spilled syrup.

I had grown up between wars; murder belonged to the realm of story, you heard about it on the radio; I had never seen a dead person, except for my grandmother, yellow and thin in her coffin. I had never imagined what a decisive argument death is! How it breaks the rules and baffles language, how explanation becomes helpless in the face of it. Death was a glimpse of how totally helpless we are in the cosmos.

8

ONE morning we received a visit from a friend of Michèle's named Charlotte. Charlotte lived around the corner, in a tiny apartment which she shared with a writer named Edmond Gilbard, who was Swiss and over ninety years old. Gilbard was thin and definite as a grasshopper; he was full of wit and had a tenuous gait that seemed to float his frail physique along like a spiritual essence. I loved to visit him, and hear him gossip about the Swiss literary life of fifty years before. He was writing his memoirs, and in the tiny living room, surrounded by cushions, crystal ashtrays and thin little vases with a couple of flowers in them, he resembled the lion of a long-vanished salon, still talking, still inexhaustibly witty. Charlotte herself, though still a young woman, was a sort of time capsule who spoke a rich French full of archaisms. She took care of Edmond and eventually married him, as if to place the last piece of a jigsaw puzzle: the France of old, where people were careful, distant, polite, intensely cultivated, and kindly. Charlotte did not seem the kind of person to bring the message she had for us.

"A friend came to see me yesterday; someone I used to know when I was a student. They're forming a support group to help the FLN. You've known about the Jeanson network? This would be similar."

A friend of Sartre's, Francis Jeanson, had formed a series of groups to support the Algerian rebels. From time to time, he gave clandestine press conferences; the photos showed him to be casual, unshaven, a little spacey, on the run. His message was that French intellectuals had a responsibility to the Third World. Frantz Fanon's *Les Damnés de la Terre* had recently been published, arguing a new morality for the old revolutionary hope: The white man had a blood debt, but had bred a fine irony in the dialectics of the blood, for the master had nourished a murderous health in his slave. He had humiliated him, crushed his elementary humanness, made him into a thing; but now, from the well of the slave's humiliation, where a secret wholeness had been brewing, the redeeming voice came. It was already coming in Algeria, the first act in the world struggle of the oppressed. It was not a war so much as a health-giving terror. In this analysis, killing was not the payment of a debt —an eye for an eye—but an act of rebirth.

Jeanson himself wasn't a terrorist, but he expressed a curiously humble sense that the possibility for a truly moral life had migrated from Europe to the Third World, that we the exploiters—white, comfortable, protected—were historically benighted and sub-stanceless. We were the "pale faces" D. H. Lawrence wrote about; the silent, suffering others possessed more reality than we did; in the new world order we were the servants. I knew the sort of thing he and his people did: carried messages, used their apartments as letter drops, created safe houses for giving shelter to FLN rebels, even carried suitcases full of money across the border. Whatever an Arab couldn't do—pass for a white man—Jeanson's people did. They were fake Arabs, impersonations; but by these means they could have a vicarious foothold in the new world. They could step over into the new morality. There was something abstruse about all this, like the working out of a logarithm. The dead man on the Rue Mouffetard was simply dead; I noticed no cleansing fire of history on that squalid sidewalk, sticky with blood, and suddenly empty, bland, quiet as an erasure. No doubt the shabby hotels there had been full of rapidly beating hearts: upstairs, men sat on their narrow beds smoking cigarettes, afraid to come down until the police had arrived in their honking van and tossed the dead man (was he someone's friend?) into the back, with a tag on his wrist. See nothing, hear nothing, let the violent purposes of others be accomplished. Don't hope, don't do anything; simply string the days together, work, drink tea.

Yet I felt that Fanon's scenario held a truth. My wretchedly complicated existence felt ghostly to me. Whether I liked it or not, I was a pale face. Listening to the clamor in my mind, compulsive and debilitating, I was ready to believe that reality had migrated elsewhere; I didn't feel very real. The master in my case had become its ghost.

Charlotte had been carrying letters and suitcases for the FLN for some time. Who could suspect this young woman from another era, wearing much-washed but impeccable dresses and high heels, her hair swept up expertly on her head, of being a subversive? She resembled a chatelaine in her chateau, its furniture looming up under dusty sheets, and she carried this air through the streets as she walked past police lines or met Arabs with code names in railroad stations. She humorously used herself as a disguise. She who was more French than anyone, who said *vous* even to her friends (a quintessence of *vieille France*) simply acted and didn't torment herself.

"Would you consider forming a reseau? Think it over. If you like, someone will be in touch with you?"

She sat with her legs together, her bust pushed slightly forward, her face kindly but almost expressionless. Her presence was like a sudden light; we realized that we had had enough of being helpless and complicated. Enough of finding things out in the newspapers, enough passive fright on the dangerous streets, with their submachine guns and their Arabs to whom, despite everything, we were cops in our souls, white men.

The war was under our skins now, like a dry itch. We contacted Maxime and his wife, Erika; Claude and his Swedish girlfriend, Connie. We were ready. We had a group; three apartments; seven people (with Lucien) ready to step beyond the pale into a world of justice and fright, perhaps violence, a world too strange for me even to imagine. This was the farthest voyage: the Jew stepping out of his skin and becoming an Arab, Semite into Semite; brother into alien brother. The odd thing is that we were all Jews, all seven of us. But Israel didn't sit very heavily on our thoughts in those days. It was a small, arrogant, curiously atheistic, brave little country. But our homeland? That seemed to me like another patriotism I couldn't swallow. Hebrew sounded like Arabic to me anyway. The Israelis I met in Paris even looked like Arabs, except for their brash, almost Germanic heavy-handedness that got on my nerves. They seemed childish, naïve. Not my people. But who were my people? Certainly not the hostile groups of Arabs standing in the street, to whom I could form no bridge, couldn't cry out: "Wait, we're brothers, I'm on your side; I'm not really a white man, you'll see." But how could they see, and what language did we have in common? What could I say that wouldn't be posing on my part, goodhearted but fatuous (with all the subtle weight of class and race of my passport, dirty and creased but powerful, like the Secret Name of the Kabala). And my people were not Michèle, or Lucien or Raymond; they were my closest friends, my lover, and yet were separated from me, from my past, which I couldn't give up without becoming nothing—separated from me by the unacknowledged certainty, deep in my mind, that one day I would go back to the United States. What would I do there? I imagined myself teaching English in some engineering college in Kansas or Oklahoma— places more foreign to me than Paris ever could be. America was like an appetite that, one day, would swallow me. Up ahead a worse anonymity, a vanishing. Yet when the time came I would go; it was written. The deeper I slipped into French, into the war and politics, into the streets, and the more Michèle was hammered into my life like a stake, the more certainly I knew, in some chamber of my heart, that my bags were already packed.

As the days passed and we waited to hear from someone, we

182

met in the evenings and talked about the pact we had made: to live outside the law; to embrace this formless, edgy war that was in our streets, the war that was destroying Algeria, creating hatred so extreme it seemed out of human proportion. Everything vanished but the waiting; the war became a home. An expectant truce reigned in the apartment. We sat on the floor beside the open windows drinking barley tea, and never had the world been painted in such contrast. On the one side white men drove black Citroën DS's through streets cleared by motorcycle police, on their way to meetings where, with polished grammar and heavy seriousness, they would decide about guns, napalm, the suspension of the rights of prisoners, ways to censor newspapers without seeming to: power, clean and relaxed, mediated by law. And on the other side were nameless men in a hurry, armed with small guns, carrying old suitcases; soldiers without uniforms, spending days in holes dug deep into the rocky ground of Algeria, coming out at night to eat in a nearby village and then to dig a mine into a military road or to rendezvous for an ambush. The war was a world; all of justice was in it; all of horror was in it. We waited for our part to begin, but already it was inside us.

We listened to raving declarations by *pieds-noirs,* read about "ratonnades," Arab hunting, in the streets of Algiers by teenagers who tore people to pieces. The extremes were almost cosmic; crazed burstings of all limits; death. The anarchists in Barcelona during the Spanish Civil War had shouted "Viva la muerte," Long live death. I knew what they meant now; I could see the same raving frustration, the same group suicide, as at Masada in old Israel: Humans going over into a kind of drunkenness, fed by little gusts of the absolute that used political language and expressed itself in human emotion but was like the bursting out of a nightmare. I was baffled and horrified by it all. The masters had gone mad. Their slaves had become deliberate and skillful. They had turned Algiers into a booby trap. For two thousand years Algeria had never been a nation. Caught between old Carthage to the east and the Moroccan empire to the west, a thin rocky strip squeezed between the ocean and the desert, it had been a kind of haven for feudal emirs and pirates. There were fierce mountain tribes that not even the Arabs had ever conquered; enclaves of Jews, in the desert, probably converted to Judaism by refugees from old Rome, fifteen hundred years ago. But now, as if horror had a plastic power, a country was being born. And this country rising out of its debris of war, out of bewilderment and anger, out of nothing, was what we saw and wanted to be part of. We became white Algerians; it was our secret. And still we waited.

I took the train to Lille once a week to teach at the university there. I wrote my thesis at the Sorbonne for a vigorous, tormented, brilliant man who made fun of my head-over-heels passion for the new intellectual modes: "Plato and Diderot managed to express complicated ideas in simple language. They don't age. While your complicated masters, with their Germanic vocabularies and their breathless baroque lingo, won't be read five years from now."

He was off by about ten years, but he was right, and it was a lesson I never forgot, although at the time I grumbled at my bad luck at being burdened with such an old-fashioned thesis director, who was closed to the vital new thoughts of Jean-Pierre Richard and Georges Poulet, René Gérard and Lévi-Strauss, and that incredible gnomic, heavy master of provocation Jacques Lacan, whose essays in *La Psychoanalysis* made me feel like the bull in the labyrinth.

Then, one afternoon, the doorbell rang. Michèle was painting. Her hands were stained with paint, her hair tied into a wild knot in back of her head. I was half reading and half looking outside, far down the hill at a round window where, I had been told, Pascal once lived, or was it Lenin, or Trotsky?

In the hallway was an olive-skinned man in a neatly cut suit. He was thin, his face was gaunt but attractive. Even before he spoke, he didn't seem to be asking for anything, he wasn't nervous; on the contrary, he gave the impression of expecting everything, a kind of alert resignation that was ready to vanish if he had got the address wrong or if some subtle sense told him we weren't who we were supposed to be. "I'm Daniel," he said. "I'm a friend of Charlotte's. She said you were expecting me."

He was carrying a canvas suitcase, and everything about him was loose, muted, as if, with a supplementary effort, he could make himself invisible.

We asked him in, and introduced ourselves. Michèle, myself, Lucien, who would be home soon, Elisabeth, his wife. Gilles was out of town with an acting company. Could he stay in Gilles's room for a few weeks, maybe longer, he wanted to know. We had expected that. We told him about Maxime and Erika, Claude and Connie. He nodded and asked for their addresses. He would go to see them himself. He left us standing in Gilles's room, took the heavy rusted key we gave him and went out.

"I'll be back later. I'm happy to know you."

From that moment and for months afterward our lives centered around Daniel, even when he was out, even when, for days, he didn't leave his room, except to go to the bathroom or take some food and eat it alone on his little table next to the window, never noticing the view. He was always well dressed; not overly so, but he was naturally stylish, as none of us were except perhaps Lucien. He seemed to come from a wealthy background. His French was perfect, without the pinchings and hesitations of the Arabic French we heard in the streets. He might not have been an Arab at all, for all anyone could tell. He even had straight hair. But his slimness and his dark skin would probably have given him away to the police, who believed they could smell out Arabs and who didn't care whom they rounded up on those brutal afternoons. So Daniel hid. Sometimes in the early evening he went out for a few hours. It was around rush hour, when the Métro and the streets were full of people hurrying home from work. We didn't know where he went, and none of us ever ran across him, even by accident. He was our guest, relaxed and friendly, but mute about anything that mattered to him. I tried to connect him, or someone like him, to the murder on the Rue Mouffetard a few months before. Someone had decided on that chain of actions. God the devourer had come down to the person who, revolver in pocket, had gone out that morning probably not knowing why but only what and who: a segmented, secure chain of command. Was killing part of Daniel's business? Only the neutral body under his boyish friendliness made me understand that it might be. People were a filmy décor in which he worked; he arranged them like a complicated set of conditions around his reason for being. The revolution gave him things to do; he probably even liked doing them. But Daniel was alone in a way that was not personal; he seemed to live at a remove from his face and his eyes. It was, I imagine, his form of sanity. We never learned his real name, not even after the war was over. We never learned what sort of life he'd led, what studies he'd done and where, whether he was married. He was a man shorn of all associations.

Sometimes, in the evening, he would come into our room and

have tea with us on the floor. We did most of the talking, but he listened, and without expressing opinions was very much part of our talk. We wanted him to like us and I think he did. The only thing we ever found out about his work was that he kept track of the families of men who were in prison or had disappeared, and saw to it that the FLN sent them a monthly indemnity. Apparently Daniel was a sort of administrator; even in the wild country beyond the law there were records and papers to fill out. The FLN were practicing to be a government, and Daniel, so suave a European, was part of that. From something he said, I gathered that he didn't speak Arabic well. He was not French, nor was he truly speaking of his own people either. He belonged to an idea, to an action. Perhaps this made him dangerous.

I saw myself in Daniel: his isolation, his foreignness and most of all his Frenchness. He was French; if he had a home, it was here. Maybe he had been raised here. His French had the slippery elegance of the Parisian; he sat with his leg over a chair arm or leaning on one arm on the floor, with the physical unconsciousness of someone full of a childlike certainty, someone whose parents had taken their best care of him and actually loved him physically. And yet a gate had slammed down between him and all he knew: maybe the great revolutionaries had experienced that. I thought of Trotsky, the Russian Jew, who had made a silence of his past, hardening himself into an instrument of thought which he wished free of swampish feelings, like an eighteenth-century mechanical toy made of cogs and pulleys, a servant of necessity and not of his own childhood and his parents, and the associations that form an impediment to action. Daniel was abstract and I too was abstract, although I lived only on the edge of action, a voyeur. Outside of his idea, Daniel too was a voyeur, I sensed. We were brothers, in these three rooms overlooking all of civilization. We had come from the swamps and prairies, from the desert; this place, overloaded with time, was a spectacle to us.

Daniel found it curious that I was an American. I suspect he tried to think of uses for me and my passport, and would have found them had there been time. But the war had become dense and it was like a glue; everything had become slow, except dying, which happened in the dirty streets of the Goutte d'Or near Montmartre, and in the wretched tin shacks that had sprung up around Nanterre—"bidonvilles," they were called—tin-can towns, made of corrugated iron, flattened oil cans, cardboard and tar paper, with rocky alleys and a couple of electric lines strung illegally overhead; water at a public fountain on a nearby street; little grocery stores, and cafés arranged around orange crates where the Algerians nursed their patience and their nervousness when they came back from the factory, half dead from the machines, and talked about their families, which had become icons of smudged photographs.

Daniel had changed our lives in another way. The war, which had become so much a part of us, was now also more distant.

"You know," he said one evening, sipping black honeyed tea on our living-room floor, "you'd better not see Maxime and Claude for a while; that way, in case anyone is being followed, the others will have more time. And don't go to political meetings or demonstrations. It's better that way."

Our job was to protect Daniel, to sever him from the war and leave him free to spin out his own connections. We too had gone underground, into a sort of safe house. We had become invisible. There was a secret heaviness of normality which we found arduous. This was our price for being at the heart of the war. Once again, Michèle and I were face to face, but in a frozen frame, the angry impersonality that seeped between us hardened now. It still had a semblance of purpose, we were side by side in the struggle; but it was no struggle, only a soundless, substanceless dance in the midst of the action. Around us were the troops in Algeria, and the civil-war hatreds of its *pieds-noirs,* the badness of spirit of the police, whom we saw as puppets of all the dark urges. The action was out there; and we—angry, disappointed, passionate—were deprived of action, deprived of ourselves. We hardly talked to each other. It's not that we weren't in love or, at least, thrown profoundly and almost dreadfully together. I think we had reached a layer that couples have to break through, or repeat themselves. We were repeating ourselves. Michèle's painting had a wild severity that I experienced, I think, as a substitute image for me, more direct than I could ever be. She was my anger, my self-assault. And I, for her? I suppose I was the foreigner. The internal exile, a ghostly sick self-restraint, the person with only one foot in the present and the other out the door. And yet we were so close. At the Volcan, in the evening, or at the little family restaurant in the Rue de l'Estrapade where we had bread soup, rabbit stew and a mashed *petit suisse* with sugar, and drank watered pink wine from unlabeled bottles, we formed an order of mute feeling that excluded everyone else.

Michèle's mouth would wrinkle with disdain, her head would lean back, as if in disbelief, and I would plunge nervously into my defense. Whatever we argued about, I felt that I was shouting "I'm here!" And Michèle, strong from her father's absence and her mother's stoniness, strong from her Alpine village and from the town history book full of ancestors going back to the eighteenth century, solid, womanly, flushed with convictions she would be willing to die for—it seemed to me Michèle was reality. Where are my ancestors? I shouted in my heart. Who am I, when the night of time rolls up almost to my present, with a bit of floating debris to let me know that somewhere in the fields of the Ukraine and the marshland of Poland my tribes had prospered, timidly, nursing an ancient German lingo written in Hebrew characters, a people of horse traders, rabbis, thieves, beggars, claustrophobia, mysteries? And America, that refuge of *shtetls* out of the past; Brooklyn, which was the negative of all my desires. What were *they?* All of this was in my nervous, precise arguments; it gave me a busy clarity. I was simply language, voice, syntax, turns of thought, quick switches of association. I burned in a twig-fire of language.

The war and Daniel held Michèle and me together. And the streets—where I could feel the hostility of the Arabs, and know that we were not brothers, although I fought on their side and belonged in their future, while I, it seemed, did without a future and wasn't in quest of one outside of my books.

Meanwhile the war had become frozen, a death dance that seemed to have no resolution. De Gaulle, with his old man's voice and his clumsy arms, wasn't a personality anymore; every gesture seemed meant to go, unedited, into the history books. It was as if the country were being governed by history, not by politics. André Malraux—yes, Malraux, the obsessed man who had once written *La Condition Humaine* and *Les Voix du Silence*—gave solemn speeches about Jeanne d'Arc in which his words seemed to be cranked out of a tin machine, full of echoing sentiment. There was a damp, cold air in it all; the vaults had opened, and ghosts were talking. The war was largely over; the army had reduced the *Moujadin* to an irrepressible annoyance. In France, the police governed by terror; policy had become a system of violence. And yet everyone knew that the FLN had won. The ghosts could go on talking, de Gaulle could go on boring his armies, Malraux could orate like a second-hand de Gaulle. Algeria was going to become a country.

Around this time something happened that made all of this visible, and almost awesome. One Saturday afternoon, coming out of the subway and buses, walking in small groups from the northern suburbs and the Goutte d'Or, and the Rue Mouffetard, from the Rue Xavier Privas and the Rue Maître Albert, coming in from the bidonvilles of Nanterre, Algerian workers began to assemble on the Avenue de l'Opéra. They assembled quietly, they knew what they were doing, they knew that no matter how many they were—ten thousand, twenty thousand—there wouldn't be as many policemen, CRS and Gardes Républicains. But they also knew that the black buses would be racing into the side streets full of pink faces and clubs, and that nothing would hold back the racial hatred —no law, no conventions. The Arabs were pure targets, they were meat; but they arrived and assembled silently, wearing their best clothes, shaved, in dense lines across the avenue. Nobody shouted slogans and held up banners. The newspapers spoke of a hushed procession. You heard the sound of thousands of feet and saw, on the brown faces, with little mustaches, and French-style berets, a look of resignation, of fright; still the men kept walking. There had never been a demonstration like this. Thousands of shy lives, far from home, used to being inconspicuous, invisible, had taken over the famous street. Not like Frenchmen, who had rights, but stolidly holding their breath, because they knew they would pay.

For weeks FLN militants had gone among them, appealing to their pride, maybe threatening them. There had been how many talks at café tables or during breaks at the factories, how many knocks on the door in the tight dark rooms where such men slept? How had they managed to fool the police informers? The surprise was total. Glued to the radio, we felt that we were present at the birth of a nation as much as at a political demonstration. The men walked up the Avenue de l'Opéra, and as they did, the neighborhood emptied out. They were alone; nobody on the street witnessed them marching through a dead city. Except the CRS swirling overhead in military helicopters and the massing army of police, who suddenly went into action, with their clubs and boots. The avenue ran with blood. There were no surprises now: the Arabs walked, fell, ran, they were dragged into buses which roared down the empty streets toward Vincennes and other anonymous suburbs. There were too many to arrest, but not too many to hurt. In a way, that was the day the war ended. The Algerians weren't protesting anything, they weren't demonstrating for higher wages or better living conditions; they were demonstrating that they existed.

Daniel didn't come out of his room that evening. He didn't want to share this with us. I could hear the tinny sound of his little radio through the door. According to the police, there had been twenty thousand demonstrators, which meant forty thousand. Through the impersonal, overly pronounced phrases of the newscaster came a sense of violation, of rape. The Arabs had raped the street. They had walked in front of the banks and the expensive shops and the solid, hewn-stone buildings with narrow balconies where the rich lived. They had walked toward the opera house, with its gilded statues and its complicated architecture. They had done something simple—walk, be. Because of this, de Gaulle had had to forgo the history book for an event, had to become an angry old man, outwitted by a young man looking out the window at the monuments of Paris, lit softly, in a gray glow.

The next morning, we found out more. Dozens of bodies had washed up from the Seine south of Paris. Dozens more were found in the forests of Meudon or dumped on the unpaved streets around the bidonvilles. Days passed, and the count went higher, a few lines in the newspapers, a statistic full of insanity. People had seen a black van on a bridge; men had been pulled out of the van and thrown into the river. Daniel was out almost all the time now. He was tracking down the missing, the dead. Establishing records. There was something almost deranged about his coolness now; he would share nothing with us. His politeness was like a weapon; he was making us not exist. He didn't have time for our leisure and our empty lives that were empty, in part, for his sake, but empty too because they were parasites feeding on an idea, his idea. Michèle's painting, my thesis, our feelings—they were like smoke to him, they had no moral weight. And we tended to feel as he did. He was real, we were not entirely real, and no amount of attractively printed pamphlets on world revolution, bought at Maspero's bookshop on the Rue de la Harpe, no quantity of testimony on torture and the dialectics of oppression, read with a shudder of recognition, as if trying to drink in life from the orderly pages with their trance of words and arguments, their silent outcries—none of this could make up the difference.

9

DANIEL vanished from our lives all at once a few weeks after the demonstration. The door to his room was partly open; in the little hallway of the apartment our old radio buzzed and crackled. We were only half listening when a program was interrupted, and an officious voice announced the smashing of a clandestine reseau in Lyon, part of the Jeanson ring. The police had found documents, money; some Frenchmen had been arrested. A name was mentioned, other arrests were expected. Daniel poked his head out the door, and listened. Then he ran back into his room. A few minutes later he looked in on us, smiling ruefully.

"I'm going. More people in Lyon. I think there's going to be trouble. Goodbye."

He left the rusty key on the hall table. He seemed to be amused, maybe relieved, at being flushed out of hiding into the world where people weren't safe. The security of our apartment had been a kind of curse, its splendid view an insult. His detachment had always had something boyish about it. The door clicked behind him, we heard the shuffle of feet on the stairs, the creaking of the varnished steps, then nothing. We never saw him again, never heard from him, or of him. He had come and gone like a lover picked up on the street without a past or a future, simply a presence, and then no one.

By late afternoon the day Daniel left, Maxime and Erika had been arrested. A day later she was at the women's prison at La Roquette and he was at La Fresnes in the political section.

As for us, we waited. "We could go to Samoëns; there's a cabin in the mountains." But we didn't do anything. I think we wanted to be arrested. We wanted something to happen, almost anything. But nothing did. There were no knocks on the door. The police didn't know about us. Or they weren't interested.

I went to Lille to teach once a week, and came back to the same ebb of feeling. Lucien's sexual irony was bouncing off the walls again. Elisabeth's shelf of drugs and nostrums was once more part of a comic opera. Her frenzied eyes and long, curly black hair took up the room. Without Daniel we all became glaringly visible to each other. One afternoon, I came home to find our mattress on the floor, the sheets torn and thrown around the room, the pillows half ripped open and a dust of white feathers lying in little pools on the floor.

At the Volcan that evening, Michèle and I decided that Lucien had done it; humorous Lucien, who swatted me with a glance, had had his little frenzy, Michèle guessed, with her cool disdain that almost made me feel sympathy for her brother. We had the impression of a glimpse into an abyss, a long-standing secret under Lucien's sexual threats. The secret was jealousy and frustration at the silence that reigned between him and his older sister. It was the family way—each of them was impregnable, steadfastly incommunicative. We never confronted Lucien, and he never indicated that he even knew what had happened. It had been an empty act or a superb one, depending on your point of view. Now that the war had left us, we had had our own little war.

"I think someone's following me, Paul," Michèle said to me one day. "A big man in a gray suit. I saw him yesterday, and he was there today too." Apparently we hadn't been entirely forgotten. The man looked like a detective in a comic strip. He wore a hat, and heavy black shoes; he was always looking into store windows and hanging around the Place de la Contrescarpe. He didn't even seem to try to keep hidden. He was simply there, as part of some tidying up, some necessary routine applied to a folder on a desk at the prefecture. We were impressed. It's flattering to be noticed, even in so pointless and slimy a way. Although we didn't take the man seriously, we all became a little paranoid. I had never been so acutely aware of strangers. Everyone, suddenly, was visible and full of secret intentions. It was as if a half-forgotten suspicion had suddenly blossomed. Were they following me to Lille? I looked behind me on the cobbled streets near the university. I watched the faces on the train and the knots of people gathered around the street stalls selling *pommes frites*. They all had opaque faces. The large man in the gray suit hung out on the street in front of our house or looked out the window of a bookshop nearby. We got used to him, and then one day he wasn't there.

The war was pretty much over now. There were negotiations at Evian, near the Swiss border. All of us had a sense of shrinkage, as if, very quickly, we were becoming smaller. Along with the peace negotiations, there was a stymied silence in the apartment. Michèle and I had never been so close, yet there was something glazed and stunned about our relationship. We had become so dependent on our daily irritations, our complicities, that we saw things through each other's eyes. We had traced a circle around us.

One day in the Luxembourg Gardens, sitting under the horse-chestnut trees at the little café, Michèle brought up the subject of children. What did I think about having a child? There was a controlled, even tone in her voice, which I knew was close to anger. A child! What did that mean? It was not a subject my mind could accept or refuse. A few years before, Michèle had become pregnant and we hadn't hesitated a minute about an abortion. The possibility had simply been too farfetched. And now, three years later, for me it was still farfetched.

Not that she wanted a child, she said. She understood our situation. We had no money, we didn't really have a place to live. Her painting came first right now. But what did I think?

The chalky light hurt my eyes, the trees thrust up, huge and dark, to a canopy of large oval leaves. I could see the boat basin beyond the balustrade, the precise patterns of its flowers in wide beds along the gravel walks. I felt an enormous passiveness. If Michèle wanted us to have a child we would have one. The thought skimmed through my mind, without substance or desire. Michèle didn't pursue the subject, but it had defined something between us. I felt a tremendous sadness, as if I were unable to change something that maybe I didn't want to change or even give a name. But it was there, as a weight, a sense of failure. I hated to disappoint Michèle. I hated to be the one who didn't give. It made me frantic, as if I had committed a crime. The crime of not wanting a child? It wasn't even that. The crime of not feeling, of indifference—or, not indifference, wanting to continue a surface sort of life: a determination to let the darkness alone. We left the Luxembourg without having made any decisions. But something had been stretched and perhaps broken between us.

And then the war played its last little game with us. While the negotiations at Evian dragged on and on, the *pieds-noirs* community in Algeria was plunged into a wild and violent despair. It was a form of collective mourning. The *pieds-noirs* had learned the Arab custom of wailing in high shrieks at a death; now they wailed at the death of what they thought of as their country. There were a million of them, and most of them weren't even French, but Spanish and Italian and Greek and Maltese. Over half a century they had become a community of hard-living sun lovers, sensual, beautiful. They were Camus's people; his sympathy for them forced him into a demoralized silence about the war and finally into the reckless despair that, one guessed, had figured in his death in an automobile accident in 1960.

As the war ended, Algiers became an apocalypse. Someone hijacked a fuel truck and drove it over a cliff into the Casbah, the Arab quarter of the city. Everybody carried guns; the army was filled with sympathetic officers, who let militant groups steal machine guns, bazookas and *plastique*, a powerful, easy-to-use explosive. Civil war was in the Paris air. Incredible paranoid fantasies were printed up on clandestine sheets and thrown about the streets. The Communists were about to take power. The Russians were sending a fleet. The *pieds-noirs* were the last patriots, the last defenders of civilization. All of which was accompanied by random murders, bombs, rumors of assassination squads sent to France to kill government officials. A *plastique* bomb went off in the storeroom of Malraux's apartment building in Paris. Leftist militants and FLN sympathizers had their apartments blown apart by *plastique*, applied like putty to their doors. The *pieds-noirs* groups seemed to have contacts in the prefecture, for people were attacked who could have been known only to the police. We organized all-night watches outside the apartments of friends who had received threats. We all felt that we were targets, and now Michèle and I thought of that gray-suited man who had been following us around. At the time, he had seemed a little comic, but it occurred to us now that we were on file somewhere, and terrorists could get their hands on the file. We were surrounded by an irrational rage and it wasn't simply the police this time, with their routines and dubious legalities.

Very early one Sunday morning, the raucous bell to our apartment rang. The sky was slate-colored, with a slight tinge of dawn on the eastern rim. It must have been five o'clock. I sat on the edge of the bed, still half asleep. The bell rang again. I went to answer it. A man and a woman were standing in the hall. He wore a dark raincoat and a hat, and had dark skin. I'd never seen him before. The woman looked nervous. She was pretty, with short curly hair and a short flowing skirt. The man asked:

"*C'est vous, M. Paul?*"

I said yes, without thinking.

"*Vous partez en voyage?*"

I looked at him. He had a blank face, a little like mine; a face without a nationality. What was he asking me? Was I going on a trip?

"I don't know what you're talking about."

It was beginning to dawn on me that two strangers had rung my doorbell at five in the morning and it hadn't been an accident. They had asked for M. Paul. In that broad accent, maybe a southern one, it sounded like the name of a gangster.

"You must be mistaken."

I shut the door softly and stood there listening in the dark corridor. They didn't say anything. They were listening to me. Then I heard the creak of stairs as they went down.

When I got back into bed, Michèle was completely awake, her face grimly expectant.

"It's obvious who they are," she said, with her instinct for threat—evil intentions were her element. She was tense, already at war; the cover hugged her as she sat up on one elbow, her breasts sagging to one side. "They're *pieds-noirs*, Fascists."

She could be right. We were close to the door. A bomb would blow the wall down on us. We crowded to the other side of the room and sat on the floor, near the open window. The cool vastness of the city was like a mockery. We waited for a while, and then, tense with fright, I tiptoed to the door, opened it slightly. There was no lumpy package, no Silly Putty for grownups with deranged minds.

"I'd better go and talk to Claude."

Claude lived around the corner. He was a dentist, whose apartment had served as a post office drop for the FLN. While Daniel was living with us, we hardly saw him; now we talked all the time, although his Marxism seemed a little hysterical to me. His apartment was filled with Marxist pamphlets about revolutions. Revolution seemed to be the ultimate sporting match to him. He had a thin, excitable voice that squeaked when he made a point. He was also a poet, but in the French manner. He didn't write bloody poems full of revolutionary sentiments. His poems were tense, abstract little diagrams for using words like *pur* and *plein*. This was poetry's deepest evolution, he claimed, with Sartre: Language had to be saved from the bourgeoisie; it had to be terrorized and abstracted, made into emotionless paradigms that refused the sentimental conquests of being simply understood.

I quickly got changed and put my shoes on. The room still smelled of our bodies and of sleep. Outside the window, the slate color of early morning gave the city a somber look. In that expanse of cubes and angles were people who wanted to harm a person named "M. Paul," who was supposed to be going on a trip. The city didn't look benign this morning.

I peered into the hall on every landing, trying not to make the steps creak. Why was I going out? Already it seemed foolish; but the anxiety of waiting was terrible. I felt an impatience to know the worst, to court catastrophe, if only to get it over with. I suppose this was another form of passiveness. The ground crunched under my feet, and then I was walking down the long alley to the street. The cobbled pavement was barely wide enough for a car; there was a tiny raised sidewalk running along one side. When a car passed, you had to step on it and hug the wall. Gray cobbles, cracked gray cement walls on both sides of the alley, which was like a vein passing through a thickness of internal organs.

I heard a car start up behind me in the courtyard; the tires crunched on the gravel, and then gave a long rumble as they bounced over the cobbles. My mind shrank to a single, paralyzed thought: *They* were in the car, the dark man in the raincoat and the pretty woman with the flouncing skirt. They had been waiting for me; and I had been stupid enough to come down. They were experts. They knew how panicky people act, they had played with me, and now, rumbling down the alley, they were going to run me down, assassinate me. It was part of the end of the world. The alley ended in a tiny opening fifty yards ahead of me. Why run, why do anything? I could feel the impact from head to toe, not a crunch of bones and flesh but a frozen, unbreathable light; my whole existence was in that light, like a marble creature full of veins and pulsing organs, a composed, incredible whole that I could see and touch. Without thinking, I stepped up onto the sidewalk and hugged the wall. The car rumbled past. A neighbor and his wife and children were getting an early start to the country. Then I was alone in the alley, still walking. Nothing had happened, and yet I had seen myself die, floating in a cold light.

And now, clear and ghostly, the world came back, huge and freezing and immobile: The mottled cement of the alley wall was full of cracks and discolorations; the cobbles shone with early morning damp; the cracks between them were dark. I could smell leaves on the trees reaching the wall; the leaves were green now in the strengthening light.

Claude, it turned out, had been visited by the dark man and his pretty friend. They had asked if he was "M. Claude," and if he was going on a trip. But Claude had had more presence of mind than I had. He had talked to them, made conversation, friendly conversation. He was puzzled, he had said, sort of disturbed at being gotten out of bed at five in the morning. What was this all about? "Going on a trip," it turned out, was a password neither of us knew. The FLN had moved its people around from place to place, had mislaid a suitcase. Now that the war was over, they were straightening out their records, making things neat. There could have been money in the suitcase, or papers, or dirty laundry. The man and the girl were knocking on doors trying to find someone who knew the password and would hand over the suitcase. The visit had been a comedy, a light touch to end the war.

PART THREE

'VE never been much good at transitions. Over the years, I have gone as if expelled, dragged or broken from one life to another, never quite willing or knowing. It has been all zigzags, changes that sprang from nowhere and became irreversible, as if I had been shunted onto another plane of life, never choosing and never prepared. What I wanted was a limited existence: an enchanted ordinariness as an engineer, living in a tract house in Queens, or as an elementary school teacher in Brooklyn, living in a tenement, with a shopping street downstairs and the smell of food in the hallway. A life close to the center, undeviating and unproblematical; a sort of immortality. But then would come the dark shove, the loose wire in my genes, and I would start on some baffling new course: a marriage, a religious conversion, an obsession that filled my life with strangeness. Like the honeybee whose eccentric flight, full of swings and surprises, results from some twist in the bee's genetic grid, I too have apparently been programmed for fuzzy swoops and teeterings beyond reason.

Therefore I was prepared, if that is the word, when several years ago another sort of shove—even darker, more arbitrary—sent me reeling. Again I found myself in a new life, but one that would never become stale or overly familiar to me; that would always be new, always just discovered. This unexplored, unchosen life was the life of the dying—the life of all life, perhaps, but starker and more intense in my case. It is, most likely, my final incarnation, and I will never become tired of it, never leave it by the pratfall of a gene or the shove of an instinct.

I entered this life on a muggy May afternoon when a doctor, feeling my neck with a hard probing touch that I have gotten to know well, discovered a small, mobile lump at the base of my neck. Within an hour, I was getting my chest and belly X-rayed. The doctor was clipped and urgent. Although X-rays showed nothing, there would have to be a biopsy. The lump, buried in the soft tissue of my neck, was oblong and somewhat flaccid. A few days later, the surgeon—again the firm probing with both hands at the base of my neck—seemed undecided. The lump was so sleepy and obscure; but what the hell, let's do it. I remember the sizzling of the electric knife; the odor of burnt blood; the pushes and clips of the tools in the freshly opened slit. I lay there as if clubbed, not thinking, not thinking. Then the doctor lifted out the rubbery clot, dropped it into a container, and went down the hall to get a quick reading by the pathologist. The tissue is sliced and quick-frozen, and then given a preliminary look which must be confirmed later when the tissue has been appropriately dyed to emphasize the structure of the cells. He was back in a few minutes, looking old and heavy.

"There's something there," he said. "We'll have to wait for the slide to be sure."

Those were the words that swung me into my new life. I had walked into the outpatient operating room of the hospital young and immortal; death had been a neurotic tune I wrote about in poems. Now suddenly it was a heaviness that dragged my legs down, a mind that wanted to dissolve back into its spoonfuls of cells, and forget, forget. The slit in my neck was the latch, and now my mortality was seeping out, a thin, freezing gas that filled the operating room. I shivered amid the cutting tools and the bottles of disinfectant, and the doctor talking to me carefully, urgently. I heard what he said, watched his lips, but his words slid off my panic, powerless to reach me in my new life.

"Don't think of this as cancer," he said. "That's a terrifying word. You have a lymphoma. That's a *kind* of cancer, but it can be treated, kept under control; maybe cured. You're not dying. People do well with a lymphoma."

"Do well" is an oncologist's term that I have heard often since then. You're doing well. He did well. It's a term that must be listened to from the perspective of this new life. Its specific meaning is not "He's well now" but "He's well for the moment"; dying has stopped for a while; he will probably live for a long time. An oncologist's "long time" measures time in the new life. It may mean a few years, which is not bad, although possibly not comforting to a forty-seven-year-old man who still daydreams, at odd moments, of a long life.

For weeks after that my body was inspected for information I never knew it contained. My urine and blood were analyzed; my bone marrow was biopsied. There were sonograms, nuclear scans and grams, X-rays. Incisions were made on the upper part of my feet, through which purple dye was injected into my lymph system. I spent a week in the hospital for some of these tests. I talked to hematologists, surgeons, oncologists, and just plain doctors. I talked to find out. I talked in the hope of hearing some word, some unintended phrase, maybe, that would release me, even for an hour, from the anxiety that spun itself into every corner of my body, deadening my face, giving a buzzing, flattened rhythm to all my thoughts. I felt like someone who had been thrown against an electric fence. Time had been cut off from before my face. The world was unchanged. The streets were full of cars and pedestrians; the sun still caught in the windows of buildings. The radio reported worldwide events. Everything was the same, but time had been removed. And without time, everything was unreal, but I was horribly real, oversized, bursting as a body bursts in a vacuum.

Listening to my doctor was delicate. I took in every shrug, every rise and fall of his voice. I weighed his words on a fine scale, to detect hope or despair. Then I called up another doctor, to hear how the words sounded in his voice. I triangulated and compared, all to find something that would shut off the terror for a while. It was as if there were a key buried in my psyche, and I had to feel around for it, probing in thick, dark waters, and then, not knowing what I'd found, finding it, then losing it again.

While my doctor gathered information, I spent my days walking. I preferred busy shopping streets: the lights and the shop windows, the double-parked cars, the people hurrying into and out of stores. There was energy, there was a present. My feelings would relax a little. I would become a temporary pedestrian, and forget my rarefied life where there was no time.

For months before all this started, my marriage had been in the process of breaking up. Already my wife was honing herself for her own version of a new life. Living with me was like being an old woman, used up, and yet she had hardly lived. It wasn't fair. For her, my lymphoma was the click of a jailer's cell closing upon her life. She boiled with guilty anger, and within a few days could hardly bear the sight of me. So I took long walks, to have something to do that kept me out of the house. Or I went to the playground with my three-year-old daughter and played in the sandbox, trying to imitate my daughter's innocence of time. In a peculiar way, my daughter and I were equals; neither of us had any time, and the irony was terrible, for I had lost mine and she hadn't acquired hers yet. Therefore we had each other. We had the work of filling a tomato-juice can with sand, had the slide polished by thousands of happy behinds. We had the soughing of the spring trees on Riverside Drive, the glow of new leaves, and the twisted, scaly trunks; the portable radios, large as suitcases, throbbing heavily as they went by; and the splintered benches, the yelps of the children, the mothers talking in their not-quite-designer jeans. My life had become a strategy for eluding terror.

It took a few weeks for the test results to be assembled. Then my doctor gave me a course in cell biology as applied to a subclass of malignancy known as lymphoma, a cancer of the lymph system. There were various kinds of lymphoma, all more or less related, more or less combined in any single illness. A given biopsy slide was likely to show several of them, with a predominance of one or another. That is why lymphomas shift and change, speed up or slow down, mysteriously go into hiding, or explode in almost sudden death. They are related also to leukemia. All in all, it is a crowded picture, full of surprises, a little like life itself, but heated up and ominous. All of this was my doctor's way of telling me that he didn't know what was going to happen to me. My particular lymphoma was actually almost benign. Its cells were "well differentiated," their histology was "good." Words like "good" made my heart leap. Anything "good" was probably on my side. There began to be some time before me. Words like "years" were pronounced. There were other words too, but I heard them selectively. Well-differentiated lymphocytic lymphomas developed slowly, but they also tended to resist treatment. They were too benign to behave like cancer cells when they were treated with chemotherapy. Therefore, they came back. And one day, one year, the doctor could run out of treatments, and the sleepy, almost inadvertent disease would expand, like an elephant rolling over you, as if by accident, not knowing you were there, and almost saying, I'm sorry.

At the time I didn't hear all this. I wanted to be cured of terror even more than of the lymphoma, which I'd never seen or touched, and now accepted as an interpretation of pages full of computer letters, graphs and a little box with glass slides in it, not as a physical fact which made my flesh more perishable.

In the end, my doctor chose a middle course. The tests had all been negative. The nodes scattered about in my lymphatic system were too small to register, even on the most sensitive tests; but that didn't mean they weren't there. The pattern of a lymphocytic lymphoma is to be scattered, not localized. A bone-marrow biopsy had disclosed a somewhat high level of lymphocytes that the pathologist called "compatible" with a lymphoma. "Compatible" is one of those cautious words doctors use to say they don't know. It meant that the lymphocytes were probably, but not definitely, connected to the lymphoma; on the other hand, they also could be normal for me. My doctor's decision was to treat with radiation, as a precautionary measure, the spot on my neck where the biopsy had been done, and not to treat the systemic disease, which was still more or less a fiction—an assemblage of data—even to him.

It was July by now, a hot, humid month. The leaves on the trees were heavy, almost flaccid. The radiologist's office was near Central Park. I went every morning at nine o'clock, and was marked with a purple paintbrush, to provide an accurate target for the machine. For twenty days, I received eight minutes and forty-seven seconds of radiation each day on my left shoulder and neck, including a small part of my jaw. The machine resembled a bulky mechanical eye that peered stolidly at the same spot on my body day after day, as if to be sure that it didn't miss anything. The radiologist's office was a warren of tiny dressing rooms, and larger rooms containing complicated machines: sonographs, gamma scanners, X-rays, hard-radiation machines. Eventually each of those machines had its turn with me, but now it was the silent, shadow-filled, almost empty room every morning, and the square, slightly battered bulk of the eye; eight minutes and forty-seven seconds of nothing, no touch, no sound. I lay on my back or stomach according to a schedule, and meditated, breathing evenly in and out. I felt solemn, detached, and then, as weeks passed, a little scared as my skin reddened, my saliva glands on that side of my mouth dried up, and the hair on my neck and jaw fell out.

Every morning, when my treatment was over, I walked to the boathouse in Central Park, and had breakfast on the terrace overlooking the lake. The Central Park South skyline was reflected in the littered heavy shine of the water; the trees tossed their willow limbs in the gusts of breeze. There were always a few regulars at the café, with their shirts off, sunning themselves or doing exercises. The boathouse became my sanctuary. From its dazzled peacefulness, I could contemplate the ruins of my marriage. I could read and write, feeling myself sink into my new life, which now had some time. The terror of the previous weeks was gone. My doctor had dispelled it with his manic, speedy talk, his words like "good" histology, and his feeling that there was "time" to use chemotherapy "if" it became necessary. The implication was that there would be a next year and, surely, other years; that my "good" lymphoma might stay asleep "for a long time." The lymphoma was simply a darker, more underscored form of life, full of life's uncertainties but not a sentence, not a doom.

I didn't exactly relax. I lived in a heavy air, I swam in muted fright; and I came "home" to the boathouse every morning, to feel the hot stillness of summer, to read my books, and to escape my wife's irritation, which increased every day. I didn't want to think about her bitter voice, her resentment at the glaring light that had suddenly fallen upon me. I had become an emissary of mortality, a messenger from further along, outside the flimsy shelter of endlessness that we spin around us when we're lucky: a portable home, a little immortality, and then suddenly it collapses.

After sitting at the boathouse all morning, I walked home through the Rambles, my shoulder and neck in a state of angry sunburn. Sunlight filtered through the trees. Isolated men sat on benches with an air of melancholy expectation. There were brooks and bridges. It was a little world, strewn with crumpled bags and beer cans, the litter of a night's sexual encounters. The men on the benches resembled night birds who had forgotten to go home. I too was a passing solitude. Time had flowed back around me. Again,

I was inside of life. I was freestanding, not thrust against a blankness.

Several times that month, my wife tried to leave me. Each time, my paper-thin peacefulness collapsed, and I became frantic, wild. The breakup of my marriage held an unreasoning terror for me. Perhaps I took it as a foreshadowing, a defeat that bespoke the unsayable defeat I tried to turn my mind from. We had been married for ten years, and for half of them things had been bad. My wife was a beautiful, slender woman, radiating calm and command. Her benign manner made her seem almost ethereal. But hard as it was to believe, this was purely theatrical; convincing, but simply a manner. In private, resentment boiled in her like life itself. Inside I feel like ashes, she would say, in rare moments of candor. I circled her bleakly, claiming to long for peace but drawn to the pitch of her nerves, which filled me with self-destructive bile. I felt like a man hanging from a cliff face. It was life on the edge, the loose wire in my genes. Our marriage had long since become Strindberg's dance of death, and we danced it like puppets; but now it was breaking up, for real death had come upon the scene and driven its neurotic imitators from the field.

When I was a boy, I used to wonder what would keep me from sinking to the level of a bum on the street. Every tramp, every stinking hulk of a drunk, was a possible destiny. Later, I saw that it wasn't so easy to sink. You had to dive, you had to work your way down. Society buoyed you up to your level; family and friends, the structure of needs driven into your flesh and psyche, do not let themselves be easily betrayed. I hadn't thought of this other stripping down, the blow of destiny that thrust from within you and then, like a bolt falling from a cloud, from without you too. I was caught in this pincers now: stripped of time, stripped even of a home; afraid that the anguish breaking around my daughter would maim her in some way. For years I had been afraid that if my marriage broke up, I would lose my daughter. It had become an obsession; it summed up all the mysterious harm I felt my wife could do to me. More than once, I had seen murder in her eyes. Lying in our bed at night, I had felt like a naked target, waiting for her rage to solidify and become a weapon. Was the lymphoma her ultimate spell? The cellular substance of her wish for me? I shunned such thoughts, partly because they were self-serving and superstitious; partly because my doctors suspected that the lymphoma had been present in its sleepy state for a number of years; and partly because it meant that I had been defeated, bewitched, skewered on rage and resentment, outwitted. Strength against strength, my wife's tunnel vision of despair and accusation had been stronger than my contradictory soul with its compulsive large-mindedness, its play of feelings and knowledge.

A month later, the marriage was over. I had come alone to the house we owned in southern France. My wife had refused to come with me, and stayed in Paris with friends. I breathed the aromatic August air like a spiritual substance. The house is a low stone building, with a roof of rough red tiles, on a hilltop far from any road. The fields of barley and alfalfa had been harvested, and a swath of yellow stubble surrounded the house. Petunias splashed brightly in a stone basin. A little way down the hill, a walnut tree dangled its smoky limbs. I sat in front of the house and gazed at the hill crest across the valley or watched the sun ignite at dusk in plumes of red mist and cloud. The days creaked with cicadas. The nights were blocks of blankness, almost a burial, except for a veil of light spilling across the sky, the Milky Way, and the bright nailheads of the largest stars. Every day I jogged down the dirt road into the valley, and walked back. Gradually, I increased the distance. It was a return among the living, a return to youth. Timidly, almost furtively—like Adam hiding his nakedness in the garden— I built the endlessness back around me. My saliva glands began to function again; the red square on my neck healed. One side of my jaw was still baby-smooth; I didn't have to shave it. It was my stigmata. But eventually that too became normal.

As days passed, it seemed that the house itself was healing me: its honey-colored stone walls and red, granular tiles; its days full of wind and somersaulting clouds. I thought of my grandparents' farm. The farm had been a model for my childhood love of empty places: the prairies, deserts and forests I read about in my favorite books; any place where the claustrophobia of emotions was dissolved, where sheer emptiness made man small, as if my genes had conjured up primeval savannas as my true home. Now I had my own house in the woods; my own romantic emptiness that overlay the earlier memories and merged with them.

One day I telephoned my wife from a neighbor's house. No, she didn't want to come down; she also didn't want to live with me anymore. It took only a few words to establish this. The phone cracked against my ear in the long gaps between the few things we had to say to each other. Suddenly there was more room than I knew what to do with. As I climbed the steep path through the woods and crossed the harvested field to the house, I could hear the brittle stubble crunch under my feet. This was ground level: no family, a flimsy life. I hadn't become a derelict, but I had hit bottom in my own way.

I am sitting at my window, looking out over the Hudson. It is a scuffed blue-gray this morning, with patches of ripples and smoke melting into each other. The Palisades directly across from me are still speckled with points of light. At river level, the abandoned factories emerge faintly from the darkness as a slightly powdered gray. The river too is dark, almost an empty trough between its banks, which here are half a mile apart.

Now it is almost full daylight. I can see seagulls wheeling close to the near shore. From this height, they don't seem to be over the river, but on it, sliding and scooting on the surface like water flies.

The far end of my living room slants to the northwest. When the sun comes up eastward over the city—the slits of the streets and the dusty black squares of the rooftops, and beyond them, visible only if I lean my head out the window, the heavy metal arches of the Triborough Bridge—there is a fringing light along the window which lasts for only a few minutes. The imperfections in the glass are heightened, a milkiness veils the sleeve of emptiness: the river; the park on this side with its leafless knobs of trees, and its baseball fields which resemble large brown vulvas; the cliff on the other side, topped by the pale rectangles of condominiums; and closing it off to the north, like a musical instrument poised to produce a humming note, the George Washington Bridge.

When I lean up close to the window, I can see a few people down below waiting for the bus. On the square of pavement, between the soggy winter turf and the benches, they resemble a scattering of grains. There is a clarity in the scene, something unspoken. The sky is blue-white. Beyond the Palisades, the New Jersey hills form parallel pleats, broken here and there by the sharp outlines of factories, gas tanks and distant neighborhoods which I will never visit, and whose names I will never know.

My living room with its five windows resembles a cage suspended from the sky, looking out on space, on the low hum of the city. Below me, the bus opens its doors and inhales the scattered grains. This morning life is distant, a brightness rimming the city.

On several occasions I have thought of jumping—half flying— from my twenty-fourth-story window; not a thought really, a fleeting image of an action. Nothing I would do, but even the image of it has given my life a new vulnerability.

During the first years after my wife and I separated, there was in the struggle between us a flow of tension that seemed rarely to let me up for air. I felt that she was a tool of destruction swinging wildly at the core of my life. Wherever I looked, I stumbled over threads of her making: threats against me, against my daughter; thrills of anger that swept through the phone or down the stairs. At times, it seemed that the only avenue of escape was out of life. And the trough of the river, even-tempered and gladly indifferent, beckoned as a kind of heaven, a busy vacancy.

I've seen every kind of storm up here. The splats of thunder; the lightning crinkling in wide swaths over the Palisades; enormous thuds of wind, snaking the water in the toilet bowl and drowning out the radio. Clouds sagged over the bridge; whitenesses of water skidded across the river, dashing up onto the highway, where cars crawled by with their headlights on, even in daylight. And the snowstorms in winter, wiping out space, crawling into my mind: a kind of death, a kind of giving up.

It is afternoon now. Reflected light from the river wavers over my wall like a watermark. There is a peculiar solitude, a nothing spinning out spokes of attention. Soon the light will turn angry, and then begin to dim, contract to a purple disc sliding behind a cluster of high-rise buildings across the river. So much space, such a contraction of time, like a balloon shielding me from what I want to avoid, but which is closer to me than thought.

During these past few months, the lymphoma has wrapped its sluggish coils around me once again. In everything I do, there is an intensity, the tunnel vision of a man making an effort. Days pass when I don't even see the river, and then, suddenly, I am buoyed by a mysterious current, something unreasonable, something like hope, rising like heat from a sidewalk grating. I have learned how to navigate this foreshortened life of mine; to ruse with panic, duck under terror. My will has become a well-exercised muscle.

In November, I made one of my bimonthly visits to the doctor. It is a dimly lighted office piled with coats. People sit demurely and read magazines, or doze. There is not much talking. All of us are self-contained and casual as we wait for our blood test—the prick in the flesh of the fingertip, the small bead of blood, the glass siphon turning pink as the blood climbs inside it, the click of the counter whirring to its level. Then we are shepherded into small, bright consultation rooms with Daumier lithographs on the wall, and shelves full of barbarously named compounds which will weaken us and make us sick, loosen our hair, disrupt the lining of our stomach, thin out our bone marrow, cause a flulike aching of the muscles, but will do even more damage to those inconspicuous additions to our bodies, the nodes, tumors and lymphocytes that gather within us to disrupt our organisms.

A year before, I had undergone a course of chemotherapy. Every few weeks, several large hypodermics of pink or transparent liquid had been injected into a vein on the inside of my elbow. There had been a cool rush in my arm and tongue; a light-headedness; then I had gone into the bathroom and smoked a joint of marijuana to keep down the nausea. The result was a cool floating feeling, as I put my coat on and waited for a cab, then walked carefully to the elevator in my building, not jiggling or shaking. I felt breakable, as if the injection had turned me into glass. All day I would sit in my reading chair and listen to music or read a novel. This was not a day for thinking, not a day to measure my adequacy to the larger questions of life. Gradually I would get tired and nauseous. By the next morning, I would be sick and try to sleep it off. Then, hour by hour, the ashen feeling in my face would lessen, the wobbly numbness in my legs would vanish. The morning after that, I would go out running, as if I were acting out a private joke: the joke of health and youth, the joke of endlessness.

As months passed, the nodes in various parts of my body shrank, and my blood count went down. My hair fell out, although I didn't become bald, only scalpy. I was hopeful and buoyant, proud that the chemotherapy didn't bother me too much. In the middle of it, I went to my house in France, and spent three weeks there. I felt that I was staring down death, although by then I already suspected that the treatment wasn't fully working. My hard little seeds had shrunk but not vanished. By this time, I knew enough about my illness to understand that those seeds would grow again, at a rate only they would determine. I knew that my doctor, for all his hard medical knowledge, observed my blood counts and my nodes as a witness to a mystery, ready to be surprised by variables that no instrument could measure. There were lymphomas that simmered for twenty years, others that "went sour" right away. The clock ticked, but no one could hear it. It was a subcase of the clock of life itself. In the four years since my lymphoma was diagnosed, my radiologist had died of a heart attack and the surgeon who had performed the lymphangiogram had drowned in a boating accident on Long Island Sound. Like me, they were young men. The fates had spun a short skein for them. And for me? Who can say? The bell curve does not favor me, but a bell curve is not destiny. Each year laboratories churn out results that may be altering the curve: new drugs, new regimens, entire new methods. Am I hopeful? Not exactly. I am trying to live until tomorrow, and then tomorrow.

Those three weeks at the house were a miracle. The winter trees resembled gray, upswept brushes; the fire grumbled all day in the fireplace. For four years I had been bending myself to a shorter arc of life. I wanted elbow room; I wanted an enlarged present, and I had managed by discipline and willpower, by selfishness, to thicken the everyday, attenuate the far-off. Normally we live in a double sphere of consciousness: a near shell reverberating with needs and hopes, full of urgency, heavy with the flesh of our lives; and a far, attenuated hood of thoughts and projects which spin us years into the future, where we pretend that there is time. The near shell is tribal and blood-real; the far, attenuated shell is glorious, flimsy; it is man's experiment with immortality, without which books would not be written and buildings would not be erected to last centuries. It is the lie of endlessness, the lie we spin out of ourselves like the "filament, filament" of the "patient spider" in Walt Whitman's poem, to give us time.

For three weeks at the house, I lived a purely tribal life. The days were empty and cold. I read long books by the fire, and felt thoughtless and happy as I jogged down the muddy road into the valley, past my neighbor's tobacco-drying shed, past the low, mossy roofs of the village, and then, laboriously, rasping and out of breath, up a long stony incline through the woods to my house. I felt that death could not harm me. I was neither young nor old. I was simply a man living alone in a stone house, surrounded by books, baking in the glowing heat of oak logs in the fireplace, feeling the sharp chill of black nights when I went outside to pee on the gravel, and heard the splatter of my urine mingling with the wind, and the reverberating hoot of an owl in the nearby woods.

Soon after that, my doctor decided to stop the chemotherapy. The most potent drug in the combination, Adriamycin, could damage my heart if more than a certain quantity was used over my lifetime. He had used about half of that, and wanted to save Adriamycin—a new kind of antibiotic which had been one of the important discoveries for cancer treatment in the 1970s—for another round of chemotherapy, "if" needed. A sonogram revealed a shadow persisting in my abdomen. No, I wasn't cured. The lymphoma had been ground down and compressed, but not extirpated. I was released into uncertainty. My outer shell of time had been broken; I would never give my thoughts to it again without an undercurrent of disbelief. Only tribal time was real to me, and tribal time was a kind of eternity. The gray smoky water of the river outside my window; the boys playing baseball on the large brown vulva that is the playing field in the park; my daughter's bony ballerina's grace, were real. Unreal were pension plans, and the conquering of cancer by the year 2000; unreal was my daughter as a young woman, a future I sometimes saw tentatively in her face. My daughter fluttered between the two times. Loving her drove holes in my body of time, and let in distance; distance that was denied me, distance I strove for and wished for without hoping, because hope devalued my one secure possession: the roomy present, which I savored best in the solitude that was the legacy of my childhood. My grandparents' farm, my house in France, my window overlooking the river.

Then, in November, came the visit to my doctor, to be palpated, X-rayed, to have my blood tested. These visits were never routine. I knew that when my doctor spoke, I would listen as to no one I had ever listened to in my life. He would push down at the base of my neck, probe under my arms and in my groin. He would feel at the margin of my rib cage on the right side and below my rib cage on the left side, for my liver and spleen. My doctor is a small, balding, energetic man. Over the years, we have gotten to know each other well. I've heard his jokes, listened to his fervent Zionism, his humorous indignation at divorce lawyers, and other favorite topics. There is a manic optimism about him, a speedy, sometimes angry intolerance. He doesn't like to answer questions, but he answers them, and I ask them. Too many of them. It is our joke. Even when I'm not sure if I want to know, I ask, and then sometimes I feel I know too much. I know how fundamentally helpless my doctor feels under his energetic manner. I know that all the clinical tests and the statistics still leave him face to face with luck every time he examines a patient in his confidence-giving little rooms. It boils down, finally, to intuition, and to ignorance. "I don't know" is the answer to many of my questions. I don't know how long you will live, if you will go into remission, if your disease will "go sour"; there are no signs, there is no text. I don't know how effective the latest combination of drugs will be; I don't know if the side effects in your case will be mild or severe; if, as a result of the treatment, you will get hepatitis, shingles or pneumonia. To him as to me, my body reveals itself sporadically, at its own pace. From it he can derive sheets full of data on the level of trace minerals in a burnt sample of my hair; on my T cell, B cell and lymphocyte counts, my red blood cells, my platelets, my sodium or glucose levels, my cholesterol. He can read my heartbeat on a graph, and my internal organs on an X-ray; test my urine; get the opinion of a pathologist on my bone marrow; perform biopsies. But finally he must say, "I don't know." And I've got to accept that my life is indeterminate; that my questions can receive only conditional answers; that no one can have the knowledge or the authority to make me safe again.

My doctor came into the consultation room holding my folder, thick with four and a half years' worth of data, including my latest platelet and white blood cell counts. He was subdued, almost casual, but he got to the point immediately without any jokes.

"I'm going to take a bone-marrow biopsy. We haven't done one in several years, and it's time to have a look. Your white count has been drifting up. I also can feel your spleen for the first time. It could be that something's up. The lymphoma may be changing over."

"Changing over" was an oncologist's phrase for something bad, that was clear.

"A lymphoma can start spilling lymphocytes into the blood," he explained, "and that may be happening here. But let's not jump to conclusions. I could be overreacting to a few numbers. Let's talk it over when we get some more data."

He brought in an apparatus equipped with a short hollow needle, anesthetized a patch of my hip, and drilled out a core sample of marrow. Despite the anesthetic, a deep, creaky pain radiated from the spot.

I felt heavy-headed and chilled as I sat on the examining table. Suddenly, all my philosophy had vanished. Again, time had been flung up close to me. I was not in remission and never had been. For months, under cover of my apparent good health, the disease had been heating up. My spleen had become a "bag full of lymphocytes," to use my doctor's phrase. When I got home, I felt under my arms, around my ribs, in my groin. There were small, inconspicuous lumps that probably hadn't been there before. I was sprouting, I was in flower. Almost immediately I began my panicky phone calls; to my doctor, first of all, in the hope that what he said would be less frightening than my imagination. This time, the truth itself was frightening. A lymphoma that "changes over" can "go sour" very quickly, or it can simmer gently. In the first case, I could be sick very soon, and he seemed almost surprised that I wasn't feeling the effects already. On the other hand, he said, that could be a good sign. I called the head of immunological oncology at the Sidney Farber Cancer Center in Boston, where I knew work was being done on a new approach to cancer treatment using something called monoclonal antibodies. I called a friend who knew doctors at Stanford who were also working with monoclonal antibodies. I called the National Cancer Institute in Washington, and spoke for an hour with a technician, who gave me all sorts of imprecise and reassuring information. I was plunged in a paradox. These monoclonal antibodies represented a radical new approach, and much of the research was being done on lymphoma. The whole field of cancer research was in an excitable state. Several lymphomas and leukemias had been traced to a virus. A type of cancer-stimulating gene, called an oncogene, had been discovered. Recombinant DNA was beginning to produce quantities of pure interferon that could represent a new form of treatment. The hope existed that malignancies could one day be turned off by genetic manipulation. Cheerful substances like vitamin A might have a normalizing effect on cancer cells. It was exciting, full of horizon. But my interest was peculiarly narrow and avid. I wanted to be saved, I wanted it now. But now there was nothing. My doctor, hardheaded, even conservative, under his manic ebullience, didn't get excited about anything that he couldn't use on the demure, patient people who sat in his waiting room. He was a pragmatist, the test was clinical usefulness.

Suddenly the wall had been shoved up close to me, and I felt bruised, as if I had been beaten with fists. Was it possible that my time was to be measured in months now, instead of years? I ran every day under the leafless November trees along Riverside Drive. The raw, moist air rasped in my lungs. The sunlight was thin, almost metallic. It was an absurd act, an act of faith, I suppose; or maybe an admission that I possessed no better kind of day than the ones I was living: teaching class, writing a book, caring for my daughter on the days that she was with me. For almost two years, I had been living with a woman, and from the start chemotherapy had been our companion, a third person that never left us alone. But now time had been brutally torn from me. I had been thrust far into the new life, where my friend couldn't follow me, where nobody could follow me. At times, while I waited for my doctor to assemble his information, it seemed to me that my fright was a way of drowning my aloneness. I had become a member of a heavy tribe, those who walked minute by minute into a blankness that ate the near distance, like the winter fog one year in Venice, unfurling in thick billows, until I walked in a blur of weight which made every step seem heavier, more obsessed. Now, too, space had clamped shut on me, except for sudden vanishing when the river, opening beyond the window, gave me room.

A week later, my doctor was ready to talk. My lymphoma had probably "changed over" to something called a lymphosarcoma-cell leukemia. If so, this was a relatively infrequent occurrence, and he was not willing to predict what would happen next.

On the other hand, looking over the flow chart of my visits to him during the past four years, he had noticed a slow upward drift of my white blood cell count all along. He had reread the original pathologist's report on my first bone-marrow biopsy, remarking a high level of lymphocytes, and remembered that a hematologist, at the time, had guessed that my lymphoma could well be accompanied by one of its near cousins, a chronic lymphocytic leukemia. By now I understood that these daunting terms—lymphoma, lymphosarcoma-cell leukemia, chronic lymphocytic leukemia—were not as definitive as they sounded. They were nets cast into a turmoil, freeze-frames of a complex flow. The conditions they referred to tended to blur into each other, and become each other. The immunological oncologists used other nomenclatures entirely, and the whole classificatory system for lymphomas was put in doubt by some scientists.

Medicine was still related to voodoo and witchcraft by one tenuous, life-giving link: it boiled down, finally, to educated guesses, habit, long practice and clinical intuition. My doctor's knowledge, extensive and up-to-date as it was, provided him not with recipes but with a kind of yoga. In a given case, he absorbed the sheets of test results, the feel of the patient's body, the years of working through similar cases, exploring life at its extremity, life at its breaking point; and then he decided, the way a baseball player swings at a fast ball. It was disturbingly close to guesswork. In my case, it meant that what I wanted to know—live or die, now or later?—would emerge over time, as the blood tests accumulated, and my state of health spoke for itself.

I lived in a suspended breath. I waited—what else could I do? —and yet I could not bear to wait. I ran harder every day, and tugged at the exercise machines in the health club. My friend Vikki and I flew up to Boston, and I had bagfuls of blood extracted by the immunologists there. I saw another oncologist, who seemed grim about my prospects, frightening me to a new pitch of tension. I called my lawyer to get my will in order. I called my ex-wife, pleading with her to take good care of our daughter. I felt an incongruous need to finish the book I was working on. Did the world need another book? I knew that wasn't the question. I felt that writing was my best self. It was, internalized, the view from my window, or my stone house on a hilltop in southwestern France. It was the cohered tensions of living made deliberate and clear. Writing, I touched the roots of my life, as I did when Vikki and I made love, or when I spent an afternoon with my daughter. But writing was stronger, more sustaining than these. Every day, I spilled words onto my yellow pad, crossed out, inverted sentences, inserted new paragraphs on the back of the page. I raced my fountain pen from line to line, in erratic humps and jags. And this crabbed hieroglyphic, curling from top to bottom of the page, was my mind climbing quietly and privately to a plane of spirit that balanced above my sick body. There my limitations were acceptable; they were the language spoken by my pen, which drank at a deep source.

I saw that a writer's immortality exists in the moment of conception, in which language has seized hold of him, and not in the posterity which few of us believe in, in these days of nuclear shadow. A work is not a life, but writing is living, and now especially I wanted to live with all my might. I wanted to fight off the shrinking effect of fear. Therefore, I wrote my book, while I waited for the blood tests to speak. And gradually they spoke, in a temporary, self-revising idiom.

"At least your count isn't shooting through the roof," my doctor said, "and that's good."

With chemotherapy the count began to come down, my nodes and spleen began to shrink again. I could see, as at the end of an alley, a brightness: the crisscrossing of passers-by, the honking and snoozing of cars; it was the bland ribbon of time that runs on, runs on.

Oh, yes, it is a flimsy ordinariness, an eroded shell. It is Vikki and her children, my daughter and me, at the Botanic Gardens, surprised by the pastel blossoms of the cherry trees like bursts of softness, in the chilly breeze of early April. It is cutting up parsnip roots, carrots and broccoli for a stew; feeding the children, and then sitting in the high shadowy living room of Vikki's apartment late at night, reading or talking. It is the old dream of an enchanted ordinariness come true in snippets and jigsaw-puzzle fragments that don't last, but lasting isn't what's important now, as long as the puzzle is real. And then, every few weeks, it is the remembering again that I'm the loose piece, the medical case with the catheter in my arm, and the large hypodermics of clear fluid; the two days of homeopathic misery; the predictable weathering of the predictable storm, a man holding on; running under trees ready to thicken into spring; looking from my window, as now, on the rim of darkness over the Palisades, and the white street lamps of the road slanting to river level; the beige necklace of lights outlining the George Washington Bridge; the river, become a nothing of black and depth, almost unreal, like a fault line burst asunder into the earth's interior.